Knowing New Biotechnologies

The areas of personal genomics and citizen science draw on – and bring together – different cultures of producing and managing knowledge and meaning. They also cross local and global boundaries, are subjects and objects of transformation and mobility of research practices, evaluation and multi-stakeholder groups. Third, they draw on logics of 'convergence': new links between, and new kinds of, stakeholders, spaces, knowledge, practices, challenges and opportunities.

This themed collection of chapters from nationally and internationally leading scholars and commentators advances and widens current debates in Science and Technology Studies and in Science Policy concerning 'converging technologies' by complementing the customary focus on technical aspirations for convergence with the analysis of the practices and logics of scientific, social and cultural knowledge production that constitute contemporary technoscience. In case studies from across the globe, contributors discuss the ways in which science and social order are linked in areas such as direct-to-consumer genetic testing and do-it-yourself biotechnologies.

Organized into thematic sections, *Knowing New Biotechnologies* explores:

- ways of understanding the dynamics and logics of convergences in emergent biotechnologies;
- governance and regulatory issues around technoscientific convergences; and
- democratic aspects of converging technologies – lay involvement in scientific research and the co-production of biotechnology and social and cultural knowledge.

Matthias Wienroth is Research Fellow at the Northumbria University Centre for Forensic Science and Visiting Researcher at the Policy, Ethics and Life Sciences research centre, Newcastle University. He studies science–society relationships and the opportunities of cross-disciplinary knowledge production for socially responsible technology development.

Eugénia Rodrigues is Research Fellow at the University of Edinburgh. Trained in sociology at the Universities of Coimbra (Portugal) and York (UK), her research interests lie at the intersection of environmental sociology and STS with a particular interest in contemporary expert–lay relations and their implications for knowledge democratization.

Genetics and Society

Series Editors: Ruth Chadwick, *Director of Cesagen, Cardiff University*, John Dupré, *Director of Egenis, Exeter University*, David Wield, *Director of Innogen, Edinburgh University,* and Steve Yearley, *Director of the Genomics Forum, Edinburgh University.*

The books in this series, all based on original research, explore the social, economic and ethical consequences of the new genetic sciences. The series is based in the Cesagen, one of the centres forming the ESRC's Genomics Network (EGN), the largest UK investment in social-science research on the implications of these innovations. With a mix of research monographs, edited collections, textbooks and a major new handbook, the series is a valuable contribution to the social analysis of developing and emergent bio-technologies.

Series titles include:

New Genetics, New Social Formations
Peter Glasner, Paul Atkinson and Helen Greenslade

New Genetics, New Identities
Paul Atkinson, Peter Glasner and Helen Greenslade

The GM Debate
Risk, politics and public engagement
Tom Horlick-Jones, John Walls, Gene Rowe, Nick Pidgeon, Wouter Poortinga, Graham Murdock and Tim O'Riordan

Growth Cultures
Life sciences and economic development
Philip Cooke

Human Cloning in the Media
Joan Haran, Jenny Kitzinger, Maureen McNeil and Kate O'Riordan

Local Cells, Global Science
Embryonic stem cell research in India
Aditya Bharadwaj and Peter Glasner

Handbook of Genetics and Society
Paul Atkinson, Peter Glasner and Margaret Lock

The Human Genome
Chamundeeswari Kuppuswamy

Community Genetics and Genetic Alliances
Eugenics, carrier testing and networks of risk
Aviad E. Raz

Neurogenetic Diagnoses.
The power of hope and the limits of today's medicine
*Carole Browner and
H. Mabel Preloran*

Debating Human Genetics
Contemporary issues in public policy and ethics
Alexandra Plows

Genetically Modified Crops on Trial
Opening up alternative futures of Euro-agriculture
Les Levidow

Creating Conditions
The making and remaking of a genetic condition
*Katie Featherstone and
Paul Atkinson*

Genetic Testing
Accounts of autonomy, responsibility and blame
*Michael Arribas-Allyon,
Srikant Sarangi and Angus Clarke*

Regulating Next Generation Agri-Food Biotechnologies
Lessons from European, North American and Asian experiences
*Edited by Michael Howlett and
David Laycock*

Regenerating Bodies
Tissue and cell therapies in the twenty-first century
Julie Kent

Gender and Genetics
Sociology of the Prenatal
Kate Reed

Risky Genes
Genetics, breast cancer and Jewish identity
Jessica Mozersky

The Gene, the Clinic, and the Family
Diagnosing dysmorphology, reviving medical dominance
Joanna Latimer

Barcoding Nature
Shifting cultures of taxonomy in an age of biodiversity loss
*Claire Waterton, Rebecca Ellis
and Brian Wynne*

Negotiating Bioethics
The governance of UNESCO's bioethics programme
Adèle Langlois

Breast Cancer Gene Research and Medical Practices
Transnational perspectives in the time of BRCA
*Edited by Sahra Gibbon,
Galen Joseph, Jessica Mozersky,
Andrea zur Nieden and
Sonja Palfner*

Science and Democracy
Making knowledge and making power in the biosciences and beyond
*Edited by Stephen Hilgartner,
Clark A. Miller and
Rob Hagendijk*

Knowing New Biotechnologies
Social aspects of technological convergence
*Edited by Matthias Wienroth
and Eugénia Rodrigues*

Forthcoming titles include:

Controlling Pharmaceutical Risks
Science, cancer, and the
geneticization of drug testing
*Edited by John Abraham and
Rachel Ballinger*

**Scientific, Clinical and Commercial
Development of the Stem Cell**
From radiobiology to
regenerative medicine
Alison Kraft

Knowing New Biotechnologies
Social aspects of
technological convergence

Edited by Matthias Wienroth and
Eugénia Rodrigues

LONDON AND NEW YORK

First published 2015
by Routledge
711 Third Avenue, New York, NY 10017

and by Routledge
2 Park Square, Milton Park, Abingdon, Oxon OX14 4RN

Routledge is an imprint of the Taylor & Francis Group, an informa business

© 2015 Matthias Wienroth and Eugénia Rodrigues

The right of the editors to be identified as the author of the editorial material, and of the authors for their individual chapters, has been asserted in accordance with sections 77 and 78 of the Copyright, Designs and Patents Act 1988.

All rights reserved. No part of this book may be reprinted or reproduced or utilized in any form or by any electronic, mechanical, or other means, now known or hereafter invented, including photocopying and recording, or in any information storage or retrieval system, without permission in writing from the publishers.

Trademark notice: Product or corporate names may be trademarks or registered trademarks, and are used only for identification and explanation without intent to infringe.

British Library Cataloguing-in-Publication Data
A catalogue record for this book is available from the British Library

Library of Congress Cataloging in Publication Data
Knowing new biotechnologies : social aspects of technological convergence / edited by Matthias Wienroth, Eugénia Rodrigues.
   pages cm. – (Genetics and society)
   1. Biotechnology–Social aspects. 2. Convergence. I. Wienroth, Matthias. II. Rodrigues, Eugénia.
   TP248.23.K59 2015
   512'.24–dc23
                  2014029200

ISBN: 978-1-138-02293-5 (hbk)
ISBN: 978-1-315-77678-1 (ebk)

Typeset in Times New Roman
by Taylor & Francis Books

Contents

List of figures ix
List of contributors x
Acknowledgements xiii

PART I
Introduction 1

1 An introduction to social convergences 3
  MATTHIAS WIENROTH AND EUGÉNIA RODRIGUES

2 Distinguishing the umbrella promise of Converging Technology from the dynamics of Technology Convergence 12
  DOUGLAS K. R. ROBINSON

PART II
Dynamics and logics 27

3 Why so many promises? The economy of scientific promises and its ambivalences 29
  MARC AUDÉTAT

4 Logics of convergence in NBIC and personal genomics 44
  CHRISTOPHER GROVES

5 The convergence of direct-to-consumer genetic testing companies and biobanking activities: the example of 23andMe 59
  HEIDI C. HOWARD, SIGRID STERCKX, JULIAN COCKBAIN,
  ANNE CAMBON-THOMSEN AND PASCAL BORRY

PART III
Governance 75

6 The messiness of convergence: remarks on the roles of two
visions of the future 77
CHRISTOPHER COENEN

7 Mapping the UK government's genome: analysing convergence
in UK policy one decade into the twenty-first century 92
ISABEL FLETCHER, STEVEN YEARLEY AND CATHERINE LYALL

8 Diagonal convergences: genetic testing, governance,
and globalization 105
CHRISTINE HAUSKELLER

PART IV
Citizens, amateurs, and democratization 123

9 Do-it-yourself biology, garage biology, and kitchen science:
a feminist analysis of bio-making narratives 125
CLARE JEN

10 Amateurization and re-materialization in biology: opening up
scientific equipment 142
MORGAN MEYER

11 Converging technologies and critical social movements:
an exploration 158
FRANZ SEIFERT

12 Rhetorics and practices of democratization in synthetic biology 174
EMMA FROW

PART V
Commentary 189

13 Considering convergences in technology and society 191
STEVEN YEARLEY

Index 196

List of figures

2.1	Convergence archetypes	15
2.2	NBIC and Converging Technology discourse and activities	15
10.1	The Open PCR machine being assembled during a workshop	150
10.2	Part of the instructions to hack the 'peltier' element for a PCR machine.	151

List of contributors

Marc Audétat is senior researcher at the Science–Society Interface department at the University of Lausanne. A political scientist by training, he has embraced the social studies of science. Fields of research: analysis of sociotechnical controversies, governance of emerging science and technology. His current work includes the promotion of public debate and the design of participatory research.

Pascal Borry, assistant professor of bioethics at the University of Leuven, researches the ethical, legal and social implications of genetics and genomics, including direct-to-consumer genetic testing, biobanking, preconceptional and neonatal screening. He is a member of the Professional and Public Policy Committee of the European Society of Human Genetics.

Anne Cambon-Thomsen, research director in CNRS, leads the group Genomics, Biotherapy and Public Health in a research unit of epidemiology and public health at the National Institute for Health and Medical Research and University Toulouse III Paul Sabatier. She is involved in several EU projects.

Julian Cockbain is a consultant European patent attorney, and partner at the British patent attorney firm Dehns. He has written numerous articles on the subject of what is or is not patentable and, with Sigrid Sterckx, has co-authored a book on exclusions from patentability under the European Patent Convention.

Christopher Coenen is a senior researcher at the Institute for Technology Assessment and Systems Analysis, within Karlsruhe Institute of Technology. As team member or project leader, he has conducted over fifteen research projects on behalf of the European Commission, parliaments and other institutions, including several projects on converging technologies.

Isabel Fletcher is a researcher based at the Global Public Health Unit in the University of Edinburgh. Her main research interests are the development of public policy in the areas of diet, nutrition and chronic disease, and the twentieth-century history of British and American epidemiology.

Emma Frow is a lecturer in Science, Technology and Innovation Studies at the University of Edinburgh. Her research focuses on guidelines, standards and governance in contemporary biosciences, with a particular emphasis on synthetic biology.

Christopher Groves's work focuses on how people and institutions negotiate and deal with an intrinsically uncertain future. He specializes in the governance of risk and uncertainty, and in ethical and political aspects of the social impact of new technologies.

Christine Hauskeller is associate professor of philosophy at Exeter University, UK. She was co-director of the ESRC Centre for Genomics in Society. Research interests include uses of DNA technologies in identity politics, science and state institutions, and methodologies and ethics of critique.

Heidi C. Howard, senior researcher at the Centre for Research Ethics & Bioethics, Uppsala University, researches ethical, legal and social issues surrounding genetics and genomics including direct-to-consumer genetic testing, whole genome sequencing and public health genomics. She is a member of the Professional and Public Policy Committee of the European Society of Human Genetics.

Clare Jen is an assistant professor in the Women's Studies Program and the Department of Biology at Denison University. Her areas of research include critical race and gender studies, feminist studies of science and health, and media studies. She is also interested in feminist science methodologies and alternative laboratory practices.

Catherine Lyall is Professor of Science and Public Policy at the University of Edinburgh and was formerly deputy director of both the ESRC Genomics Forum and ESRC Innogen Centre. She publishes on the governance of the life sciences and more broadly on research policy, including interdisciplinarity and research impact.

Morgan Meyer is lecturer in sociology at Agro ParisTech and associate researcher at INRA. He was guest professor at Vienna University, a visiting fellow at the University of Edinburgh and co-edited 'Intermediaries between science, policy and the market' (*Science and Public Policy*, 40(4)) and 'Epistemic communities' (*Sociological Research Online*, 15(2)).

Douglas K. R. Robinson is Managing Director of TEQNODE Limited (Paris, France) a contract research firm and consultancy focusing on the analysis and management of emerging and potentially breakthrough technologies and related innovation processes (including societal uptake of new innovations).

Eugénia Rodrigues is research fellow at the University of Edinburgh. Trained in sociology at the Universities of Coimbra (Portugal) and York (UK), her research interests lie at the intersection of environmental sociology and STS

xii *Contributors*

with a particular interest in contemporary expert–lay relations and their implications for knowledge democratization.

Franz Seifert is a biologist, political scientist, and lecturer at the University of Vienna. His major fields of interest are technology and rural controversies such as the controversy over agricultural biotechnology; the linkage of local and global political dynamics; cross-national comparisons; and the democratization of technology policies.

Sigrid Sterckx, Professor of Ethics at Ghent University, focuses on ethical aspects of bio-banking, organ transplantation and patenting of human body material; ethical issues regarding human enhancement; medical decision-making at the end of life; environmental justice and governance; and ethical aspects of the patent system.

Matthias Wienroth is research fellow at the Northumbria University Centre for Forensic Science, and Visiting Researcher at the Policy, Ethics and Life Sciences research centre, Newcastle University. He studies science–society relationships and the opportunities of cross-disciplinary knowledge production for socially responsible technology development.

Steven Yearley is Professor of the Sociology of Scientific Knowledge at the University of Edinburgh and was director of the ESRC Genomics Forum from 2006 until 2013. He works on Science and Technology Studies topics in relation to environmental and to genomics issues.

Acknowledgements

This book is the direct upshot of a workshop held in the autumn of 2012 at the ESRC Genomics Policy & Research Forum, in Edinburgh. The engaging discussions undertaken by participants on convergence in contemporary societies were the trigger to further debate and analysis. Two years on, we are publishing this collection of what we believe to be reference studies on the theoretical, conceptual and empirical dimensions of Social Convergences. It was both a long and exciting project.

At the workshop, we wanted to hear participants' views on current developments in the field of technological convergence and were guided by two main lines of enquiry in planning the meeting: to widen the dominant – though conceptually restrictive – debate on Converging Technologies in order to render visible the social and cultural processes, practices and logics that are actively involved in the production of contemporary technoscience, and, in so doing, to grant a place to the so-far overlooked side of Social Convergences.

The book represents not only the work of those involved in the initial meeting – in fact, some of the authors only joined the book project at a later stage and some of the participants in the workshop did not take part in the book project for various reasons – but also the results of the work, goodwill and encouragement of many people who at different moments encountered this project.

The workshop drew on a variety of resources, human and otherwise. Our thanks go to the office team at the Genomics Forum that helped with the practicalities of running the workshop, and to the Genomics Forum overall, for the encouragement and financial support. Thanks are also due to the ESRC for their support of the ESRC Genomics Policy & Research Forum through grant RES-145–28-005.

For the production of the book we benefited from the input of many colleagues and friends: thanks to our authors for accepting the challenge of rethinking convergence; and to a great number of scholars who provided their time as peer reviewers of the chapters: both the editors and the authors are very grateful for their insightful comments. At an earlier stage the project of the book was helped by the suggestions of the editors of the ESRC Genomics Network (EGN) Genetics and Society Book Series (particularly Adam

Hedgecoe at Cesagen in Cardiff and the series editors Ruth Chadwick, John Dupré, Dave Wield and Steven Yearley) and the recommendations of two anonymous referees. Our thanks also go to Helen Greenslade, the EGN editor that accompanied the first steps of the book, and to Mel Evans who supported us in the following period. At Routledge we benefited from the professional aid of the editorial team, especially Emily Briggs, who oversaw the first stages of the manuscript, Alyson Claffey, and Ruth Bradley who accompanied the book to publication.

Finally, we are in great debt to Steven Yearley who, both as director of the Genomics Forum and editor-in-chief of the Genetics and Society book series, was always happy to support, advise and encourage this project throughout.

Matthias & Eugénia

Part I
Introduction

1 An introduction to social convergences

Matthias Wienroth and Eugénia Rodrigues

Introduction

The notion of Converging Technologies has been part of national science policy discourses across the globe since the late 1990s. The unifying idea of these has been that the coming together of different compatible technologies will produce wide-ranging and beneficial social and economic changes. In order to foster technological convergences, and generate societal benefits upon application, proponents of the Converging Technologies (CT) discourse have called for considerable public funding to be made available to research, particularly in the fields of nano-, bio-, and information and communication technologies as well as cognitive science (this is the 'NBIC' dimension of the CT discourse; further discussion of this theme is available especially in Chapters 2 and 6 of this volume). In the last decade, the CT discourse has somewhat lost its drive due to a lack of significant and apparent impact from technological convergences, and the issue of still outstanding all-encompassing and game-changing societal benefits. This applies as much to the NBIC discourse as it does to genomic aspirations that were developed in the emergence and functioning of the Human Genome Project. While funding policy and research practice have aimed to associate research into social and ethical aspects of technoscience with publicly funded CT research projects, the focus on technological convergence within the CT discourse has neglected other kinds of convergence that occur in and around technoscience. This volume proposes a novel approach to thinking and analysing the very promissory concept of Converging Technologies: to focus on social aspects of technology discourses and practices, and to develop an understanding of social aspects as not only accompanying but, moreover, significantly contributing to technological convergences.

From workshop to book

On 27–28 September 2012, the ESRC Genomics Policy & Research Forum in Edinburgh, UK, organized a workshop inviting a variety of scholars from

Europe and North America to discuss the 'The Messiness of Convergence'. The aim of the event was:

> to advance and widen current debates in Science and Technology Studies and in Science Policy concerning 'Converging Technologies' by complementing the customary focus on technical aspirations for convergence with the analysis of the practices and logics of scientific, social and cultural knowledge production that constitute contemporary technoscience. In case studies from across the globe, contributors discuss the ways in which science and social order are linked in areas such as direct-to-consumer genetic testing and do-it-yourself biotechnologies.
>
> (workshop abstract)

While the notion of 'convergence' remained contested throughout the two-day event, the discussion of case studies in the context of Converging Technologies quickly directed attention to the apparent overlooking of the significance of social convergences in both shaping and constituting technological (or: technoscientific) convergences. The discussions inspired the publication of this volume, and its outlook in terms of the three aspects of (1) logics and dynamics of social convergences; (2) implications for governance; and (3) social convergences in technoscientific appropriation by scientific amateurs outside academia, state laboratories, and industry. The empirically informed and fully peer-reviewed chapters in this book put forward different approaches to understanding these convergence processes and their governance in relation to the new biotechnologies, using in particular the examples of personal genomics and do-it-yourself biotechnology (including synthetic biology).

This prefatory chapter is divided into three sections: this introduction, a proposal for approaching the understanding of social convergences, and an overview of the chapters and their contributions to the discussion of social convergences and the CT policy discourse.

Understanding social convergences

Convergences enact technoscience. Scientific understanding develops not only through the elaboration of existing disciplines but through placing existing knowledges in novel combinations and new relationships. Sometimes new opportunities for knowledge development and for the creation of new products and technologies arise from these convergences. And science policies may build on this idea by trying to stimulate and fund work at promising intersections of knowledge, though such investments and interventions in the path of science are seldom unanimously agreed. Such was the case with the Human Genome Project (HGP). The HGP and the transcription of DNA have enabled a considerable number of research projects, and the development of a variety of applications. The original promise of the HGP was to provide the building plan for the human body, and via this knowledge to pretty much instantly enable the development of therapies and cures for a broad range of genetic diseases. This promise has not been fulfilled, yet; instead, the complexity of the genome and its interactions with the environment have become more apparent; and emerging genetic research has enabled the development of a variety of other applications including forensic phenotyping (for use in the criminal justice system), genetic testing for predispositions to certain diseases (for example as a commercial product), and anthropo-geographic mapping of human migration (towards an understanding of the interaction of genome and culture in human development). All of these can eventually contribute to the overall aim of developing genome-based therapies and cures.

Convergence describes transformative processes that lead to the creation of something novel beyond the sum of those aspects that are converging: knowledges, practices, stakeholders, artefacts, or spaces. While the notion of interdisciplinarity may lie at the heart of the CT discourse (Nordmann, 2004) as recently reaffirmed in a report by the US-American National Academy of Sciences (Board on Life Sciences, 2014), convergence does not simply equate to disciplinary synergy, and encompasses more than knowledges and skills. In this book we highlight the distinctively social dimensions of convergence. Social convergences can lead to new social formations (see Glasner *et al.*, 2006). More specifically, this edited volume engages with convergences in the socio-political loci of technoscientific discourses and practices, potential and actual applications, promises, and imaginaries (see, for example, Chapters 3 and 6 in this volume). These social convergences constitute social elements such as stakeholder identity; defining-power (the power to participate in meaning- and decision-making); alliance building; forms of data collection, sharing, and use; socio-technical anticipatory governance and other forms of regulatory management and governance. Thus, in our view convergence describes social and technological practices that prepare the ground for changes; social convergences are moments at which new social identities, organizations, and relationships emerge. The concept reminds us that socio-technoscientific boundaries are diffuse and dynamic.

Strikingly, convergences need not be limited to collaborations between existing technoscientific actors. They may provide opportunities for new kinds of social actors, though the convergence process can also shape the conditions for those actors' participation. Material manifestations of social convergence include home-based genetic-mapping kits for inferring the user's biogeographic ancestry where the level of informativeness and the practical use of such information are not apparent to the consumer beyond the notion of identifying one's genetic heritage. Here, ideas and practices of commerce, research, and healthcare come together in a context that seems to require close governance but in practice depends on non-specific regulation instead. A more widely used application is the home pregnancy test as a domesticated health service and instrument (see Chapter 8 in this volume). Both tests are anticipatory, and engage users' expectations about their personal and social identity, their obligations, and their involvement in research and production that is remote from the user, may include her in these processes but does not provide any feedback. We find a similar convergence of identities, roles, spaces, and uses reflected in the shift from treating illness to anticipating illness and treating expectations in the healthcare system. Personal genomics has had an effect on consumers, with them (for example) taking medication in order to try to avoid falling ill with future medical conditions implied by readings of their genome. This is a convergence of personal genomics, healthcare, and commerce, and individual consumer and healthcare behaviour in which all three are changed.

Another example of social convergence is the way that public views of science, and involvement in science, shape scientific enquiry and the public articulation of science by researchers:

> Recent decades have seen an increased demand from citizens, civic groups and non-governmental organisations for greater scrutiny of the evidence that underpins scientific conclusions. In some fields, there is growing participation by members of the public in research programmes, as so-called citizen scientists: blurring the divide between professional and amateur in new ways.
>
> (Royal Society, 2012: 7)

These so-called 'citizen scientists', or science amateurs, are slowly gaining some recognition from academics, and indeed there are cases of collaboration where the work does not consist of simply using citizens as calculating machines nor drawing on the computing power of citizens who own PCs, but where 'citizens' collect data as a distributed research community. Beyond that, and primarily in the do-it-yourself community, science amateurs develop and conduct their own experiments (see, for example, Chapter 10 in this volume).

In a highly competitive research environment, citizen scientists find themselves enrolled in the boundary work of academic scientists in which one hypothesis or practice of work is bounded against another along the lines of 'scientific' and 'non-scientific' or 'serious science' and 'storytelling'. This is a practice academic scientists engage in with colleagues as well as with non-academic researchers, including commercial players such as personal genomics companies who offer biogeographic ancestry testing. Publics' scientific interest and literacy are aspects of this constant negotiation of new and emergent science and technology. A *Guardian* article by Prof. Mark Thomas ('To claim someone has "Viking ancestors" is no better than astrology', 25 February 2013), and the response to it by Prof. Martin Richards and Dr Vincent Macaulay ('It is unfair to compare genetic ancestry testing to astrology', 8 April 2013), engage in negotiating science in and for society. They each make evaluative, boundary-defining statements about the scientific work of commercial stakeholders who offer biogeographic ancestry genetic testing, and the impact of such commercial use on the role of science. While Thomas's argument largely adheres to the well-rehearsed line of des-interested science as 'real science' (see Ziman, 2002), his article – unwittingly – traces social convergences in concerns about the representation of scientific ideas in the public domain (here, in response to a BBC Radio 4 interview with Alistair Moffat, managing director of commercial provider BritainsDNA, about commercial biogeographic ancestry genetic testing), about the informativity of emergent scientific technologies, their early commercial uptake, and the nature of customers' self-identity formation through consuming such technologies. Richards and Macaulay, on the other hand, view ancestry genetic testing as a public technology to raise interest in science, and they see scientific enquiry as part of creating a grand narrative about humanity, and interpretation of data – rather than an insistence on 'pure fact' – as a key aspect of technology use. For our purposes, the discussion provides an example of how the appropriation of emerging technoscience impacts on expectations of stakeholders about the further trajectory of related scientific enquiry, how such enquiry is related to changes in the social fabric of technology use and discourse.

Book overview

Grounded in case studies and alert to current theoretical treatments of the issues at stake, the contributing authors provide insightful discussion of these and other examples of social convergence in more depth. While some authors focus on their respective examples, others also provide a thorough reflection on existing Converging Technologies discourses such as NBIC as the basis for developing critical understandings of social convergences in the context of technological convergence – what overall might be described as *technoscientific* or, with Christopher Groves in Chapter 4, as *socio-technical convergence*.

Following the current chapter, Douglas Robinson provides an introduction to the narrative history of the CT programme with a focus on the notion of NBIC, leading him to attend to the disconnection between the policy programme and vision of CT and technological convergence in research and product development. Tropes addressed in this chapter are taken up throughout the book, beginning with Part II on the logics and dynamics of social convergences.

Part II Logics and dynamics

The concept of social convergences encapsulates a diversity of dynamics, logics, and processes that form part of the production of new and hybrid social identities and relationships – for example of new and proactive consumers of personal genomics at the interface of research, commerce, and healthcare. Part II on the logics and dynamics engages with the key groundwork of understanding what is meant by social convergences; it explores how these can be made accessible from different angles.

Marc Audétat in Chapter 3 approaches the discussion of CT from the viewpoint of the Sociology of Expectations. The rhetoric of promise and potential futures is carefully analysed in his chapter, presenting the reader with one discursive dynamic for the CT discourse by comparing various promissory technology communities and embedding the CT discourse in the context of a long tradition of technological hype.

Christopher Groves in Chapter 4 attends to the conceptual nature of convergence. His chapter explains the weak and strong definitions of technological convergence to then distinguish a third form of convergence, one that he describes as socio-technical. This third form is then explicated as a discursive element in the meaning-making processes of anticipating and governing emerging technologies, bringing together social and technological evolution. Groves suggests that the master narrative of personal genomics represents a key example of such socio-technical convergence.

Heidi Carmen Howard and her co-authors in Chapter 5 present the example of Direct-To-Consumer genetic testing, specifically the case of the USA-based online provider 23andMe, in a discussion of various dynamics of convergence. The authors pay particular attention to the social and ethical issues arising from the dual role of 23andMe as a commercial service provider and a research-conducting biobank in the context of an under-regulated setting and market for such convergent activities.

Part III Governance

The policy programme of CT, and, indeed, the governance of technological convergence – for example, funding decisions and the support for research-and-development infrastructure – are shaped by the visionary and promissory nature of the CT public discourse, as Robinson and Audétat have suggested. Simultaneously, developing governance for potential applications has generally been difficult and contentious, leading to various kinds of attempts to steer the emergence of applications through technology assessments (e.g. Grunwald, 2000; Schot and Rip, 1997), modularized foresight (e.g. Fisher and Mahajan, 2006), and anticipatory governance (e.g. Guston, 2014) including the concept of responsible research and innovation (e.g. Owen et al., 2012). By exploring the idea of social convergences and particularly by examining their ability to shape and even constitute technological convergences, the chapters in Part III suggest ways of understanding and conceptualizing governance approaches to convergence.

Understanding the messiness of convergence through an analysis of the CT discourse, Christopher Coenen in Chapter 6 suggests that two streams of thought have shaped CT and related discourses and their governance: transhumanist views, and ideas about the unity of science. By interrogating these two underlying grand narratives, Coenen proposes that a discursive convergence is exercising a significant impact on the CT programme, a programme that is itself a governance device.

Isabel Fletcher and colleagues in Chapter 7 set out to study a further aspect of social convergence by tracking the genome in the present-day UK government, in order to ascertain the impacts that genetic and genomic technologies have had in the governance sphere. Through detailed analysis of departmental and allied websites and documents, Fletcher, Yearley, and Lyall map the way the genome is governed in the UK and demonstrate how widely spread genomic knowledge and genomic technologies are in UK policy agencies. They observe that the first decade of the twenty-first century has produced a 'unique case of convergence around a specific set of technologies that have attained an iconic status within the policy arena', while still concluding that neither the 'genomicisation' of government nor the announced transformative impact of genomic technologies has taken place. This exploratory study furthermore offers a basis for international comparative work.

Christine Hauskeller in Chapter 8 provides a philosophical approach to convergence focusing on analysing processes and shifting power structures. In her chapter, she develops a critique of the CT programme as resting on an obsolete understanding of governments' ability to shape and manage technological development and societal use. Instead, using the example of DTC genetic testing, she argues that social convergences change the way technological use can be governed. CT programmes' focus on the technological overlooks the cultural context of technological developments, thus tending to diminish the capacity for governance and therefore counteracting the original idea of CT as a programme of Foucauldian governmentality.

Part IV Citizens, amateurs, and democratization

Citizens have generally been the least visible actor in mainstream debates on convergence. But, as demonstrated by the principal case-study technological examples referred to in this book (synthetic biology, do-it-yourself biology, bio-making narratives, and nanotechnology), citizen and civil-society groups are commonly granted a role or – indeed – have demanded or invented one.

If, as we propose in this book, technological convergence is underpinned and shaped by social convergences, then attention has to be given to the place that citizens are granted or adopt. It is not for scholars to explore the question of 'whether' there is a place for citizens in the heart of processes of technoscientific convergence; rather, their job is to document and analyse the roles that citizens fulfil. The chapters in Part IV make an excellent start in this analysis of how citizens (diversely framed) are challenging existing conceptualizations of convergence and of the place that citizen as 'consumers' should occupy.

Chapter 9 by Clare Jen adopts a feminist and practice-oriented approach to analyse the forms of critique that have been offered to key convergent technologies. In particular she is interested in the way that movement actors have responded by trying to appropriate the new technologies for their own social objectives.

Morgan Meyer, in turn, analyses the tools that citizens (whom he presents in this regard as amateurs) use in their dealings with biology, particularly the do-it-yourself kind (DIY-bio) in Chapter 10. Through a vivid account of the socio-technical processes that distribute information about and produce core equipment for the practice of DIY-bio, Meyer demonstrates the process of *amaterialization* through which various – and sometimes contrasting – logics and dynamics (e.g. the ethics of hacking versus open source) converge. He argues that, crucially, the new kinds of equipment that result from the 'works' of DIY-bio practitioners do not just enable them to engage in scientific practice; more importantly, they enable practitioners to perform socio-political work as well.

Franz Seifert's chapter is concerned with the civil-society and social movement activity focused on convergent technologies (Chapter 11). He charts the development of social-movement organizations within various European countries and explores whether it is existing organizations who adopt these roles or whether new groups are brought into being. He also uses the CT case to reflect on the adequacy of theories of 'new social movements' for analysing citizen engagement with innovative, converging technologies.

In the final chapter of Part IV, Emma Frow discusses how the discourse of democratization, commonly associated with the development of the young field of synthetic biology, has been matched by practices that, to start with, were intended to fulfil that democratic ambition. As the aim of creating an accessible area of scientific knowledge is proclaimed by many of synthetic biology's key actors and advocates, traditional notions and barriers associated with how science is produced come into question. It is then pertinent to ask, as Frow does in this book, 'how democratization is being discussed and enacted in synthetic biology'. Two main interpretations are identified, one directed at the democratization of innovation and the other concerned with the democratization of governance within the field.

The book concludes with Part V: a reflective commentary by Steven Yearley (Chapter 13); he examines the enduring appeal of the very idea of convergence and investigates the implications that talk of convergence tends to bring with it. Using cases from the book, he then considers how the research summarized in this volume poses an alternative to mainstream views by – for example – identifying the different kinds of actors who can be responsible for convergence and highlighting the different ways in which technical processes can converge. He emphasizes the value of this volume's chapters in stressing the open-endedness and negotiability of convergences.

References

Board on Life Sciences (2014) *Convergence: Facilitating Transdisciplinary Integration of Life Sciences, Physical Sciences, Engineering, and Beyond*. Washington, DC: National Academy of Sciences.

Fisher, E. and R. L. Mahajan (2006) 'Midstream Modulation of Nanotechnology in an Academic Research Laboratory', *ASME 2006 International Mechanical Engineering Congress and Exposition* (American Society of Mechanical Engineers): 189–95.

Glasner, P., P. Atkinson and H. Greenslade (2006) *New Genetics, New Social Formations*. Abingdon: Routledge.

Grunwald, A. (2000) 'Technology Policy between Long-Term Planning Requirements and Short-Ranged Acceptance Problems: New Challenges for Technology Assessment', in J. Grin and A. Grunwald (eds) *Vision Assessment: Shaping Technology in 21st Century Society* (Wissenschaftsethik und Technikfolgenbeurteilung 4), Heidelberg: Springer, pp. 99–147.

Guston, D. H. (2014) 'Understanding "Anticipatory Governance"', *Social Studies of Science* 44(2): 218–42.

Nordmann, A. (2004) *Converging Technologies – Shaping the Future of European Societies*. Interim report of the Scenarios Group, High Level Expert group.

Owen, R., P. Macnaghten and J. Stilgoe (2012) 'Responsible Research and Innovation: From Science in Society to Science for Society, with Society', *Science and Public Policy* 39(6): 751–60.

Richards, M. and V. Macaulay (2013) 'It is unfair to compare genetic ancestry testing to astrology', *Guardian*. Available at: www.theguardian.com/science/blog/2013/apr/08/unfair-genetic-ancestry-testing-astrology [accessed 21 May 2014].

Royal Society (2012) *Science as an Open Enterprise. Royal Society Science Policy Centre report 02/12*. London: Royal Society.

Schot, J. and A. Rip (1997) 'The Past and Future of Constructive Technology Assessment', *Technological Forecasting and Social Change* 54(2): 251–68.

Thomas, M. (2013) 'To claim someone has "Viking ancestors" is no better than astrology', *Guardian*. Available at: www.theguardian.com/science/blog/2013/feb/25/viking-ancestors-astrology [accessed 21 May 2014].

Ziman J. (2002) *Real Science: What It Is and What It Means*. Cambridge: Cambridge University Press.

2 Distinguishing the umbrella promise of Converging Technology from the dynamics of Technology Convergence

Douglas K. R. Robinson

Introduction

The concept of 'Converging Technology' emerged as an umbrella term in the early 2000s, entangling visions around a number of key enabling technologies and their application to improving human performance and well-being. With projections of significant contributions to human enhancement[1] and, more recently, by promising potential solutions to societal grand challenges, Converging Technology (as an umbrella promise) has been promising the possibility to add value through the integration of different scientific disciplines and their technological applications with anticipated transformative changes to industry and society. Nanotechnology and biotechnology in particular have been identified by some as a cornerstone in various visions of Converging Technology.

What is unclear is what are the *actual* research and innovation activities linked to convergence? What specific trajectories of development are actually occurring (can be identified), and what are the policy, governance and societal challenges involved?

This short chapter provides a first step towards exploring these questions (which are explored further in the accompanying chapters in this volume). This is done by:

1. exploring the historical emergence of the umbrella promises/labels 'Converging Technology' and 'NBIC' (nano-bio-info-cogno);
2. making clearer the distinction between 'Converging Technology' and 'technology convergence'; and
3. considering what might be the broad policy, governance and societal implications related to technology convergence.

The main point of this chapter is to highlight that discussions on the future promises and scenarios based on the umbrella terms of 'NBIC' and 'Converging Technology' mostly involve speculative ethical reflection (uncontrolled speculation) and that, especially from a policy-making perspective, there is a need to shift the approach to focus on more concrete issues of technological convergence. The chapter gives a glimpse at what these issues of technological convergence may be, where other chapters in the book will elaborate this point further.

Converging Technologies and NBIC as policy-level visions

The debate around convergence of technologies precedes the Converging Technology and NBIC promise icons, for example, in the rise of materials science since the 1950s, and in the idea of technology fusion, for example in *Mechatronics* (Kodama, 1992). Information and communication technologies (ICT), starting in the 1970s, and biotechnology, emerging since the 1980s, have both been presented as part of the Converging Technology vision (Antón et al., 2001). One can also see the uses of the term in the 1990s, revolving around the convergence of telecommunications, broadcasting infrastructures and services, particularly anticipating the role of the internet.

There has been high visibility since the early 2000s of the particular *umbrella-term* 'Converging Technology' as a research-and-technology policy initiative in the United States, a term which was then used elsewhere. More than a decade later, there still is no agreed definition of Converging Technology with the term often being used interchangeably with the acronym NBIC.[2] The NBIC initiative in the United States in the early 2000s was put forward as way of capitalizing on Converging Technology. Some have proposed that it was set up as a means to argue for further financial support for nanotechnologies by providing 'visions' rather than genuine roadmaps for the development of converging technologies, or a 'new renaissance of science'.[3] Though more of a visioning exercise than a specific observation of a trend in science and technology, the NBIC promise triggered much debate and was closely tied to the forward-looking activities related to nanotechnology, particularly around the vision of human enhancement applications. Such debate remains there today in discussions of ethical and societal aspects of NBIC, which often still refer to the concept of human enhancement (Béland, 2011; Ferarri et al., 2012). As Ferrari et al. and Swierstra and colleagues describe, the activities of social scientists, particularly from the field of science and technology studies, have been very large, particularly around the vision of NBIC for human enhancement, with much speculation.

Linked to the NBIC activity in the US, the research arm of the European Commission (what was then called DG Research) responded to the excitement that was generated in the US and went further in developing more specific descriptions of Converging Technology. It initiated an activity that led to the 2004 CTEKS report (Nordmann, 2004), a report which extended 'converging' to all sciences and technologies and developed the concept of a governance approach. A similar approach to convergence was taken up in a report commissioned by the European Parliament and executed by the European Technology Assessment Group (ETAG, 2006). That report emphasized that convergence was already occurring in laboratories and that investigation of convergence was required at that stage of the innovation process (in addition to examining the strong future visions in circulation at the time (e.g. NBIC and human enhancement)).

Elsewhere in the world, for example in Middle East, South America and Asia, there has been less use of the terms Converging Technology and NBIC. One example in Israel was a programme promoting converging sciences and technologies. This activity was initiated by the National Science Foundation of the Israeli Academy in cooperation with the Israeli National Committee for Converging Technologies. In this programme, convergence was taken as a mode of interdisciplinarity, and convergence could include more than the nano, bio, info and cogno elements of NBIC. Around the same period, other actors began discussing topics related to converging technologies. In 2006, the International Risk Governance Council (IRGC) included converging technologies in its *White Paper on Nanotechnology Risk Governance*. Other activities included the European Group on Ethics and social science researchers, who explored the societal and ethical consequences of converging technologies relating to NBIC, including debates on human enhancement and the boundaries between health technologies and cosmetics (Swierstra *et al.*, 2009).

More than a decade after publication of two widely referenced reports (Roco and Bainbridge, 2002; Nordmann, 2004), NBIC continues in the activities of NBIC2.[4] NBIC2 has broadened the original term to include more disciplines and to consider the issues of convergence on much greater scales than research or technological development alone. For example, at the recent NBIC2 meeting in Belgium[5] convergence was described in terms of platforms at a variety of levels including: (1) foundational tools (NBIC+); (2) earth scale platform (earth systems); (3) human scale platforms (social–infrastructural systems such as mega cities); and (4) societal-scale platforms (how societies behave). The priority-setting role of the NBIC vision remains, albeit with different ideological aims. This meeting, and the associated discussions and reports, have created the new term: Converging Knowledge and Technologies for Society (CKTS). It provides an opening and a reflection on some dynamics of convergence, but is still located at the level of policy discourse and invited experts. What is interesting, is the rhetorical power of such positioning of NBIC and now CKTS, with notions of generations of convergence and the positioning of different actors in this world, including different modes of governance (see Figure 2.1).

Figure 2.2 shows a schematic representing the roll of rhetoric and activities in and around NBIC and Converging Technology from the early 2000s until today. The cloud represents the excitement around discussions about NBIC and Converging Technology. As described previously, both labels (often used interchangeably) are seen as guiding and mobilizing resources, particularly for funding mechanisms but also in stimulating interest from researchers and industrial actors.

The promise of Converging Technology 15

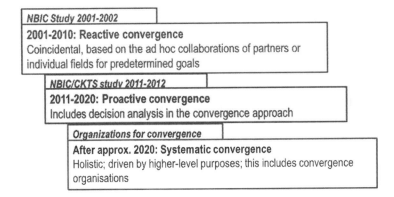

Figure 2.1 Convergence archetypes.

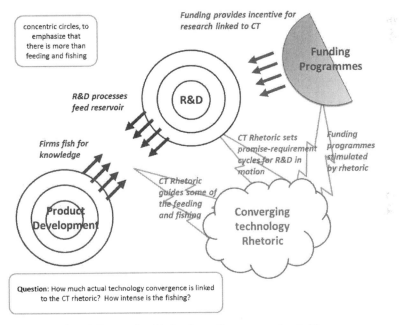

Figure 2.2 NBIC and Converging Technology discourse and activities.

What is not clear is how much actual knowledge creation and product development is linked to the excitement and discussions around the umbrella terms Converging Technology, NBIC and CKTS. What is clear is that very little is directly linked to the vision of converging technologies, but instead that the notion of *technology convergence* – a characteristic in some emerging fields of research and innovation – should be the entrance point to understanding actual activities and value creation. The next section explores this further.

Technology convergence in new fields of research and innovation

Converging Technology and NBIC can be distinguished from the broader notion of Technology Convergence, where technology convergence is more than just a combination of different disciplines or technologies. Value is gained through convergence resulting in completely new ideas, methods and outputs. I therefore propose a broad definition to guide us in this chapter:

> Technology Convergence occurs where scientific disciplines or key enabling technologies combine with other disciplines or enabling technologies to promise new or added value beyond synergism.

Technology Convergence therefore reveals itself as a key dynamic, leading to new and promising fields. This is evidenced, for example, in a recent project *Making Perfect Life* (van Est and Stemerding, 2012; Douglas and Stemerding, 2014), funded by the Science and Technology Options Assessment (STOA) body of the European Parliament, that explored converging technologies – engineering and biotechnology – by looking at two bio-engineering megatrends relating to convergence. In this project they observe two trends in the convergence of biology and engineering. Trend 1 describes biology as becoming a technology, where promises of controlling biological systems to perform functions to perform work abound (this includes cells, organs, the brain, up to and including the human body). Trend 2 describes technology as becoming biology, where biology, cognitive and socio-inspired technologies are applied to human bodies and brains. These would shape societal dynamics (ways of living), manufacturing processes and improve/augment technical devices. This includes artificial constructs made to behave like living systems (van Est and Stemerding, 2012: 7). These trends resonate with a general idea of technology convergence being the transformation of multidisciplinary activities to interdisciplinary activities.[6]

In interdisciplinary activities, previously separated disciplines come together synergistically to form a new type of activity to create more than can be achieved through merely shared projects or shared facilities. This gives it an originality and potential beyond multidisciplinary activities with experimental synergies. Interdisciplinarity within technology convergence can result in previously unexplored areas of experimentation and new ways of working. Taking the results of technology convergence from the laboratory into development, demonstration and deployment can bring industry into new realms of manufacturing and offer new products, which in turn can have new and unforeseen benefits for society if developed in a responsible manner.

This idea of technology convergence described here is particularly evident in the United States, for example, the Massachusetts Institute of Technology (MIT) produced a white paper on the convergence of the life sciences, physical sciences and engineering (MIT, 2011). The paper distances itself from the NBIC term, and explores the evidence and promise of the convergence of the life sciences, physical sciences and engineering. The paper describes such convergence in terms of interdisciplinarity and the added value that could be gained from technology convergence. In its closing paragraphs, the MIT report points out that, alongside providing new combinations and transformative technologies, technology convergence has the potential to speed up scientific discovery.[7] In the same vein, the National Institute of Advanced Industrial Science and Technology (AIST)[8] in Japan is addressing technology convergence in its Photonics-Electronics Convergence System Technology programme, where electrical engineering, photonics and material/fabrication sciences have been organized to support the convergence of electronics and photonics for advanced chip design. Looking at another example, in India there is a strong focus on specific areas of technology convergence within the broader domain of ICT. In the area of research and higher education, the Centre for Converging Technologies at the University of Rajasthan[9] has developed a Ph.D. and master's programme that explores particular examples of convergence. In their programmes they tinker with the NBIC acronym and expand it; the 'b' to include bioinformatics and biotechnology and the 'c' to incorporate cognitive science and neuroscience.

Following on from the examples given already, it is reasonable to suggest that the umbrella terms Converging Technology and NBIC may in fact be particular visions of transdisciplinary[10] forms of *technology convergence.*

Technology convergence in research and product development

Although this short chapter cannot be exhaustive regarding the characteristics and dynamics of technology convergence, what I intend to do is to provide some illustrative vignettes to show the *types* of issues that are already clear instances of technology convergence with regards to research and development and some challenges already evident in the analysis of technology convergence.

Coordination challenges in multi and interdisciplinary research

Interdisciplinarity has been at the heart of the Converging Technology discussions since the early 2000s (Nordmann, 2004). An example of an emerging interdisciplinary field is synthetic biology (Benner and Sismour, 2005; Andrianantoandro *et al.*, 2006; Purnick and Weiss, 2009). In synthetic biology, a variety of disciplines come together in a variety of ways with the overarching idea of applying an engineering approach to biological systems, describing biological systems as living machines, and building devices from standardized biological building blocks. Thus, synthetic biology can be described as applying engineering principles to describe and construct biological systems and processes. There are a wide variety of tools, approaches and ideas regarding the most promising research directions and, although the community is not as yet fully formed, one can identify locations where research is published and events where results are shared.[11] Synthetic biology has been enabled by the decreasing cost and speed of DNA sequencing resulting in a dramatic increase in the availability of biological building blocks to explore and combine. Over the past ten years, a number of devices have been developed (Drubin et al., 2007).

What is clearly visible in synthetic biology are the emergence of the tools and equipment necessary to conduct research, which we describe as technology platforms for research.[12] As opposed to production platforms (Gawer and Cusumano, 2002), which place an emphasis on the standardization of interfaces to allow compatibility, technological platforms here appear as enablers of R&D, as families of technological options and as addressing successive product development actions. These platforms are critical for many research areas that emerge out of the process of convergence, for example Peerbaye (2004) has shown how genomics platforms emerged in R&D institutions and some R&D companies (e.g. micro-arrays) but took on a further feature in France when public financing was made available. Why bring up this issue for technology convergence? An important organizational issue for technology convergence is that technology platforms for research are not just a collection of equipment – they enable and constrain further actions, dictating the research lines possible (Robinson and Boyle, 2007). This characteristic relates to the nature of the actual instrument, what it has been designed for and what can be explored with it. It also relates to the research protocols and methods that accompany the platforms and associated techniques. Thus at the level of the organization of research, the recognition of the possibility of such platforms incites actions to realize them, actions by research institutions and by governmental agencies. This has been particularly visible in the field of nanotechnology (ibid.).

Examples of technology convergence are instances of the combination of a variety of disciplines, as well as many industries and value chains, and they will shape the existing industry structures and research infrastructures. The colocation of the scientific and technological activities, particularly around technology platforms (what some have labelled technological agglomeration)[13] reinforces the development of convergence. It also involves large investments in infrastructure, such as Genopole (Peerbaye, 2004) and the British Synthetic Biology centres. Enabling convergence in areas such as nanobiotechnologies and nanobiomaterials, for example, requires bigger and better clean rooms than other sciences.

One challenge for any sort of convergence-based R&D is the availability of skilled technicians. Skilled technicians are a key element in research settings and are often missed out in discussions of technology convergence. They are crucial for research, particularly in complex multidisciplinary environments, and must be factored in when discussing the skills and expertise necessary for areas of technology convergence. Such technicians have to combine skills and knowledge from multiple fields to be able to construct, test and apply scientific tools, devices and machinery in the laboratory. One example is in biomaterials, where material science meets living materials, creating an overlap of different research protocols and ways of creating scientific research equipment. Since such facilities are expensive and take some time to construct, they need high investment (both financially and in training personnel) over a period of time.

Intellectual property challenge

The example of synthetic biology is useful to explore collaboration challenges in technology transfer and product development for converging technologies. Computation and biotechnology play major roles in the story of synthetic biology convergence and synthetic biology carries characteristics inherited from its parent disciplines. Similar to one of its parents, the field of biotechnology, rapid discovery processes are currently in place for synthetic biology and the number of 'biological parts' being developed is ever increasing. It has been noted that the situation of rapid discovery has reached a point where protecting intellectual property through patenting seems an inappropriate means of intellectual capital management (Klein, 2012). In contrast with its biotechnology parent, an important characteristic of the field of synthetic biology research is the open access culture, with shared accessibility to the data that is being produced in laboratories. This is very visible in another of synthetic biology's parent fields, the field of computational sciences. Since its early stages in the mid 2000s, much effort has gone into creating a Registry of Standard Biological Parts[14] to facilitate sharing of knowledge, supported by the iGEM[15] community and the BioBricks foundation[16] making it increasingly possible to develop biological assembly standards and open databases (Knight, 2003; Anderson *et al.*, 2010). The culture of openness and sharing (open source), in combination with the 'inappropriateness' of patenting as a means of intellectual capital management has created an interesting situation in synthetic biology: if knowledge from synthetic biology research is to be transformed into applications for the market, how will this intellectual property be appropriated? Such appropriation is important if commercialization is to take place (Rai and Boyle, 2007). Perhaps synthetic biology will follow a similar path to that of the mobile phone industry, a case where no one firm has the monopoly on intellectual property (patents) and thus for the industry to flourish, firms have to work together through cross-cutting licences. Another alternative to patents for appropriating value could be through copyright. This idea has been put forward by Kumar and Rai (2007) where synthetic biologists could make the argument that DNA segments could be thought of as source code for living systems, similar to source code for a computer programme. Therefore, like for software, DNA parts could be covered by copyright. Copyright is an illustrative example in synthetic biology, as is open access and the suggestion of licensing similar to that of the mobile phone industry. How does this work out for other areas of convergence? Also, will the situation evolve, for example in bioprinting?

Product development and market infrastructures when value chains converge

For new products to emerge, the development of manufacturing capability, creation and testing of new business models, and standards is needed – all of which require dedicated and coordinated efforts. For example, new combinations of materials and functionalities which emerge from previously separate industries with different regulatory worlds, for example, tissue production through additive manufacturing, provide considerable challenges for the creation of stable and functioning value chains. A well-known example of an evolving industry over the past decades is the semiconductor industry. Tasks involved in the creation of chips include: integrated circuit design; manufacturing of integrated circuits; and the integration of these circuits into a chip or system (Lee and von Tunzelmann, 2005). In the early days of this industry, all of these tasks were located in each individual firms. However, the complexity and the increasingly high cost of production has meant that the various elements that make up computer chip development have become organizationally separated, so that different companies addressed different parts of the production process (for example design houses; wafer companies; foundries; and electronic packaging). However, the pressure to reduce cost and power consumption and the increasing complexity and performance requirements is again changing the traditional landscape for chip development towards more system-level integration in the chip design itself (systems on a chip). Thus there is convergence in terms of how different elements of a system is designed (not fully integrated more than the circuit, but whole parts of devices) but also how the industry itself is structured.

This example reveals that the process of technology convergence may thus lead to organizational convergence in the design and manufacturing process, requiring an increasing amount of coordination, and shifts in the industry structures. Joint research and development are necessary, shared between organizations and actors that were previously separate.

Regulation challenges

Criss-crossing disciplines and previously separated value chains, which are characteristic of technology convergence, bring with them serious challenges for regulation, for example in the area of nanomedicine, which is already entering/stimulating value chains and in some cases entering markets (D'Silva et al., 2012). There are also holes in regulation around emerging technologies which could be taken advantage of. Desmoulin-Canselier (2012) provides an example of a loophole in the potential regulation of technology convergence by showing that previous measures to prohibit human cloning refer much more to the actual 'doing, that is to say the production permitted by techniques' than 'the knowledge' itself. In this example, the prohibition does not affect the freedom of research nor does it restrict the dissemination of the knowledge (but it does restrict discussion and dissemination on the techniques and means of cloning). This provides a real challenge at the heart of regulating technologies based on convergence that may be used for unethical applications as policy-makers need to consider what should be regulated – regulating the *'doing'* versus regulating the *dissemination of knowledge.*[17] For areas of technology convergence such as synthetic biology, and some areas of additive manufacturing, it is predicted that this difference between regulating the doing and regulating the knowledge will become a key focus point in future discussions. Of equal importance is that legislation strategies are based on the idea that evolutions occur in a single linear trajectory, with an evolving technology, where regulation is adapted accordingly in a reactive way. Technology convergence promises evolution on multiple routes and at a rapid pace, and thus it may be necessary to create regulations and other governance instruments to be able to respond rapidly and on multiple fronts, D'Silva *et al.* (2012) touch on this point.

An emphasis on speculative ethics?

From the very early days of NBIC, discussions focused on human enhancement through improving human performances (both individual and social) and continue today. The healthcare promise of providing implants, such as deep-brain stimulators, prosthetic limbs and artificial organs, was often blended with the idea of improving performance of clinically healthy persons to move beyond what is classed as a healthy human. A particularly visible example was when Kevin Warwick of the University of Reading became the first person to have a computer chip implanted into his forearm and connected to his nerves to allow the control, via the internet, of a robotic hand situated in another location. Kevin Warwick labelled this demonstration of a prototype technology as an 'upgrade' to his human body.[18] The ethical discussions around human enhancement encompasses everything from the use of implants and their role in improving the quality life of the physically and mentally impaired to issues around transhumanist ideals of upgrading the body and increasing human performance.

This 'human upgrade' example reveals that there are real issues concerning human enhancement today. But what is surprising is that much of the discussion around human enhancement and Converging Technology still lies firmly rooted in the future, with studies anticipating on what will be the future situation if such human enhancements proliferate. What *is* clear is that there was a swift focus on issues of human enhancement in the social science studies of Converging Technology, perhaps at the expense of questions about what could actually happen in the *near* term.[19]

By placing the discourse of technology development and its impacts firmly in the future, the interest garnered by the NBIC vision in the 2000s provided rich resources to discuss Converging Technology at the level of the umbrella promise, somewhat disconnected from actual technology convergence activities in public and private research laboratories. This emphasis is echoed in

Nordmann and Rip's plea for less speculative ethics. They propose that there is a 'a market' for the ethics of new technologies and that ethicists, philosophers and social scientists have reacted with an over-supply of *speculative ethics.* They define *speculative ethics* as follows:

> Speculative ethics leaps ahead in time. It focuses ethical concern on future worlds full of advanced materials, theranostics, smart dust for ambient intelligence and human enhancement. 'If-and-then' statements begin by suggesting possible technological developments and then indicate consequences that seem to demand immediate attention. What looks like a merely possible, and definitely speculative, future in the first half of the sentence (the 'if'), turns into something inevitable in the second half (the 'then'). As the hypothetical gets displaced by a supposed actual, the imagined future overwhelms the present.
>
> (Nordmann and Rip, 2009: 273)

Nordmann and Rip show that promoters of speculative ethics refer to a broad requirement that society (including industrialists, policy-makers, researchers, etc.) should reflect on the potential changes that may be on the horizon at early stages, even if they are remote possibilities. They also emphasize that that there is a cost of raising irrelevant concerns and that this is often positioned, by promoters of speculative ethics, as less than the cost of finding ourselves unprepared. The main argument by Nordmann and Rip is that such arguments overlook the opportunity costs, that there are limited resources for such activities which in turn limits the breadth and scope of what one can actually reflect upon and further articulate.

Concluding remarks

It is clear that policy shapers cannot afford to neglect the promise of converging technologies (for example see the interest in the recent WTEC conferences), even if they recognize the possibly unrealistic claims made in some application areas. The challenge is what to do, beyond the challenges posed by specific application areas. In summary, technology convergence rather than Converging Technology (or NBIC) should be the entrance point for policy intervention and this requires consideration of further levels of convergence and the issues this will present. But there remain issues and concerns, and opportunities for further inquiry. (For example, the generations of umbrella labels), although useful for creating priorities, may inhibit technology convergence in research and in product development if there is too much emphasis on the umbrella labels and the associated umbrella promises.) This is evidenced by the emphasis on speculative ethics, which arguably has drawn resources away from near-term ethical and societal issues as argued by Nordmann and Rip (2009). What is visible in many areas of technology convergence (in additive manufacturing, neurotechnologies and synthetic biology) in research is the coordination challenge. Coordination is necessary to create the infrastructures that support the production of knowledge and the articulation of strategic agendas (for example in industry roadmaps). Other challenges described in this chapter include overlapping and conflicting regulatory and intellectual property landscapes. Such challenges are not unique to technology convergence but are particularly prominent in areas where convergence between previously separated disciplines occur and each manifestation may require different coordination approaches.

Notes

1 The technological augmentation of human capabilities and modification of the human body and intellect.
2 NBIC is an acronym of the coming together of nanotechnology (N), biotechnology (B) information and communication technologies (I) and cognitive technologies (C).
3 CONTECS Final Report (2009) http://cordis.europa.eu/documents/documentlibrary/124377001EN6.pdf.
4 http://wtec.org/NBIC2.
5 Roco (2012) Methods and global investments for converging technologies. Converging Technologies for Societal Benefit, Leuven, 20 September 2012.
6 Here I position *multidisciplinary* R&D as activities drawing on knowledge from different disciplines but which stays within the boundaries of one particular discipline. In contrast, *interdisciplinary* R&D brings disciplines together into a coordinated and coherent whole (a new field glued together by shared goals and R&D processes).
7 Parallels can be drawn to other areas of scientific discovery that have been accelerated by convergence. One example is the development of X-ray crystallography during the 1940s which stimulated a large-scale shift of chemists and physicists into the field of biology, leading to revolutions in molecular biology, which led to the discovery of DNA.
8 www.aist.go.jp/index_en.html.
9 www.uniraj.ac.in/cct.
10 Transdisciplinarity, integrates the social, natural and health sciences in a humanities context transcending traditional disciplinary boundaries with a focus on a common societal goal or challenge (Nowotny, 2004). One could argue that the discussion of Converging Technology, NBIC and CTEKS focus on a transdisciplinary form of technology convergence. This is particularly evident in the recent NBIC2 discussions.
11 A key event for sharing results and experiences is the BioBricks Foundation Synthetic Biology Conference Series. http://sb6.biobricks.org/about.
12 This is particularly the case for nanotechnology R&D, where control and manipulation of molecular processes at the nanoscale requires many different types of technical instrumentation (Robinson et al., 2007).
13 Ibid.
14 http://partsregistry.org/Main_Page.
15 http://igem.org/Main_Page.
16 http://biobricks.org.
17 In response to earlier comments on this chapter requesting this to be elaborated, prohibiting cloning as an act does not prohibit sharing knowledge about cloning. Freedom remains to describe cloning even if freedom to actually clone is inhibited.
18 www.kevinwarwick.com.
19 For more details see Nordmann (2004), Swierstra et al. (2009) and Ferrari et al. (2011).

References

Anderson, J. C., J. E. Dueber, M. Leguia, G. C. Wu, J. A. Goler, A. P. Arkin and J. D. Keasling (2010) 'BglBricks: A Flexible Standard for Biological Part Assembly', *J. Biol. Eng.* 4(1).

Andrianantoandro, E., S. Basu, D. K. Karig and R. Weiss (2006) 'Synthetic Biology: New Engineering Rules for an Emerging Discipline', *Molecular Systems Biology* 2(1).

Antón, P. S., R. Silberglitt and J. Schneider (2001) *The Global Technology Revolution. Bio/Nano/Materials Trends and Their Synergies with Information Technology by 2015*. Santa Monica, CA: RAND.

Béland, J. P., J. Patenaude, G. A. Legault, P. Boissy and M. Parent (2011) 'The Social and Ethical Acceptability of NBICs for Purposes of Human Enhancement: Why Does the Debate Remain Mired in Impasse?', *NanoEthics* 5(3): 295–307.

Benner, S. A. and A. M. Sismour (2005) 'Synthetic Biology', *Nature Reviews Genetics* 6(7): 533–43.

D'Silva, J., D. K. Robinson and C. Shelley-Egan (2012) 'A Game with Rules in the Making – How the High Probability of Waiting Games in Nanomedicine Is Being Mitigated through Distributed Regulation and Responsible Innovation', *Technology Analysis & Strategic Management* 24(6): 583–602.

Desmoulin-Canselier, S. (2012) 'What Exactly Is It All About? Puzzled Comments from a French Legal Scholar on the NBIC Convergence', *NanoEthics* 6(3): 243–55.

Douglas, C. M. and D. Stemerding (2014) 'Challenges for the European Governance of Synthetic Biology for Human Health', *Life Sciences, Society and Policy* 10(1): 1–18.

Drubin, D. A., J. C. Way and P. A. Silver (2007) 'Designing Biological Systems', *Genes Dev.* 21: 242–54.

ETAG (2006) *Technology Assessment on Converging Technologies*. Report commissioned by the European Parliament implementing Framework Contract IP/A/STOA/FWC/2005-28.

Ferrari, A., C. Coenen and A. Grunwald (2012) 'Visions and Ethics in Current Discourse on Human Enhancement', *NanoEthics* 6(3): 215–29.

Gawer, A. and M. A. Cusumano (2002) *Platform Leadership*. Boston, MA: Harvard Business School Press, pp. 252–4.

Klein, D. A. (2012) *The Strategic Management of Intellectual Capital*. Abingdon: Routledge.

Knight, T. (2003) *Idempotent Vector Design for Standard Assembly of Biobricks*. DSpace. MIT Artificial Intelligence Laboratory; MIT Synthetic Biology Working Group. Available at: http://web.mit.edu/synbio/release/docs/biobricks.pdf [accessed 6 June 2014].

Kodama, F. (1992) 'Technology Fusion and the New R&D', *Harvard Business Review* July–August: 70–8.

Kumar, S. and A. Rai (2007) 'Synthetic Biology: The Intellectual Property Puzzle', *Texas Law Review* 85: 1745–68.

Lee, T. L. and N. von Tunzelmann (2005) 'A dynamic analytic approach to national innovation systems: The IC industry in Taiwan', *Research Policy* 34(4): 425–40.

Merz, M. and P. Biniok (2010) 'How Technological Platforms Reconfigure Science-Industry Relations: The Case of Micro- and Nanotechnology', *Minerva* 48(2): 105–24.

MIT (2011) *The Third Revolution: The Convergence of the Life Sciences, Physical Sciences and Engineering*. Boston, MA: Massachusetts Institute of Technology.

Nordmann, A. (2004) 'Converging Technologies – Shaping the Future of European Societies', *HLEG Foresighting the New Technological Wave*. Luxembourg: European Commission.

Nordmann, A. and A. Rip (2009) 'Mind the gap revisited', *Nature Nanotechnology*, 4(5): 273.

Nowotny, H. (2004) 'The Potential of Transdisciplinarity', in *Rethinking Interdisciplinarity*. Available at: www.interdisciplines.org/medias/confs/archives/archive_3.pdf [accessed 16 March 2013].

Parandian, A., A. Rip and H. te Kulve (2012) 'Dual Dynamics of Promises, and Waiting Games around Emerging Nanotechnologies', *Technology Analysis & Strategic Management* 24(6): 565–82.

Peerbaye, A. (2004) 'La construction de l'espace génomique en France: La place des dispositifs instrumentaux', Ph.D. thesis, École Normale Supérieure de Cachan.

Purnick, P. E. and R. Weiss (2009) 'The Second Wave of Synthetic Biology: From Modules to Systems', *Nature Reviews Molecular Cell Biology* 10(6): 410–22.

Rai, A. and J. Boyle (2007) 'Synthetic Biology: Caught between Property Rights, the Public Domain, and the Commons', *PLOS Biology* 5(3): 389–93.

Robinson, D. K. R., P. Le Masson and B. Weil (2012) 'Waiting Games: Innovation Impasses in Situations of High Uncertainty', *Technology Analysis & Strategic Management* 24(6): 543–47.

Robinson, D. K. R., A. Rip and V. Mangematin (2007) 'Technological Agglomeration and the Emergence of Clusters and Networks in Nanotechnology', *Research Policy* 36(6): 871–9.

Roco, M. C. (2012) 'Methods and global investments for converging technologies', Converging Technologies for Societal Benefit, Leuven, 20 September 2012.

Roco, M. C. and W. S. Bainbridge (eds) (2002) *Converging Technologies for Improving Human Performance. Nanotechnology, Biotechnology, Information Technology and Cognitive Science*. Arlington, VA: National Science Foundation.

Roco, M. C., D. Rejeski, G. Whitesides, J. Dunagan, A. MacDonald, E. Fisher, G. Thompson, R. Mason, R. Berne, R. Appelbaum, D. Feldman and M. Suchman (2013) 'Innovative and Responsible Governance of Converging Technologies', in M. C. Roco, W. S. Bambridge, B. Topnn and G. Whitesides (eds), *Convergence of Knowledge, Technology and Society* (Science Policy Reports). Dordrecht: Springer, pp. 433–89.

Swierstra, T., R. van Est and M. Boenink (2009) 'Taking Care of the Symbolic Order: How Converging Technologies Challenge our Concepts', *Nanoethics* 3(3): 269–80.

van Est, R. and D. Stemerding (2012) *Making Perfect Life – European Governance Challenges in 21st Century Bio-engineering*. Final Report. European Governance Challenges in Bio-Engineering, Brussels, European Parliament.

van Lente, H., C. Spitters and A. Peine (2013) 'Comparing Technological Hype Cycles: Towards a Theory', *Technological Forecasting and Social Change* 80(8): 1615–28.

Warwick, K. and M. Gasson (2004) 'Extending the Human Nervous System through Internet Implants Experimentation and Impact', *Systems, Man and Cybernetics, 2004 IEEE International Conference* 2: 2046–52.

Part II
Dynamics and logics

3 Why so many promises?

The economy of scientific promises and its ambivalences

Marc Audétat

Introduction

The discourse of the convergence of technology, in the examples of genomics and nanotechnology, is addressed here to highlight the driving forces producing and supporting scientific promises and the ambivalences that arise. The sustained hype that often accompanies research is explained by the highly competitive turn taken by the 'regime of technoscientific research' (Joly *et al.*, 2010). The subject is approached with the concepts of 'situatedness' and 'performativity' of the sociology of expectations (Brown and Michael, 2003). Nevertheless, I have opted for the term promise, because it is less neutral than vision and expectation and allows for discussion of questions of credibility and ambivalence raised by the convergence of technology.[1]

Hype/disillusionment patterns

A recent study of the predictive capacity of personal genomics that surveyed thousands of twin pairs for 24 diseases came to pessimistic conclusions (Roberts *et al.*, 2012); its release in the press provoked a controversy. The headline in the *New York Times* read, 'Study says DNA's power to predict illness is limited'.[2] Although not a surprise to geneticists, these results allowed anyone to understand that the chances of gene tests bringing relevant advice to patients affected by common diseases in the near future are low. A medical geneticist commented:

> It is a barrel of cold water on the promises of gene tests. Everyone is discouraged and bothered by this study. There are large infrastructures of sequencing for which new justifications will have to be found.

A couple of months later, *Science* published a study designed to estimate the abundance of rare variants in the population of genes involved in the efficacy of drugs (Nelson *et al.*, 2012). One of its authors, a clinician who is involved in several promissory research projects using large sequencing infrastructures, explained and commented on the results in the local press:

> It is a surprise, we must confess: there are more mutations in the human genome than we anticipated ... And the problem is that so many are contributing to illnesses that it is going to be difficult to attribute a meaning to all of these mutations. All this casts doubts on the concept of personalised medicine.

One thus comes to understand that personal genomics is more complex than anticipated and therefore not within close reach as is often suggested. Consequently, the promises of gene tests have given rise to some kind of ambivalence. The convergence of informatics and genetics does not deliver results simply by itself. The promise that Moore's law in DNA sequencing (increasing speed at decreasing costs) will – naturally so to speak – bring about personal genomics is no longer credible. Meanwhile, many signs tend to indicate that parts of the public believe that the promises of gene tests are already effective, helping people to live better and longer (Henneman et al., 2012).

These ambivalences are matters of the sociology of expectations that investigates the relationships that future visions and scientific promises have with research and innovation processes (van Lente, 1993; Brown et al., 2000; Borup et al., 2006). It illustrates a particular moment when a discrepancy becomes apparent between promises and feasibility. The hype over personal genomics is in difficulty; the actors in this 'community of promise' – including researchers, clinicians, the pharmaceutical industry, decision makers and patient organizations – seem disoriented. Projects that focus on DNA analysis will have to cope with this disillusionment and help to restore the excitement about this road of research.

Ten years ago, Brown and Michael (2003) observed a recurring pattern when current expectations are compared with memories of previous expectations. At the time, a profound sense of disappointment over xenotransplantation and gene therapy was taking place. The stakeholders themselves had retrospectively deemed the promises of the previous decade for these areas of research to be naïve. Interestingly, at the same time, personal genomics was entering its own decade of hype (see Tutton, 2012), and the promises of embryonic stem cells were being touted in the scientific community as well as in the media. Today, embryonic stem cells have been replaced in therapeutic research by somatic induced stem cells, and it appears as though our confidence in the promise of personal genomics has been shaken. Thus, a pattern keeps repeating itself, as if each new rash of promises has inevitably to entail subsequent barrels of cold water. Will this same course of events happen with current discourses heralding revolutionary innovations that are supposed to be within reach thanks to nanotechnology, synthetic biology, brain sciences, or big data? It would be too easy to answer that ambivalence and disappointment are necessary parts of any research endeavour. Indeed, as we shall see, these different cases are linked by their technoscientific character and by the regime of research funding in which they are involved. The latter explains this tendency to sell technological future as real, well before tangible results would authorize such claims. The hypothesis is that scientific promises reflect the regime of research funding and of promotion of sociotechnical change (Felt *et al.*, 2007; Joly *et al.*, 2010).

Hype/disillusionment fluctuations and ambivalences of promises constitute matters of concern in the process of innovation. Emerging science and technology (EST) need undetermined periods of promises before research and development (R&D) trajectories are able to provide their own impetus and deliver results. However, too much hype can be risky. Gene therapy, which was promoted with great fanfare in the 1990s, later failed to deliver. Is this glitch on the hype curve not due to the level of overoptimistic expectations? This case shows that exaggerating promises can risk the reputation of an entire emerging field. Another matter of concern is that, once it is largely shared on a collective level, a promise may act as a requirement for innovators (Borup *et al.*, 2006). Furthermore, when a situation of ambivalence is uncovered, misunderstandings become apparent; differences of expectations, and the reasons why some research is funded as a priority, become visible across social groups. However, these moments that most stakeholders fear provide rare opportunities to discuss, contest, evaluate and reorient science policies. The idea of this chapter is to show that the convergence of technology discourse (inadvertently) steers such kind of opportunity.

Contemporary features of scientific promises

'We are accustomed to being daily bombarded with' scientific promises, wrote Brown (2003: 3). Off-the-record comments criticizing 'exaggerated hype', 'inflated technological optimism', 'stratospherically high expectations', 'hyperbolic' or 'extreme futures' and so forth have become widespread (Brown, 2003; Borup *et al.*, 2006; Pollock and Williams, 2010). Since around 2000, when a sociology of scientific promises was felt to be necessary, another outbreak of promises erupted that was seemingly larger than the previous one; it reshaped old unfulfilled promises and encompassed the technological changes envisaged in 'grand stories' of the future. A decade of renewed expectations followed, the start of which can arbitrarily be pinned to the launch of the US National Nanotechnology Initiative in 2001 and the publication by the National Science Foundation (NSF) of Converging Technologies for Improving Human Performance (Roco and Bainbridge, 2002). Here the idea of convergence is that the technologies operating on the nanoscale are inevitably going to merge: nanotechnology, biotechnology, information technology and cognitive sciences (NBIC). These converging technologies were proposed 'for improving human performance', an idea associated with striking popular images of 'enhancing individual sensory and cognitive capabilities', 'brain-machine and brain-to-brain interaction', implants using 'neuromorphic engineering' and extending life expectancy (Roco and Bainbridge, 2002; Renn and Roco, 2006). An account of these science policy ideas, origin, influences and issues has been given by Christopher Coenen (2007, 2010; and Chapter 6 in this volume).

Ever since the idea of Converging Technologies was presented as a series of disruptive technologies that will deeply challenge society in the near future, it has become a matter of concern and enquiry. 'Converging Technologies' steered an uncomfortable European reaction: the Commission of the EU appointed a group of 'high level experts' to foresee 'the new technological wave' and 'relate the converging technologies to European environment and policy goals' (Nordmann, 2004: 6). Although especially 'inspired' for an official document of science policy, the vision of Roco and Bainbridge is not isolated and is part of a large wave of scientific promises. Thus, before examining what converging technologies mean or could mean, it is crucial to highlight the factors pushing the production of scientific futures which are brought to public attention.

Scientific promises have a long career in modern society that can be traced back to Francis Bacon, whose *New Atlantis* (1627) contains early and explicit ideas of the 'prolongation of life', of physical and cognitive enhancement and of fabricating new species and new materials. The recent wave of promises is reminiscent of the Futurism movement that was popular around 1910, as well as the 'biofuturism' of the 1920s and 1930s, which led Aldous Huxley to write his novel *Brave New World* (1932). More recently, after the Second World War, the promise of the exponential production and widespread availability of energy was considered a certainty for decades. The fact technoscientific promises and visionary futures have always accompanied modern science and progress does not explain their present features and propensity for escalation. The tide of promises the NBIC convergence is part of prompts a discussion of factors and trends that explain it.

Contemporary scientific promises often have an air of déjà vu and sometimes appear as though they were involved in a mirror game with popular images and stories of science fiction (SF). Indeed, this literary genre has long explored emerging technologies. Following recent studies, borrowings from science to SF have been more important than one might think (Milburn, 2002). And these days it has become common to read that 'the future is going to be more than what SF has ever envisioned' (*New Scientist*, 12 October 2008). SF authors have been called on to draw the future to nanotechnology, to sketch visions of its societal environment. The boundary between science and science fiction, once used to delineate realism from fairy tales, seems to have vanished.

To begin with, the fact technoscientific research is considered and funded as a promoter of economic growth explains to a large extent the pace and most features of contemporary scientific promises (see section below). Converging Technologies belongs to a wave of promises that holds the success of information technology and Moore's law to be the exemplar. Information technology is the only indisputable technological revolution and offers many examples of achieved convergence like the PC, the Internet, or the smart phone. It is because Moore's law has aligned the roadmaps of so many actors so many times that it has become a matrix of contemporary scientific promises.

In the recent production and circulation of promises, new networks of actors are also taking part including writers, philosophers, and futurologists, offering other networks in which ideas circulate and are enriched. The circulation of promises has massively increased in the press, in movies, in advertisements, and throughout the Internet. The blogosphere, which came into existence around 2000, has become a privileged place for many discussion forums occupied with the future of technology and therefore represents a privileged place to study promises. The blogosphere is also seen as a place where a certain kind of democratization is going on. Theoretically, anybody may participate in discussions about technological change by posting comments and engaging in debates, so that the discussion about technology and the future no longer seems to be restricted to experts. The circulation of promises happens as though everyone can share a piece of the dream. Indeed, discussing and circulating promises involves reinvention, rewriting, additions, reflection.

Yet, the actors who have critically amplified scientific promises are the numerous intermediary ones such as industry analysts and business media who have 'specialized in the production, commodification and selling of future oriented knowledge' (Pollock and Williams, 2010: 525). In summary, promises have always been a part of science and technology, but today, arguably, their production and circulation differ greatly. Scientific promises are highly situated in present networks of actors. Contrasting with the technologies of the distant future they often evoke, they are meant for short-term goals. Promises are devices used in the competition for capital investments in R&D. This fact links two critical factors that stimulate the production of promises, the context of the world economy and the evolution of the regime of research funding.

The economy of promises and the regime of research

The sociology of expectations explains that visions are needed to provide guidance, encouragement and orientation to professional researchers, science policy makers, capital risk takers and investors, managers and customers. They create a 'shared belief' and a 'protected space' for innovation to take place (Ruef and Markard, 2010). As attempts to build networks of actors around innovation, expectations are also subject to tests of legitimacy and credibility (Joly, 2010). In this way visions and promises enable the development of new science and technology. Furthermore, the dynamics of expectations and innovation are framed by a context that binds competition in the globalised economy with the competition for research funds.

Scientific research has long been considered to be of strategic value, a matter of competitiveness and of defence, which therefore connects it to geopolitics. From this point of view, the present context differs in a very important point: the everyday assertion of power of emerging countries. Emerging economies are now competing with the most advanced ones in all domains. Most 'big' laboratories remain in advanced countries, but for how long? Since this shift has been well anticipated, investments in science and technology must be understood to be part of a competition that is considered tougher for developed countries. This prospect is part of Europe's commitment to a 'knowledge economy' (Lisbon Agenda, 2000). Nanotechnology has been promoted as a way for advanced countries to retain some technological leadership. In this context, the large priority research programmes and their promotion would appear to be demonstrations of strength, with the bubble of promises as a by-product.

Another factor that has progressively pushed the production of promises is the evolution of research policy: research funds have become ever more competitive. The severity of the competition is indicated by the average rate of success of research applications in the US and in Europe (granted projects), which is estimated to be about 20 per cent. As a consequence, laboratories are investing more in 'communication' to maintain the hype needed to ensure the funding of research.

Competition for research funds for EST is organized by state intervention and is justified as a means of increasing the practicality of research. Priority research and large programmes promoting technosciences are highly competitive. Scientific entrepreneurs are producing discourses of legitimization more and more, and in ways that create unease among researchers who are often more cautious. Professionals frequently complain about the expected results they have to outline beforehand in grant applications, about the pressure for justifying the usability of research. Promises are everywhere in the workflow of research; they are used to attract and to maintain capital flows and to support the trajectory of research facilities.

Is this inherent to the ensemble of emerging technosciences or of priority research? Obviously not. Other kinds of research have since engaged in the business of promises in order to climb up the list of funding priorities or to draw attention to neglected fields of science. The open coffers for scientific research now belong to a golden age. Areas of science that have the bad luck of being labelled as 'fundamental' in the research funding categories have found it more and more difficult to justify their budget share. How many grant applications for research that is considered 'basic science' have argued for some potentially striking innovation it will bring about? How many have tried to fall under the categories of 'applied' or 'priority' by propagating promises?

The competitive regime partly explains this kind of escalation of promises and prospects. The EU flagship scheme for Future and Emerging Technologies, in place in Europe since 2010 (with the tagline 'science beyond fiction'), is now adding to this treadmill, with billions of euros being allocated to winners for ten-year periods. The tendency to overplay promises beyond considerations of feasibility has become a common feature, and the research policy and funding system also bears significant responsibility in this evolution of contemporary science. All factors mentioned so far have combined to create a market of promises which acts like a financial and speculative one on top of research and innovation.

Scientific promises are to a large extent the result of the increase in competition at different levels: geopolitical, economic and in research funding. In her in-depth analysis, Bensaude-Vincent (2009) came to reconsider the contemporary history of research policy with regard to technosciences. The fields of materials science, nanotechnology, biotechnology, life sciences, information technology and neurosciences, the products of which end up in society, are the result of decades of technology push policies. She explains how technosciences became the paradigm of priority funding and how it came to dominate the whole regime of science and technology research. The dominant regime of technoscientific promises is also widely contested, its efficiency criticized together with the division of labour between public and private research. The key issue is what Joly (2010) calls the 'problematisation' of research, that is, the junction with a (societal) problem or demand. From this point of view, the lesson of the controversy about genetically modified organisms (GMOs) divides into those holding it as a failure of communication and those considering it rather as a failure of problematization. Furthermore, many promises appear to stem from poor problematization, or even as substitutes to problematization. Joly, Rip and Callon (2010) explain how 'the regime of technoscientific promises' is challenged by an alternative, vibrant model of innovation they call 'the regime of collective experimentation'. This regime features research that is more distributed, democratized, demand–pull or society driven, aiming at open source rather than traditional intellectual property. Summarizing, promises and future visions must be understood as elements of strategies in a context of competition which also opposes different models of sociotechnical change.

Convergence: matters of definition, matters of strategies

The visionary report of the NSF *Converging Technologies*, written as a blueprint for human enhancement, apparently inspired by a transhumanist and a military research agenda, and presented as a new renaissance which can bring 'world peace, universal prosperity, and a higher level of compassion and accomplishment' (Roco and Bainbridge, 2002: 6) meant the crossing of a threshold to many observers and resulted in a number of comments and controversies. It also raised the question of how to set priorities in technology assessment and in science and technology studies. These discussions had to deal with the question of some definition of convergence of technology.

Many historical precedents can be found of this kind of discourse. In the 1950s and 1960s, cybernetics was a powerful discourse promising to bring nature, machines, society and information on the same level of analysis. Prophetic imaginaries of this kind have appeared throughout the history of modern science, such as the idea that there is a science of the sciences or a science governing the entire technical world. Converging Technologies can be seen as a contemporary version of old creeds.

Scholars began to interpret the facts supporting 'NBIC convergence'. Following Roco and Bainbridge's own ideas, studies involved asking questions such as, 'How do disciplinary boundaries move?', 'Are specialist areas of research merging?', 'Where does convergence occur?' Various authors reviewed this programmatic discourse; in many policy documents they found that convergence of technology is meant not as something that is actually occurring or that is going to occur, but rather the opposite. That is, convergence is often employed as a response to the lack of interdisciplinary work and as a metaphorical encouragement to technologists to look towards other domains and join in interdisciplinary platforms. This mundane use of convergence is indeed widespread in the vocabulary of scientific entrepreneurs. 'Yes, we need this discourse. It is good. It is stimulating research.' answered P. Aebisher, President of the Federal Institute of Technology (EPFL), Switzerland, who would later win the 2013 flagship Human Brain Project, in a 2010 radio interview. Schummer concludes that the NBIC convergence is a 'teleological concept' (2010: 66).

According to Miège and Vinck (2012), there are perhaps three different types of convergence to consider: the nanoscale itself, what it is supposed to allow in terms of connecting (or merging) living matter with the machine, and the hybridization of disciplines together with the networks and collaborations actors make (from science, industry, society, etc.). This approach takes its prophetic functions of convergence together with its programmatic functions. To check their hypothesis, they looked at the map of disciplines by means of a scientometric analysis of publications, and to laboratories and technological parks; they conducted a case study of the domain of micro-electro-mechanical systems (MEMS). Their first observation was that the nanoscale clearly does not create convergence by itself. Furthermore, the analysis of publications since 1995 suggests strategies of differentiation at work within disciplines. Capitalization on the appealing character of the nanoworld is widespread.

These studies tend to show that promises like 'convergence' and 'nanotechnology' are often part of larger strategies to shift the boundaries of domains. Convergence of disciplines cannot be excluded as a possibility, although it seems that differentiation is much more significant and real.

Therefore, convergence should be considered mostly as an 'accompanying imaginary'. Its vagueness and impossible definition is precisely what allows it to work: it is a non-binding imaginary. Convergence might refer to the value of interdisciplinary work, to the merging of different specialist fields that are dedicated to the development of certain instruments (like bioinformatics), or to the fusion of technology and the body – whatever the exact meaning, convergence acts as a source of inspiration and helpful narratives.

Accompanying imaginaries work as a means of feeding the promotion of as well as the funding and enthusiasm for emerging fields and their challenges. Convergence of technology is to be understood as a 'rational myth' (Miège and Vinck, 2012: 44), which acts as a mobilizing discourse. It has to convey a structuring story about the direction science is supposed to take in order to provide guidance on agency for stakeholders.

In the end, convergence is perhaps to be understood as the confluence of actors and means towards definite goals instead of the confluence of disciplines or technologies. The European understanding of the convergence of technologies underlines that 'convergence requires deliberate agenda settings' (Nordmann, 2004: 15). There are many examples of disciplines closely collaborating to overcome technological challenges and to develop complex devices (for example labs-on-chip and nanovectors). Other examples involve dual-use research (mixed civil and military purposes), which allows for more funding than the competitive regime alone. Therefore, convergence of technology is hardly conceivable without actors and strategies, and in turn raises the question of the problematization of research: how do promises pass tests of credibility, enrol actors and create alignment.

Converging Technologies pertains to promises which seemingly differ from the way the 'biotechnology revolution' was predominantly promoted in the 1980s and 1990s. Grand stories of technological utopia stand in contrast to the flat discourses of expected usability and competitiveness that dominates research policy. But the NBIC convergence has been drafted for the same agenda as that of conventional science policy. Its narratives and paternalistic paradigm of science–society relations make it an archetype of promises in the regime of technosciences. Technological change is heavily naturalized by a flow of assertive declarations: radical new technology will necessarily come into being, and society either has no role or must adapt; the ethics of this paradigm states that it would be unethical not to advance these technologies.

Nanotechnology or 'scientific promises as a literary genre'[3]

Nanotechnology has proved to have a particularly inspiring character. Following its early stages, this field steered the extraordinary visionary effort of engineer Eric Drexler, who sketched an entire future with and for nanomachines in his *Engines of Creation* (1986). This wave has been shadowed by significant developments in the 1990s – for example, in chemistry (associated with Richard Smalley) and materials science – which gave a real impetus to innovation and the way nanotechnology is marketed today (Selin, 2007) before the notion of Converging Technologies took over and envisioned such an outstanding new future. 'Nanonarratives' (Milburn, 2002) have filled books, magazines, websites, blogs, academic reports and movies. In contrast to the high level of promises of nanotechnology, the production of nanoparticles as well as the numerous and mundane nanoproducts directly available to consumers raised a series of 'classical' governance issues such as risk and uncertainty, standardization, soft law versus regulation, and so forth. In this way, the production of visions and promises of nanotechnology has been such that it became a matter of concern in itself and an object of study (Berube,

2005; Chateauraynaud, 2005; Jones, 2008; Kjolberg and Wickson, 2010; Maestrutti, 2011).

Nanotechnology has primarily been a battleground over definition. Its gift for inspiring narratives and its popularity have been used intensively as a strategy in the competition for research funds. Arie Rip (2006) proposes that we speak of 'folk theories' of technologists. The 'folk theories of nanotechnologists' follow many different creeds that can be identified and tracked. Their rationale cannot be understood in an isolated manner; they have to be considered as 'narrative strategies' in the struggle over meanings in the orientation of science and research efforts. These struggles pit, for instance, those who restrict the definition of nanotechnology to the physics of (near) quantum properties against those who adopt a more flexible definition that encompasses other chemical properties. They place established paths to innovation, like 'the pursuit of miniaturisation' (electronics) and 'the discovery of new properties and new materials' (materials science), at variance with challengers who promote 'the creation of nanomachines and nanorobots'. They foster opposition between common top-down industrial processes to obtain nano-objects and newer ones that employ bottom-up, 'atom by atom' or self-assembly processes. They divide visionaries of radical new technologies, such as 'connecting to the nervous system', and pragmatists who promote improvements to existing technologies and markets like 'connecting the world of objects (and humans)'.

Folk theories also reflect competing paradigms of sociotechnical change, which are contained in narratives like 'one cannot escape the nanoworld, it is only a matter of time', naturalizing technological change (see Mody, 2004), or 'nanotechnology as an opportunity not to repeat the fiasco of GMO', or 'as an opportunity for responsible innovation', reflecting a more open science policy (see Kaufmann et al., 2010).

Sociologists have observed disciplines reshaping their public image and repositioning themselves by engaging in the nanosciences. They have witnessed domains realizing suddenly that they have always been 'nano', and others, not working at the nanoscale, such as microtechnics, capitalizing on the appeal of the nanovocabulary (Vinck, 2009b). Multiple laboratory breakthroughs are fighting for relevance by inventing their own visions of the future. All these strategies have used nanotechnology's gift for narratives in order to attract research funds. As a result of these strategies and struggles for significance, 'nanotechnology' has become an umbrella term for untold numbers of technologies in multiple realms of application. And it is indeed impossible to limit its definition to strictly technical terms or to explain what nanotechnologies consist of without referring to narratives.

The value of the approach of expectations in terms of rational myth or folk theories is that it does not take into account feasibility or plausibility of the envisioned technology beforehand – a myth is true because one believes it. This anthropological perspective means that nanotechnology or convergence are what actors believe it is, what they hope, dream, fear or bet it will be. It allows for the study of expectations' performativity.

In the end, it has to be acknowledged that scientific promises form a literary genre of their own (Rip, 2008). As a consequence, it is necessary to mix cultural and literary analysis with social studies of science. Both bring critical methods that, when combined, allow for the analysis and critique of scientific promises. It leads to discuss the narratives, including the iconography and repertoires, as well as the *mise-en-scène* that are employed. It is also critical in identifying the models of science–society relations in order to characterize the imaginary that is implied. This kind of analysis also holds the potential to introduce visions and expectations into discussion; it helps scientific promises to be denaturalized, compared and contested.

Finally, the so called convergence, beyond its role of narrative artefact, is to be understood as the convergence of actors of research and innovation towards particular goals. Examples abound. The success or failure in building networks of actors depends, then, on multiple 'tests of strength in various arenas' that promises undergo (Joly, 2010).

Discussion

Our 'risk society', and the pace of the economy of scientific promises, are generating a lot of concerns for the future. As a result, we are presented with multiple possible futures, sometimes diametrically opposed. The self-fulfilling prophecy that converging technologies will solve all our problems and bring prosperity stands in opposition to prophecies emphasizing precaution and sustainable development and to dystopian views of nanotechnology leading to a future of totalitarian control. As others have already noticed, the proliferation of possible futures 'makes the future more rather than less opaque' (Brown and Michael, 2003: 6). And the proliferation of scientific promises makes science policy, research and innovation, more opaque. As with issues of risk and uncertainty, there is a tendency for technoscientific promises to tell a different story to publics and stakeholders than is told behind the scenes. The difference between what is actually considered plausible by technologists and promoters and what the public and politicians are led to believe is a potential source of problems (Nowotny and Felt, 1997; Swierstra and Rip, 2007). This problem has been explicitly addressed for example in an official report with regard to 'nanomedicine' (NANOMED Roundtable, 2010).

'Science is supposed to be the main beneficiary of its promises, but it can also be one of its first victims' reflected a geneticist. Following the opinion of many scientists, the time spent on competition for research funds and the means necessary to do so has become a vast drain on resources. These same scientists often acknowledge their fear of an erosion of trust in science among the public as a result of promises becoming too commonplace. These concerns are linked with the fact that large sections of the public perhaps know more about science through its promises and narratives than anything else (e.g., facts, theories, history).

One of the key societal issues raised by the proliferation of possible futures has to do with society's understanding of progress and technological change. Short-term competitiveness and financial wherewithal dictate technological innovation and undermine collective faith in a better future. Today, promises seem decoupled from reality and disenchanting because they are performed mainly in the service of short-sighted goals. These conclusions and discussions are adding to Isabelle Stengers's plea for 'slow science' (Stengers, 2013).

The naturalization of technological change contained in commonplaces like 'If we don't invest in this technology, others will and take our place' remains the dominant paradigm. It tends to prevent other futures from being imagined and to avoid discussion of science and research policy. Using the example of GMO in agri-biotech, Joly (2010) illustrates that in order to promote a technology, one has to overshadow other possible options, and to create some irreversibility. The naturalization of scientific and technological change conveyed by the 'NBIC Converging Technologies' for instance obscures the choices to invest in a particular science and technology over others.

Among the public, including scientists and engineers, it is often assumed that knowledge progresses serendipitously. But technosciences and their societal issues are rather the result of defined priorities. So who decides these priorities? How do we bridge scientific promises and societal expectations? Science and technology policy is often still decided within very narrow circles. It then follows that putting scientific promises into discussion opens up a space for critique, reflection and public debate. It favours the participation of citizens in science and technology 'upstream', that is, before research trajectories become irreversible. It invites exploration of convergence by participative problematization of technoscientific research.

Finally, for sociologists of science as well as for ethicists and researchers in the field of ELSI (ethical, legal and social issues of EST), there is also ethics at stake, since engaging with scientific promises may help grant them importance and reinforce their legitimacy. Exploring the ethics of a technoscience while ignoring the manufacture of ambivalence could lead one to take part in this ambivalence. The opportunity for 'speculative ethics' is put into question when it means the exploration of ethical issues of scientific promises taken at face value (Nordmann and Rip, 2009). Social studies of science have a role to play in conducting research on scientific promises and articulating it with ethical considerations. Promises must be decoupled from the cognitive authority of science so as to open up space for reflection and debate. The empowerment of people and stakeholders, including scientists, to greet new promises with the requisite critical skills must be encouraged.[4]

Notes

1 This contribution builds on recent publications and discussions in the social studies of science. The interviews of the four medical geneticists have been conducted at the Science–Society Interface of the University of Lausanne. The case studies of

nanotechnology, the analysis of science policy reports, and the reflection about the governance and the promises of technoscience have taken place within two projects, *Internorm*, platform of participation of civil society organisations to international standardisation (University of Lausanne, 2009–13), and *Nanopublic*, a project dedicated to interdisciplinary research and the promotion of dialogue between nanotechnology and society (Science–Society Interface, since 2008).
2 *New York Times*, by Gina Kolata, 3 April 2012, p. D5.
3 Rip, 2008.
4 Special thanks to Alain Kaufmann, Arie Rip, Christopher Coenen, Claude Joseph, Dominique Vinck, Gaïa Barazzetti, Stephan Elkins, Tiziana Boni.

References

Bensaude-Vincent, B. (2009) *Les vertiges de la technoscience. Façonner le monde atome par atome*. Paris: La Découverte.
Berube, D. M. (2005) *Nano-Hype. The Truth behind the Nanotechnology Buzz*. Amherst, NY: Prometheus Books.
Borup, M., N. Brown, K. Konrad and H. van Lente (2006) 'The Sociology of Expectations in Science and Technology', *Technology Analysis & Strategic Management* 18(3–4): 285–98.
Brown, N. (2003) 'Hope against Hype – Accountability in Biopasts, Presents, and Futures', *Science Studies* 16(2): 3–21.
Brown, N. and M. Michael (2003) 'The Sociology of Expectations: Retrospecting Prospects and Prospecting Retrospects', *Technology Analysis and Strategic Management* 15(1): 3–18.
Brown, N., B. Rappert and A. Webster (2000) *Contested Futures: A Sociology of Prospective Techno-Science*. Aldershot: Ashgate.
Chateauraynaud, F. (2005) *Nanosciences et technoprophéties. Le nanomonde dans la matrice des futurs*. Paris: GSPRH-EHESS.
Coenen, C. (2007) 'Utopian Aspects of the Debate on Converging Technologies', in G. Banse, A. Grunwald, I. Hronszky and G. Nelson (eds), *Assessing Societal Implications of Converging Technological Development*. Berlin: Sigma.
——(2010) 'Deliberating Visions: The Case of Human Enhancement in the Discourse on Nanotechnology and Convergence', in M. Kaiser, M. Kurath, S. Maasen and C. Rehmann-Sutter (eds), *Governing Future Technologies: Nanotechnology and the Rise of an Assessment Regime* (Sociology of the Sciences Yearbook 27). Heidelberg: Springer, pp. 73–87.
Drexler, E. K. (1986) *Engines of Creation: The Coming Era of Nanotechnology*. New York: Anchor Books Edition.
Felt, U. and B. Wynne (eds) (2007) *Taking European Knowledge Society Seriously*. Report of the Expert Group on Science and Governance, Luxembourg, Directorate General for Research, European Commission.
Henneman, L., E. Vermeulen, C. G. van El, L. Claassen, D. R. Timmermans and M. C. Cornel (2012) 'Public Attitudes towards Genetic Testing Revisited: Comparing Opinions between 2002 and 2010', *European Journal of Human Genetics* 21(8): 793–9.
Joly, P.-B. (2010) 'On the Economics of Techno-Scientific Promises', in M. Akrich, Y. Bethe, F. Muniesa and Ph. Mustar (eds), *Débordements, Mélanges offerts à Michel Callon*. Paris: Presse des Mines, pp. 201–21.

Joly, P.-B., A. Rip and M. Callon, (2010) 'Re-inventing Innovation', in M. Arentsen, W. van Rossum and A. Steeng (eds), *Governance of Innovation. Firms, Clusters and Institutions in a Changing Setting*. Cheltenham: Edward Elgar, pp. 19–32.

Jones, R. (2008) 'The Economy of Promises', *Nature Nanotechnology* 3: 65–6.

Kaiser, M., M. Kurath, S. Maasen and C. Rehmann-Sutter (eds) (2010) *Governing Future Technologies: Nanotechnology and the Rise of an Assessment Regime*. (Sociology of Sciences Yearbook). Heidelberg: Springer.

Kaufmann, A., C. Joseph, C. El-Bez and M. Audetat, (2010) 'Why Enrol Citizens in the Governance of Nanotechnology?', in M. Kaiser, M. Kurath, S. Maasen and C. Rehmann-Sutter (eds), *Governing Future Technologies: Nanotechnology and the Rise of an Assessment Regime* (Sociology of Sciences Yearbook 27). Heidelberg: Springer, pp. 201–15.

Kjolberg, K. L. and F. Wickson (2010) *Social Perspectives on Nanoscale Sciences and Technologies*. Singapore: Pan Stanford Publishing.

Maestrutti, M. (2011) *Imaginaires des nanotechnologies. Mythes et fictions de l'infiniment petit*. Paris: Vuibert.

Miège, B. and D. Vinck, (2012) *Les masques de la convergence. Enquêtes sur sciences, industries et aménagements*. Paris: Editions des archives contemporaines.

Milburn, C. (2002) 'Nanotechnology in the Age of Posthuman Engineering: Science Fiction as Science', *Configurations* 10: 261–95.

Mody, C. C. M. (2004) 'Small, But Determined: Technological Determinism in Nanoscience', *International Journal for Philosophy of Chemistry* 10(2): 99–128.

NANOMED Round Table (2010) *A Report on the Nanomedicine Economic, Regulatory, Ethical and Social Environment*. Seventh Framework Programme.

Nelson, M. R., et al. (2012) 'An Abundance of Rare Functional Variants in 202 Drug Target Genes Sequenced in 14,002 People', *Science* 337(6090): 100–4.

Nordmann, A. (2004) *Converging Technologies – Shaping the Future of European Societies*. Report, European Communities.

——(2007) 'If and Then: A Critique of Speculative Nanoethics', *NanoEthics* 1: 31–46.

Nordmann, A. and A. Rip (2009) 'Mind the Gap Revisited', *Nature Nanotechnology* 4: 273–4.

Nowotny, H. and U. Felt (1997) *After the Breakthrough: The Emergence of High-Temperature Superconductivity as a Research Field*. Cambridge: Cambridge University Press.

Pollock, N. and R. Williams (2010) 'The Business of Expectations: How Promissory Organisations Shape Technology and Innovation', *Social Studies of Science* 40(4): 525–48.

Renn, O. and C. M. Roco (2006) 'Nanotechnology and the Need for Risk Governance', *Journal of Nanoparticle Research* 8: 153–91.

Rip, A. (2006) 'Folk Theories of Nanotechnologies', *Science as Culture* 15: 349–65.

——(2008) 'Scientific promises as a literary genre', paper presented at the session Future Science, Present Fiction, 4S/EASST International Conference, Rotterdam.

Roberts, N. J., J. T. Vogelstein, G. Parmigiani, K. W. Kinzler, B. Vogelstein and V. E. Velculescu (2012) 'The Predictive Capacity of Personal Genome Sequencing', *Science Translational Medicine* 4(133):133–58.

Roco, M. C. and W. S. Bainbridge (2002) *Converging Technologies for Improving Human Performance. Nanotechnology, Biotechnology, Information Technology and Cognitive Science*. NSF/DOC-sponsored report. Arlington, VA: National Science Foundation.

Ruef, A. and J. Markard (2010) 'What Happens after a Hype? How Changing Expectations Affected Innovation Activities in the Case of Stationary Fuel Cells', *Technology Analysis and Strategic Management* 22(3): 317–38.

Schummer, J. (2010) 'From Nano-Convergence to NBIC-Convergence: "The Best Way to Predict the Future Is to Create It"', in M. Kaiser M. Kurath, S. Maasen and C. Rehmann-Sutter (eds), *Governing Future Technologies: Nanotechnology and the Rise of an Assessment Regime* (Sociology of Sciences Yearbook). Heidelberg: Springer: 57–71.

Selin, C. (2007) 'Expectations and the Emergence of Nanotechnology', *Science, Technology and Human Values* 32(2): 196–220.

Stengers, I. (2013) *Une autre science est possible! Manifeste pour un ralentissement des sciences*. Paris: La Découverte.

Swierstra, T. and A. Rip (2007) 'Nano-ethics as NEST-ethics: Patterns of Moral Argumentation about New and Emerging Science and Technology', *NanoEthics* 1: 3–20.

Tutton, R. (2012) 'Personalizing Medicine: Futures Present and Past', *Social Science & Medicine* 75: 1721–8.

van Lente, H. (1993) 'Promising technology: The dynamics of expectations in technological development', Ph.D. thesis, Twente University, Delft: Eburon.

Vinck, D. (2009a) *Les Nanotechnologies*. Paris: Le Cavalier Bleu.

——(2009b) 'Le passage au nano. Comment un laboratoire s'arrange avec des incertitudes majeures', in Y. Chalas, C. Gilbert and D. Vinck (eds), *Comment les acteurs s'arrangent avec l'incertitude*. Paris: Editions des Archives Contemporaines, pp. 23–39.

4 Logics of convergence in NBIC and personal genomics

Christopher Groves

Introduction

'Technological convergence' is a concept that can be used analytically in very different senses. It also makes its presence felt in different ways in the promissory rhetoric that surrounds emerging technologies, and with diverse consequences. As an analytical concept, convergence comes in weaker and stronger forms. One common 'weaker' version views it as the combination of one or more different technologies in order to perform a given task (as in the case of e-book readers) with enhanced functionality. In such cases, convergence is driven by function and intention. A 'stronger' form of convergence has been used to understand the emergence of enabling technologies upon which a range of technological capabilities may depend. What drives convergence in this sense is a dynamic that lies deeper than designers' intentions or particular functions, one rooted in an epistemological compatibility between the research programmes associated with particular technologies or, in some cases, in the ontological basis of the technologies themselves.

This stronger sense of convergence, although derived from concepts employed by innovation scholars to describe and explain the evolution of technologies, has been taken up and used in ways that go beyond either description or explanation. Whereas it has been used in innovation studies to understand past instances of technological change, it has been deployed in a future-oriented, promissory context by technological 'enactors' (e.g. researchers, representatives of industry, technology strategists and so on) (Garud and Ahlstrom, 1997). As enactors' rhetoric about nanotechnology, biotechnology, information technology and cognitive science convergence (nano-bio-info-cogno, or NBIC) in particular demonstrates, the (often implicit) use of a strong concept of convergence to help articulate the promise of a technology or technologies can play a performative and also a political role. It can help to legitimate and mobilize support for particular visions of the future, thus activating these technological expectations in the present as attractors for funding and catalysts for the development of research programmes (Brown, 2003). Like technological expectations more widely, convergence can help create both material and symbolic realities here and now. The symbolic efficacy of convergence can be particularly evident in how it can help define what counts as legitimate ethical and political debate about converging technologies (Nordmann, 2007; Hanson, 2011).

In this essay, I distinguish the two aforementioned analytical senses of convergence from a third, which I isolate by examining the future visions constructed by personal genomics (PG) companies around their products and services. The vision of convergence implicit in these visions differs markedly from either weak or strong technological convergence. Specifically, it has two mutually supporting sides that mark it as a concept of what might be called socio-technical, rather than technological, convergence. On the one hand, technological capabilities such as genomic scans, methods for their interpretation, and networked social media (Lee and Crawley, 2009) are projected as converging. On the other, the social roles of patients and health professionals are also interpreted as convergent (Prainsack *et al.*, 2008). Each side of the convergence, technological and social, is a necessary condition of the other. I develop this socio-technical concept of convergence by contrasting it with the strong sense of convergence deployed within NBIC rhetoric, and show how it remains promissory in nature, while also preserving a sense of the contingency of the future, contrasting with the technological–determinist image of the future that inhabits NBIC rhetoric – an image that is derived from the strong analytical concept of convergence.

I suggest that, although the term 'convergence' is not explicitly used by PG enactors, the concept of convergence that can nevertheless be traced implicitly at work within their rhetoric echoes certain analytical themes within Science and Technology Studies (STS), and that of 'co-construction' in particular (Bijker *et al.*, 2012). Finally, in the Conclusion, I examine how the promissory use of convergence within NBIC and PG rhetoric, despite the different logics of convergence at work, serves a similar function in either case. Convergence serves as a kind of master narrative (Jasanoff, 2008) in each case for making sense of uncertainty, for constructing a knowable future that resonates with technologically mediated patterns of affect, emotion and desire, and which helps to frame debates about the appropriate ways to regulate and govern emerging technologies.

'Weak' and 'strong' analytical concepts of convergence

The weaker form of convergence, as noted above, is driven by design needs and intended functions. An example is the combination of books and display technologies ('electronic paper') to produce e-readers like Kindles (Murphy, 2004: 90). Here, the functionality of a book is seen as enhanced by the novel combination of two established, socially embedded technologies. Modifications to these technologies may be necessary, but they provide affordances to each other that enable them to work together.

The second, strong interpretation of convergence depicts devices and artefacts with different technological functions increasingly becoming reliant on the same 'enabling' technological capabilities, as novel and more effective forms of these capabilities are developed. An example is the evolution, since the 1970s, of telecommunications networks built on digital hardware and software systems which allow voice, image and data to all be transmitted using the same infrastructure (Duysters and Hagedoorn, 1998). Whereas the first kind of convergence is a process shaped by pre-existing purposes and explicit intentions, the second kind is theorized as being driven by the evolution of enabling technological capabilities, and the way in which they may, without conscious direction, increase the combinatory potential of technologies that rely on them. As in the case of telecommunications, this is a process that may involve both material and conceptual re-engineering. Reconstructing infrastructures on which different functions rely often goes hand in hand with conceptual shifts that may create new connections between innovation processes and research programmes in different technological or scientific fields. These shifts may be driven by the development of new metaphors that allow the ontological basis of technological capabilities – the nature of the 'things' they manipulate – to be re-conceptualized. A shift of this kind, it has been argued, contributed to convergence in telecommunications by unifying theories of communication across different media, based on the concept of information provided by information theory (Hilbert and Cairo, 2008). The development of such connective metaphors can help to organize what Sheila Jasanoff calls a 'master narrative', a 'compelling and frequently repeated story about the way the world works that takes hold of our imaginations and shapes the ways in which we perceive reality, as well as our possibilities for collective action' (2008).

For supporters of the strong concept, however, what drives convergence is innovation itself, the production of new artefacts that support new capabilities (Duysters and Hagedoorn, 2008). New artefacts instigate or continue evolutionary dynamics that conceptual work may then reinforce or speed up. Future possibilities opened up by innovation are seen as being seized upon and activated in the present, assisted by conceptual re-engineering. The material and conceptual convergence of technologies may be viewed as having value in itself, over and above particular artefacts and capabilities. In such cases, strong convergence is viewed, not just as adding value to existing technological capabilities but as an evolutionary dynamic that opens up for exploration new territories of future value.

This future promise of unforeseen potential drives how concepts of strong convergence have been used explicitly by a variety of technology enactors and supportive commentators involved with strategic nanotechnology policy, particularly as part of the USA's National Nanotechnology Initiative (NNI). Some of these actors have promoted NBIC convergence as a strategic vision for nanotechnology and the other fields included in the acronym, describing it as, at once, an inevitable outgrowth of current trends and as a strategic societal goal (Gordijn, 2006). Their vision of convergence is closely related to other perspectives on the future horizons of nanotechnology first articulated in the late 1990s, as described in the US National Science and Technology Council's brochure

Shaping the World Atom by Atom in 1999 (Nordmann, 2004), and in the writings of supporters of visions of 'molecular manufacturing', precision control over the structure of matter made possible by new nanoscience techniques:

> Total (or near total) control over the structure of matter will intrinsically revolutionise our lives. No aspect of our daily living – let alone other technologies – will remain untouched.
> (Dinkelacker, 2002: 2)

The harmonies between these visions arise from how they extend informational metaphors already extant in molecular biology (Garcia-Sancho, 2007) to inorganic structures, thus 'informationalising matter' itself (Kearnes, 2008). This use of informational metaphors supports a hypothesis that is articulated as the justification for developing nanoscience as an essentially interdisciplinary research programme – namely, that macro-scale organization in nature is based upon information-bearing structural patterns at the nanoscale that guide processes of self-organization (Nordmann, 2004). Discovering these informational 'building blocks' will, it is hoped, create the basis for perfecting technical control over natural processes, leading to a point in the future where natural constraints on human volition can largely be overcome.

A research programme based on this extension of informational metaphors is forcefully expressed by champions of NBIC convergence, M. C. Roco and W. S. Bainbridge, who have promoted the strategic value of this vision in a series of publications since the early 2000s. They see research in nanoscience and nanotechnology as driving the development of enabling techniques and technologies for applications that link biotechnology, information technology and cognitive science, creating in the process new interdisciplinary research initiatives that will see researchers 'combining research methods and results across these provinces' (Roco and Bainbridge, 2002: 2). These initiatives will in turn lead to novel applications in manufacturing technologies, neuro-engineering for cognitive enhancement, life extension and other radical and potentially highly socially disruptive applications, and will support the reconceptualization of nature across these scientific domains comprising 'closely coupled, hierarchical systems' (ibid.: 14) through which the ontological 'unity of nature' will finally be understood through the exploration of the nanoscale (ibid.: 281). The discovery of the unity of nature provides a 'master narrative' for NBIC research and innovation alike, one that echoes visions of the 'unity of science' with origins reaching back through the Standard Model of particle physics to the Enlightenment and earlier (Dupuy, 2007):

> The unity of nature at the nanoscale provides the fundamental basis for the unification of science, because many structures essential to life, computation and communication and to human thought itself are based on phenomena that take place at this scale.
> (Roco and Bainbridge, 2003b: 54)

As Jose Lopez shows, the extension of extant informational metaphors in NBIC convergence supports a narrative of the future based upon a complex, though disguised, temporal logic, in which radical futures promises allow an equally radical retroactive extension of technological determinism as an explanatory logic for historical change. This narrative posits a future *novum*, a discovery that will mark the point at which multiple streams of research and technological development condense into a revolutionary moment of acceleration. Beginning from the assumption that this *novum* will demonstrate the reality of the unity of nature, the narrative then uses the concept of the unity of nature retroactively to interpret the motive forces behind the whole of human history. History is reconceptualized in technologically determinist terms as a series of human successes and failures in understanding the unity of nature, and in achieving technical control over it (Lopez, 2004), which have reshaped human societies. Ethical and political debates over inequality and other issues within human history to date will, once the *novum* is passed, be shown to have only been epiphenomena of our limited ability to remodel the world and ourselves. With the master narrative of the 'unity of nature' to guide us, social and ethical questions become viewable from the present as engineering problems, a matter of '[c]hanging the societal "fabric" towards a new structure' (Roco and Bainbridge, 2002: vii).

In NBIC narratives, a strong technological determinist concept of convergence is thus used to articulate the future promise of current research and innovation. It is also, however, used to legitimate this future promise by retrospectively baptizing all human technological achievements as partial successes in revealing and exploiting the informational unity of nature. These past achievements have, of necessity, led us to the present, from which the convergent future, as the destiny of technological humanity, can be glimpsed. By utilizing the concept of strong convergence from innovation theory to, in effect, construct a theory of history, NBIC narratives disguise, as Lopez (2004) and Sparrow (2007) have argued, the political role of promises and expectations in driving and legitimizing a research programme, the ultimate results and outcomes of which remain subject to a huge degree of uncertainty. By adopting a particular interpretation of technological convergence from innovation theory, NBIC convergence constructs a radically disruptive future vision based on speculative interpretations of current research. These interpretations are then extended via the use of informational metaphors into a master narrative of the discovery of the unity of nature. NBIC convergence then presents this narrative as the only story in town when it comes to understanding the collective future of humanity, with the aid of a totalizing interpretation of history.

Promise, uncertainty and affect

The role of expectations and promises in the NBIC narrative requires closer examination. Research in the sociology of expectations has explored how technological expectations, defined as 'real-time representations of future technological situations and capabilities' (Borup *et al.*, 2006), act on processes of innovation in the present. Researchers in this field have explored the extent to which expectations and promises can be performative, helping to actually constitute future trajectories of technological evolution in the present. Expectations articulate a vision of a future, a 'future present' (Adam and Groves, 2007) that provides an imaginary vantage point from which phenomena here and now can be viewed in, as it were, the future perfect tense. In the case of NBIC, by the time the *novum* arrives, all foregoing achievements in nanoscale engineering 'will have been' the necessary stepping stones towards its realization. Expectations and promises thus help to stabilize the contested meaning of scientific artefacts in the present, presenting them as precursors of an imagined future. By stabilizing the meaning of technoscientific artefacts in relation to a particular future vision, they can also help to stabilize them materially, shaping the direction of technological evolution by linking it to specific research programmes and the resources that underpin them.

The political significance of expectations thus lies in the extent to which they are tools for domesticating an uncertain future. They perform this function by helping to construct and reproduce regimes of truth within which statements about the future (including ethical and political ones) can be treated as reliable or legitimate. In doing this, they exploit particular forms of expertise (technology forecasting, futures studies, innovation economics), invoking for themselves the epistemological legitimacy associated with formalized ways of representing narratives about the future, such as cost–benefit analysis, innovation scoreboards, integrated assessment models and so on. However, the epistemic effects of expectations cannot be separated from values, affect and emotion: regimes of truth are inseparable from regimes of hope (Brown, 2005), but as well as hope, uncertainty may awaken fear, desire or anxiety. These affective and emotional components of future orientation constitute, for the individuals who are involved in the circulation and reproduction of expectations, elements of a lived future (Adam and Groves, 2007: 128) through which affiliation to particular promises and expectations is mobilized.

The evaluative, affective and emotional dimension of NBIC rhetoric is registered in the analysis provided by Bechmann and colleagues (2009), who affirm that strong convergence is deployed within NBIC narratives as a symbol of a 'new renaissance' accompanied by 'world peace, universal prosperity and an evolution to a higher level of compassion and accomplishment' (citing Roco and Bainbridge, 2003a: 140–2). The promise of NBIC appears to be nothing less than the total domestication of uncertainty through technical control. The confirmation and exploration of the unity of nature through interdisciplinary NBIC science will transform the human condition. From these hardly unambitious imaginings it is evident that a complex mix of hope, fear and desire is implicit in the production and reproduction of NBIC. The sociology of expectations suggests that the intensity of technological determinism present in the NBIC narrative may be directly proportional to the degree of contingency to which it, through the very grandiosity of its central promise of triumph over uncertainty, exposes itself. In Brown's (2005) terms, the vast breadth of the hope it seeks to evoke pulls with it a powerful desire for a regime of truth in which hope can be shown to be more than just hope.

Convergence of a third kind: personal genomics

NBIC narratives rhetorically exploit the analytical concept of strong convergence to mask their own promissory nature, using it to suggest that their projected future is, in fact, inevitable. We now turn to personal genomics (PG), in order to explore a form of convergence narrative that is based, in contrast, on the co-dependence of social and technical systems and of the contingency of their co-evolution. In this way, the difference between the strong conception of convergence and the one that can be traced working implicitly within the rhetoric of PG enactors mirrors the distinction between technological determinism and the social construction of technology as competing theories within science and technology studies. Convergence within PG rhetoric retains a fragile, contingent character – and, as a result of having this character, has its own strategic, political uses.

Since 2007, a number of companies (particularly in the USA) have offered genetic susceptibility testing for a variety of common health conditions. These tests represent a new wave of mass-market genetic testing, distinct from previous generations of susceptibility testing that were based on testing a limited number of genes for monogenic conditions. These new tests build on socio-technical developments such as the genome-wide association study (GWAS), which explores correlations between the incidence of particular variations at single points on an individual's genome (single nucleotide polymorphisms, or SNPs) and the presence of particular phenotypical traits (including pathological ones). After subjecting customers' biosamples (typically, saliva or material from a buccal swab) to a scan of areas where significant variation is known to occur (rather than full genome sequencing), personal genomics companies compare the results with data from a library of GWAS studies. Proprietary algorithms are then used to produce risk profiles from this data for a variety of health conditions. Unlike earlier generations of susceptibility tests, personal genomics tests are subject to a significant degree of regulatory ambiguity, which has stimulated concern over when and how these tests may be used, how reliable they may be, and what clinical value (if any) they may possess (SACGHS, 2010).

The vision of convergence articulated in PG (generally without using the word 'convergence', which has to date only been explicitly used by analysts studying the field, e.g. Lee and Crawley, 2009) largely lacks the kind of determinist logic that characterizes NBIC narratives. The future projected by PG enactors' rhetoric is one that promises the transformation of healthcare, but recognizes that, at the same time, what is needed in order to create this future is the building of coalitions across various socio-technical and social domains, as well as technical advances. Social movements and interest-based

Logics of convergence 51

alliances, as well as research programmes, are required to make it a reality. In what is arguably its most developed form, as articulated by the company 23andMe, this PG narrative represents the steps necessary for bringing about this projected future as (a) the convergence of genomics, genome interpretation services and networked social media, and (b) enlisting customers as co-producers of research and healthcare, and enrolling healthcare professionals as enablers of new forms of patient autonomy.

The convergence being implicitly articulated here is not the weaker variety analysed above, in which increased efficiency is sought through new combinations of existing technologies. Nor is a technologically determinist logic invoked, in which revolutions in enabling technologies are represented as the inevitable destiny of technological evolution. Promises and expectations of a radical future are explicitly made a key part of PG rhetoric, with this future represented as one in which it is technological capabilities and social practices that will converge, mutually conditioning each other. The master narrative of PG is that of 'personalized medicine', through which is represented a future in which genomic information is used to tailor drugs to individuals and thus avoid side effects, and – most relevant for the business models of PG companies – to profile genetic risks of developing rare or common health conditions, thus enabling physicians to prescribe prevention programmes and customers to change risky health behaviours, where appropriate. This envisioned goal is presented as only being possible through the co-evolution of social practices, on the one hand, and technologies on the other. This marks a clear difference between the promissory rhetoric of PG on the one hand and that of NBIC on the other. It also distinguishes the visions presented by PG companies from earlier future visions associated with genomics, in which genetic determinism was a key trope (Fortun, 1999).

Despite this avoidance of determinism, the master narrative woven as part of PG rhetoric depends, as does NBIC, upon the extension of informational metaphors originating in molecular biology, interlocking with what has been called the 'informationalisation of healthcare' (Nettleton and Burrows, 2003). The expectations which drive this narrative often concern connections between genetic information and autonomy, made via imagery of mapping and prophecy, through which genomics is envisioned as providing the information needed to avoid particular futures and to realize others (Groves, 2013). Many more radical versions of the visions of personalization feature a strong participatory element focused on individual access to and informed interpretation of data (Weston and Hood, 2004), a vision developed furthest by advocates of self-quantification (Cline, 2009; Wolf, 2010), in which the narrative of personalized medicine is also that of the 'democratisation of data' (MacDonald and Walton, 2009). Such radically participatory visions of personalization view technological artefacts and capabilities as tools for creating new forms of sociality, communities of inquiry that may make possible new forms of counter-power to challenge 'the generalities of official knowledge' (Wolf, 2010), creating 'a revolution in the balance of power between patients and today's healthcare systems' (Smarr, 2011). At the same time, new, technologically enabled social networks and their emergent practices are seen as making possible the development of new technological capabilities through collective experimentation and 'tinkering'.

What is notably absent both from more mainstream and from radical personalization narratives is any expectation that the development of technological capabilities alone will unlock a personalized medicine future. What we find instead are instances where key loci for change are identified as being essential to progress towards personalized medicine, without these loci being either technical objects or technological capabilities.

For example, on 16 December 2010, 23andMe published a press release containing the following:

> One of 23andMe's research goals is to identify novel pharmacogenetic associations using web-based phenotyping of efficacy and toxicity ... If this project is successful in yielding replications, it will set the stage for rapid, well-powered and cost-effective research on many medications.

The project in question utilized an opt-in system for customers, whereby those using 23andMe's services are invited to register for web-based surveys as part of a programme subsequently entitled '23andWe'. In this specific case, social media infrastructure provided by the company and a new concept of 'crowdsourced' research, made possible by social sharing of data, served as the basis for a pharmacogenetic study. Decisions made by individual consumers to purchase tests are seen as contributing to genomic research for the public good – in the manner of Adam Smith's invisible hand. What is more, this desire of customers to act on and exploit personal genetic information for its personal rather than strictly clinical utility is expected to catalyze transformations in *clinician–patient relationships*. These relationships, and the pursuit of personal utility, are seen by PG companies as constituting two important loci for change upon which personalized medicine will depend. I examine these in the rest of this section.

Expectations within the PG industry that broad social and regulatory acceptance of the personal utility of PG testing will be vital for progress towards personalized medicine have been examined by Groves and Tutton (2013). Personal utility, Groves and Tutton argue, has been rhetorically positioned by PG companies as a new regulatory object (Lezaun, 2006), separate from traditional concepts of clinical utility. By 'personal utility' is meant benefits of the information produced by genome scans that cannot be reduced to the utility of test results for improving clinical decisions (Foster *et al.*, 2009). Information about genetic risk may, it has been argued, have positive effects on a consumer's sense of identity, on their sense of responsibility and control over their future, on 'family dynamics', and on coping strategies. This can exist, it is argued, even in the absence of clinical utility (Hsu *et al.*, 2009), and can be produced through 'bottom-up' research facilitated by social media.

Logics of convergence 53

The case for considering personal utility as an appropriate object for regulatory attention was made at a seminar convened by federal agencies in December 2008. Invitees included medical academics, geneticists, representatives from other federal bodies, the Personalized Medicine Coalition (PMC), public health institutions, along with 23andMe, and other companies such as deCODEme and Navigenics. A report from the seminar gave qualified support to the idea of personal utility as an appropriate regulatory object, noting that stakeholders should work together to 'explore individuals' and population subgroups' notions of perceived personal utility' and to 'assess whether personal utility may impact measures of CU [clinical utility]' (Khoury et al., 2009: 7). The support given was only qualified due to the difficulties of measuring something as inherently diverse ad subjective as personal utility. Nonetheless, the report recognizes that these benefits may be a reason for regulators not to over-regulate personal genomics, a point also stressed in an earlier report from the same seminar (Fraker and Mazza, 2008: 14, 18, 40).

The second leverage point resides in the transformation of patient–clinician relationships. 23andMe stressed the 'empowering' effect of the personal utility of genomic information in testimony to a House of Representatives Committee on Energy and Commerce hearing on personal genomics on 22 July 2010:

> Customers empowered with this information have made lifestyle changes aimed at reducing their risks of developing disease and have provided information to their doctors to aid in diagnosis and treatment. These actions have improved and even saved lives.
>
> (Gould, 2010)

The future contribution of PG to personalized medicine is seen as being dependent upon patients collaborating more with their doctors as well as in autonomously developing new ways to exercise more control over health behaviours that amplify any existing genomic risks. A further shift in social relationships is expected to affect the genomic research infrastructure itself across public and private domains, connecting consumers of personal genomics to scientists performing association studies, as in the 23andWe research programme mentioned above:

> It starts with self-quantification, but those people who are measuring themselves can contribute their own data – genetic, medical, behavioral and environmental – to science.
>
> (Cline, 2009)

> we believe in empowering individuals by helping them understand their genetic make-up and actively engaging them in the development of new ways to accelerate research.
>
> (23andMe, 2008)

This survey of regulatory objects and patient–clinician relationships as leverage points for progress towards personalized medicine suggests that PG rhetoric embeds within its master narrative specific expectations regarding the convergence of social and technical elements. This convergence, it is implied, is key to the production of personalized medicine as a new material and symbolic reality. Around personal utility and clinician–patient relationships, enactors' rhetoric sets out how innovation in PG is dependent upon the co-construction of social and technical elements implicated within each of these leverage points. The technological production of risk profiles makes possible new socialities, while at the same time requiring active participation from customers in the production and interpretation of data and its use in healthcare. The 'democratization of data' is not simply presented as a freeing of genetic information, but as the creation of the social infrastructure needed to interpret its meaning and to put it to work. For NBIC proponents, the massive technological, economics and social transformations expected to result from informationalising matter are solely a matter of technical change – the first domino which, when pushed, topples all the others. By contrast, from the standpoint of personal genomics, convergence is an inherently complex, social process of 'informationalising medicine'. It is based on the exploitation of 'big data' (Howe *et al.*, 2008), which is expected to render individual health futures legible and controllable. But this will require social change motivated from *within* social relationships, in order to create the relationships, technological capabilities and practices needed to make work data over into an object that is of genuine utility.

Conclusion

In this chapter, I have explored three different ways of understanding technological convergence. The first, weak form is manifest in intentional combinations of existing technologies. NBIC narratives, as we have seen, exploit a particular analytical concept of strong technological convergence, which deals with fundamental technical changes within enabling technologies, and identifies efforts at conceptual 're-engineering' that accompany such changes. The promissory rhetoric of these narratives develops convergence in a technologically determinist direction, subsuming under its internal logic processes of social change as well as technological evolution.

By contrast, the master narrative of PG implies a concept of convergence that represents personalized medicine as the co-construction of social relationships and technological capabilities. Yet this narrative remains one of technological convergence, in so far as these co-constructed assemblages are viewed as the 'enabling technologies' for personalized medicine, a set of tools for making the future legible and actionable. This implicitly co-constructionist perspective is, as we noted above, closer to social constructivist theoretical tendencies within STS than it is to technological determinism.

PG's promissory dimension is similar to that of NBIC narratives, however, in so far as it is politically significant. NBIC narratives are stories about the strategic priorities that must be fulfilled in order to achieve a particular technologized vision of human destiny. As such, they are deeply connected with anxiety and hope in the face of the uncertainties to which an intrinsically uncertain future exposes human beings. They construct uncertainty in particular ways in order to tame it, proposing particular actions that are required from the US federal government, regulatory agencies, scientists and businesses so that opportunities may be exploited and risks avoided. The NNI provides the main arena in which these strategies can be settled, institutionalizing linear views of innovation.

PG, too, constructs uncertainty in particular ways in order to domesticate it and enlist technology 'selectors' (Garud and Ahlstrom, 1997) in supporting specific technologies. The contingency that attaches to the individual and group agency that companies represent as essential to the evolution of PG make this evolutionary potential inherently fragile. The concepts of personal utility and changing clinician–patient relationships have been used by companies to articulate the future promise of PG. Where the determinism of NBIC is mirrored in the grand strategy approach of the NNI, the implicit co-constructionism of PG is mirrored in the arguments of its enactors about dangers of over-regulation. Where each new technical advance is seen by proponents of NBIC as another inevitable progressive step towards a revolutionary future, PG rhetoric sees progress as open, fragile and dependent on 'intelligent' regulation, as well as on experimentation and 'tinkering' that may expand the uses and utility of the technologies on which PG relies. A tone of anxiety was evident in PG companies' public representations to the US House of Representatives Committee on Energy and Commerce in July 2010, one perhaps appropriate to the fragile future constructed in their wider rhetoric.

None of this means that strategic variation is impossible in NBIC or PG convergence rhetoric. For example, it is as easy to find individual examples of NBIC advocates arguing that progress is imperilled and fragile due to constraints on funding or to the public's aversion to risk (Sparrow, 2007) as it is to find personal genomics companies representing their industry as one in which '[t]he train may have left the station, but it's never too late to get on board' (Hsu et al., 2009: 2). However, these kinds of rhetorical tactics represent local improvisations within broader strategies in which the uncertain future is constructed in particular ways and not in others (McGoey, 2012), in the hope of eliciting responses from other social actors that fall in behind enactors' master narratives of convergence, rather than undermine them.

References

23andMe (2008) '23andMe launches web-based Personal Genome Service™ outside U.S.', *23andMe Media Centre*, 22 January. Available at: http://mediacenter.23andme.com/press-releases/23andme-launches-web-based-personal-genome-service-outside-u-s [accessed 19 July 2013].

——(2010) '23andMe receives funding from the National Institutes of Health to evaluate web-based research on the genetics of drug response', *23andMe Media Centre*, 16 December. Available at: http://mediacenter.23andme.com/press-releases/23andme-receives-funding-from-the-national-institutes-of-health-to-evaluate-web-based-research-on-the-genetics-of-drug-response [accessed 19 July 2013].

Adam, B. and C. Groves (2007) *Future Matters: Action, Knowledge, Ethics*. Leiden: Brill.

Amato, I. (1999) *Nanotechnology: Shaping the World Atom by Atom*. Washington, DC: National Science and Technology Council.

Bechmann, G., C. Büscher and S. Pfersdorf (2009) 'Converging Technologies and NBIC as Topics for "Knowledge Politics"', in *Knowledge Policies and Politics and the NBIC Field*, pp. 91–103. FP6 Project, Knowledge Politics and New Converging Technologies: A Social Science Perspective. Available at: www.converging-technologies.org.

Bijker, W. E., T. P. Hughes, T. Pinch and D. G. Douglas (2012) *The Social Construction of Technological Systems: New Directions in the Sociology and History of Technology*. Cambridge, MA: MIT Press.

Borup, M., N. Brown, K. Konrad and H. van Lente (2006) 'The Sociology of Expectations in Science and Technology', *Technology Analysis and Strategic Management* 18: 285–98.

Brown, N. (2003) 'Hope against Hype – Accountability in Biopasts, Presents and Futures', *Science Studies* 16: 3–21.

——(2005) 'Shifting Tenses: Reconnecting Regimes of Truth and Hope', *Configurations* 13(3): 331.

Cline, E. (2009) '23andme ... and me: Interview with Esther Dyson on 24 June'. Available at: http://spittoon.23andme.com/2009/12/07/23andme%e2%80%a6-and-me-interview-with-esther-dyson [accessed 12 July 2013].

Dinkelacker, J. (2002) *Transition to Tomorrow: Social Institutions at the Threshold of Nanotechnology's Molecular Epoch*. Palo Alto, CA. Available at: http://sunarcher.org/jamie/pubs/Transition_To_Tomorrow_2002.pdf.

Dupuy, J. P. (2007) 'Some Pitfalls in the Philosophical Foundations of Nanoethics', *Journal of Medicine and Philosophy* 32(3): 237–61.

Duysters, G. and J. Hagedoorn (1998) 'Technological Convergence in the IT Industry: The Role of Strategic Technology Alliances and Technological Competencies', *International Journal of the Economics of Business* 5(3): 355–68.

Fortun, M. (1999) 'Projecting Speed Genomics', in M. Fortun and E. Mendelsohn (eds), *The Practices of Human Genetics*. Dordrecht: Springer, pp. 25–48.

Foster, M., J. N. Mulvihill and R. Sharp (2009) 'Evaluating the Utility of Personal Genomic Information', *Genetics in Medicine* 11(8): 570–4.

Fraker, M. and A.-M. Mazza (2008) 'Personal genomics: Establishing the scientific foundation for using personal genome profiles for risk assessment, health promotion, and disease prevention'. Paper presented at the Joint NIH–CDC Seminar, Bethesda, MD. Available at: http://epi.grants.cancer.gov/phg/docs/personal_genomics.pdf [accessed 15 August 2011].

Garcia-Sancho, M. (2007) 'The Rise and Fall of the Idea of Genetic Information (1948–2006)', *Genomics, Society and Policy* 2: 16–35.

Garud, R. and D. Ahlstrom (1997) 'Technology Assessment: A Socio-cognitive Perspective', *Journal of Engineering and Technology Management* 14(1): 25–48.

Gordijn, B. (2006) 'Converging NBIC Technologies for Improving Human Performance: A Critical Assessment of the Novelty and the Prospects of the Project', *Journal of Law, Medicine and Ethics* 34(4): 726–32.

Gould, A. (2010) Testimony of Ashley C. Gould, General Counsel, 23andMe, Inc. 'Direct-to-consumer genetic testing and consequences to the public health', Committee on Energy and Commerce, Subcommittee on Oversight and Investigations, U.S. House of Representatives. Available at: http://democrats.energycommerce.house.gov/documents/20100722/Gould.Testimony.07.22.2010.pdf [accessed 20 June 2011].

Groves, C. (2013) 'Road-maps and Revelations: On the Somatic Ethics of Genetic Susceptibility', *New Genetics and Society* 32(3): 264–84

Groves, C. and R. Tutton (2013) 'Walking the Tightrope: Expectations and Standards in Personal Genomics', *BioSocieties* 8(2): 181–204.

Hanson, V. L. (2011) 'Envisioning Ethical Nanotechnology: The Rhetorical Role of Visions in Postponing Societal and Ethical Implications Research', *Science as Culture* 20(1): 1–36.

Hilbert, M. and O. Cairo (2008) 'From the binary digit to technological convergence'. Paper presented at the WSEAS International Conference. Proceedings. Mathematics and Computers in Science and Engineering, 22–24 July, Heraklion, Greece.

Howe, D., M. Costanzo, P. Fey, T. Gojobori, L. Hannick, W. Hide and S. Y. Rhee (2008) 'Big Data: The Future of Biocuration', *Nature* 455(7209): 47–50.

Hsu, A. R., J. L. Mountain, A. Wojcicki and L. Avey (2009) 'A Pragmatic Consideration of Ethical Issues Relating to Personal Genomics', *American Journal of Bioethics* 9(6–7): 1–2.

Jasanoff, S. (2008) 'The Facts of the Matter', *How Science Speaks Truth to Power – Experts and Politics*, Presentation at Cornell University, 2 September, Ithaca, NY.

Kearnes, M. (2008) 'Informationalising Matter: Systems Understandings of the Nanoscale', *Spontaneous Generations* 2(1): 99–111.

Khoury, M. J., C. M. McBride, S. D. Schully J. P. A. Ioannidis, W. G. Feero, A. C. Janssens and J. Xu (2009) 'The Scientific Foundation for Personal Genomics: Recommendations from a National Institutes of Health-Centers for Disease Control and Prevention Multidisciplinary Workshop', *Genetics in Medicine* 11(8): 559–67.

Lee, S. S. and L. Crawley (2009) 'Research 2.0: Social Networking and Direct-to-Consumer (DTC) Genomics', *American Journal of Bioethics* 9(6–7): 35–44.

Lezaun, J. (2006) 'Creating a New Object of Government', *Social Studies of Science* 36(4): 499–531.

Lopez, J. (2004) 'Compiling the Ethical, Legal and Social Implications of Nanotechnology', *Health Law Review* 12(3): 24–7.

MacDonald, C. and N. Walton (2009) 'Personal Genomics: Democratization, or Empowerment, or "Something"', *American Journal of Bioethics* 9(6–7): 46–8.

McGoey, L. (2012) 'Strategic Unknowns: Towards a Sociology of Ignorance', *Economy and Society* 41(1): 1–16.

Murphy, P. C. (2004) 'Books Are Dead, Long Live Books', in D. Thorburn, H. Jenkins and B. Seawell (eds), *Rethinking Media Change: The Aesthetics of Transition*. Cambridge, MA: MIT Press, pp. 81–93.

Nettleton, S. and R. Burrows (2003) 'E-scaped Medicine? Information, Reflexivity and Health', *Critical Social Policy* 23(2): 165–85.

Nordmann, A. (2004) 'Nanotechnology's Worldview: New Space for Old Cosmologies', *IEEE Technology and Society Magazine* 23: 48–54.

——(2007) 'If and Then: A Critique of Speculative NanoEthics', *Nanoethics* 1: 31–46.

Prainsack, B., J. Reardon, R. Hindmarsh, H. Gottweis, U. Naue and J. E. Lunshof (2008) 'Personal Genomes: Misdirected Precaution', *Nature* 456(7218): 34–5.
Roco, M. C. and W. S. Bainbridge (2002) 'Converging Technologies for Improving Human Performance: Integrating from the Nanoscale', *Journal of Nanoparticle Research* 4(4), 281–95.
——(2003a) *Converging Technologies for Improving Human Performance: Nanotechnology, Biotechnology, Information Technology and Cognitive Science*. Dordrecht: Kluwer.
——(2003b) *Nanotechnology: Societal Implications – Maximizing Benefit for Humanity*. Arlington, VA: National Science Foundation.
Secretary's Advisory Committee on Genetics Health and Society (SACGHS) (2010) *Direct-to-Consumer Genetic Testing*. Bethesda: Department of Health and Human Services.
Smarr, L. (2011) 'Quantified Health', *Strategic News Service*, 30 September. Available at: www.stratnews.com/recentissues.php?mode=showandissue=2011-09-29 [accessed 30 September 2011].
Sparrow, R. (2007) 'Revolutionary and Familiar, Inevitable and Precarious: Rhetorical Contradictions in Enthusiasm for Nanotechnology', *Nanoethics* 1: 57–68.
Weston, A. D. and L. Hood (2004) 'Systems Biology, Proteomics, and the Future of Health Care:? Toward Predictive, Preventative, and Personalized Medicine', *Journal of Proteome Research* 3(2): 179–96.
Wolf, G. (2010) 'The data-driven life', *New York Times*, 28 April. Available at: www.nytimes.com/2010/05/02/magazine/02self-measurement-t.html [accessed 6 June 2014].

5 The convergence of direct-to-consumer genetic testing companies and biobanking activities
The example of 23andme

Heidi C. Howard, Sigrid Sterckx, Julian Cockbain, Anne Cambon-Thomsen and Pascal Borry

Introduction

Direct-to-consumer (DTC) genetic testing (GT) involves the advertising and/or the offer of genetic tests directly to the public. Available tests include both health or disease-related testing (which will be the focus of this chapter) as well as non-health-related testing, such as for paternity or genealogy and ancestry. The offer of health or disease-related DTC testing has been of particular interest to stakeholders, since they are often provided without any involvement from a health care professional (HCP). This relatively novel model of provision and the commercial basis of the offer, along with the new types of testing offered (i.e. genome-wide testing), have made this phenomenon a popular topic of debate for different stakeholders including geneticists, ethicists and policy makers. Along with the sale of genetic tests, some DTC genetic-testing companies are also creating their own databases or biobanks of genetic information based on the data from consumer genotypes and phenotypes in order to conduct research. In essence, companies are creating biobanks or databanks very similar to the more traditional genetic biobanks established by universities and/or hospitals. In this way the research goals of companies converge with those of university researchers in that they both want to find gene–disease associations that can help in the understanding and/or prediction of the development of diseases. However, the biobanks created by DTC GT companies and the subsequent research performed, cause a blurring of the limits around our traditional understanding of consumers and research subjects. They highlight important questions with respect to the adequacy of consent and the issue of transparency and trust in research. In this chapter we aim to describe the phenomena of DTC GT for health or disease-related testing and the biobanking and research activities of some of these companies, using the company 23andme as our main example. We further discuss the consequential problems with respect to consumers consenting to research, as well as with potential problems with transparency and trust.

Direct-to-consumer genetic testing

What is it?

Direct-to-consumer (DTC) genetic testing (GT) has been defined as the offer and/or advertising of genetic tests directly to consumers outside of the traditional health care system and often without the intermediary of an HCP (Genetics and Public Policy Center, 2006, 2008). That being said, the discussion about DTC genetic testing has revolved mostly around the model of a direct *offer* without the involvement of an HCP (Vorhaus, 2012b). Admittedly, more and more companies are now making it mandatory for consumers to consult with an HCP before ordering a test and/or receiving the results (Howard and Borry, 2012a). Although, strictly speaking, DTC genetic testing is not new, the phenomenon really gained popularity with a number of private for-profit companies emerging in 2007–08 (Francke, 2013). Since then, the field of DTC GT has been very dynamic and populated with a heterogeneous group of companies and services (Ducourneau *et al.*, 2013). In the past couple of years, many new companies have appeared, others have closed or stopped their DTC services (i.e. deCode, Navigenics) (Vorhaus, 2012a). Yet other companies have changed the ways in which they operate, or have altered the types or the list of tests they have on offer. Furthermore, different types of tests are sold by different companies. Although most companies study the actual DNA in very similar ways, the different tests (are meant to) provide information about different types of traits or phenotypes; for instance some genetic tests provide information about the chances of developing a certain disease whereas other tests will provide information about non-disease-related phenotypes like hair colour. Furthermore, the test results obtained from DTC GT companies can be used for different purposes or ends. Some tests can provide results that can be used to diagnose diseases or to provide a probability of developing a disease while a person is still asymptomatic. Other test results can offer information about a person's capability to metabolize certain drugs; these are referred to as pharmacogenetic or pharmacogenomic tests. DNA test results can also be used for ancestry or genealogy purposes. Some companies claim to offer tests that can help in finding the perfect cream for your skin (dermatogenetics) and others claim to use DNA testing results in romantic matchmaking (http://scientificmatch.com). Moreover, companies sell tests in different ways or in different packages. Some companies sell one single test for one trait, others sell numerous tests for a group of traits (i.e. cardiovascular associated traits), and yet other companies perform genome-wide testing (also known as genome scanning) whereby hundreds of thousands to millions of different genetic variants (often single nucleotide variants (SNPs)) are tested and results are returned for a large number of different traits. One of the most well-known companies which sells such testing, and the main example used in this chapter is 23andme (23andme a).[1] 23andme is a privately owned company founded in 2006 by Linda Avey, Paul Cusenza, and Anne Wojcicki (23andme c). It has received 'funding from several prominent technology and health science companies, strategic angel investors and venture capital firms, including Yuri Milner, Johnson & Johnson Development Corporation (NYSE: JNJ), MPM Capital, the Roche Venture Fund (Swiss: RO.SW), Google Ventures (NASDAQ: GOOG), and New Enterprise Associates, among others' (23andme c). By September 2013, 23andme had 400,000 consumer genotypes in their database (Fast Company). As for other DTC GT companies, in August 2011, the Genetics and Public Policy Center (USA) published a list of 27 DTC GT companies, the large majority of which operate from the USA (Genetics and Public Policy Center). Although a bit outdated (indeed, a number of the companies listed no longer sell genetic tests DTC) it does give a good overview of the different types of companies and the phenotypes for which testing is offered.

Much of the ethical, legal and social issues debates have centred around companies that sell genome-wide testing, however it is important to remember that all companies that advertise or offer genetic testing directly to consumers (whether it be for one or hundreds of genetic variants) are included in DTC activities. This is especially important to keep in mind when thinking of guidelines, best practices and potential ways to better regulate DTC GT activities. Given the large amount of heterogeneity in this area, it has been mentioned that a one-size-fits-all way of regulating these activities may not be the best approach (Hudson *et al.*, 2007). For our purpose in this chapter focusing on the biobanks or databases produced from consumers' samples and data, this is also important, since the possibilities of further uses of such data may be strongly influenced by the way in which consumers/research participants are recruited and the purposes of the original tests purchased.

What are some of the ethical and social issues of DTC genetic testing?

The potential benefits of offering genetic testing DTC include increased access to genetic testing for the public, increased awareness and education regarding genetics and genomics, as well as support for consumer and individual autonomy (Berg and Fryer-Edwards, 2008). Furthermore, companies highlight that consumers can participate more actively in the creation, storage and protection of their personal genetic information and in this way there may be a greater guarantee of privacy (Foster and Sharp, 2008). Some companies also claim that if consumers know their genetic risks for developing certain disorders this will encourage them to modify their lifestyle in order to achieve better health (Howard and Borry, 2009).

On the other hand, the concerns surrounding DTC genetic testing include the absence of individualized medical supervision (Hogarth, Javitt and Melzer, 2008) as well as absence and/or the quality of pre- and post-test genetic counselling (Wade and Wilfond 2006). The consent procedures as well as the potentially inappropriate genetic testing of minors have also been called into question (Borry *et al.*, 2009, 2010). Concerns have also been voiced over the degree of protection for privacy (Anastasova and Rial-Sebbag, 2012; Knoppers, 2010) and the possibility of overburdening the public health care system (McGuire and Burke, 2008). Finally, the concerns on which we focus in this chapter revolve around the research and biobanking activities of DTC GT companies (Howard, Knoppers and Borry, 2010).

Whether perceived as a positive or negative phenomenon, the advent of DTC GT services has, at the very least, incited stakeholders in genetics to face some important questions regarding the established standards, and the ideals strived for in genetics, both in the clinic and in research. How should genetic tests be offered and by whom? Where do different genetic tests fit into our view of medical services and consequently what are the best practices, guidelines and regulations for genetic tests? Should these apply to all genetic testing or should different guidelines be established for different subsets of tests? Do we believe that DNA ancestry testing necessitates the same standards as genetic testing for diseases; and if not then why? Furthermore, given this new DTC context, do we want to rethink the acceptable standards for the provision of genetic information and genetic counselling before and after testing, for informed consent in research, for transparency regarding conflicts of interest, and for genetic testing in children? These are all issues that stakeholders in genetic testing (HCPs, patients, lawyers, ethicists, policy makers, consumers, etc.) need to address seriously, given the current offer of DTC genetic testing services.

DTC genetic testing: different levels of convergence

First, the type of convergence we make reference to here is the joining or coming together of traditionally different realms or activities in genetics, namely consumer services and research activities. As such, we do not discuss the convergence of technologies that are coming together to make new (better) technologies, but rather the use of the same technologies (for genome testing) used for two different purposes by companies: selling a genome service to individuals, and the use of this genomic information for biomedical research. We focus on how this convergence of company activities confers on (some) clients (i.e. those who take part in research) the dual and potentially very different roles of consumer and researcher subject. We highlight the fact that this convergence of activities creates uncertainties regarding the types of procedures and institutions that are (or can) be put in place to responsibly support the research activities of companies. In particular, we discuss the impact of this convergence of activities on the process of consent, the need for transparency and its (potential) effects on public trust.

The phenomenon of DTC genetic testing joins together aspects from typically different and relatively distinct realms. For example, these activities bring together the commercial, health care and research spheres. Although these spheres have been joined together in the past (i.e. in pharmaceuticals, imaging technologies), specifically for the field of genetics, this is the first instance whereby all three realms are present on the individual level (as a consumer or patient or research subject). There are two main areas of convergence in this context, each resulting in the blurring of different boundaries and each raising a number of questions and concerns.

The first area of convergence (which we will only briefly mention here as it is not the focus of this chapter) is created by the fact that DTC GT companies offer some health and disease-related genetic tests similar to those offered in the traditional clinical setting but in a commercial context, often without an HCP. Moreover, companies selling these tests claim that they are not selling medical services but purely informational services (Cambon-Thomsen, 2009). The confusion or blurring that may arise at the individual level is because the person purchasing DTC GT is not necessarily engaging in genetic testing as a patient or proband, which is the case in the traditional clinical setting, but as a consumer. It has been said that this type of commercial offer of genetic testing is catering to the 'worried well' as opposed to patients or probands who have family or clinical histories indicative of the need for genetic testing. Yet, these 'non-patient' customers will still be receiving information that may provide potentially important indications about their health. A main question this raises is whether the individual obtaining the genetic test should be 'treated' as a patient or consumer (Anastasova and Rial-Sebbag, 2012; Chassang, Rial-Sebbag and Cambon-Thomsen, 2011). An important factor here is the fact that some companies which sell genome-wide testing offer the possibility of purchasing genealogical testing and/or health testing. Hence a consumer who originally meant to purchase only these services for genealogical purposes and who purchases the 'complete package' (of genealogy and health testing) may not fully realize that they may receive potentially serious health information regarding disease or reproductive health information. Related to this is the issue of regulation of, and guidelines for, these activities. There is also a blurring and potential double standard with respect to how DTC GT services should be viewed: are they health services or commercial/recreational services? Should commercial companies offering DTC genetic tests have to follow clinical guidelines already in place for clinical genetics, or should they be allowed to function outside of this realm? And, if so, why?

Second, and the focus of this chapter, is the convergence of these companies' offer of genetic testing with their biobanking/research activities. At the individual level, a person can be a consumer when he/she clicks the 'order' button on a company website; that person can then become, with minimal extra steps, a research subject since companies use consumers' genotyping data to conduct disease–genotype association studies. Hence there is a convergence of commercial and research activities that is new in the field of genetics. As stated by Tobin *et al.* (2012: 833), 'The subtle nature of this transition (from customer to research participant) has implications both for consumers and for the research enterprise in general.' This convergence raises important questions with respect to the issues of consent, transparency and public trust in genetic research. We now elaborate further on these themes.

DTC GT companies as biobanks and their research activities

Biobanks have been defined as an 'organized collection of biological samples and associated data' (Cambon-Thomsen, 2004: 866). There are many different types of biobanks with variations including (but not limited to) the collection size, the main purpose of the collection (clinical vs. research vs. forensic), the method of participant recruitment, the degree of accessibility to samples and data, and the types of institutions (public or private) in charge of and/or funding the biobanks (ibid.). Biobanks have become a mainstay of biomedical research, including genetic and genomic research. As stated by Cambon-Thomsen, as far back as 2004, the prevalence of biobanks was increasing in all countries. Cambon-Thomsen attributed this increase mainly to the following three factors: (1) more biomedical research has meant an increase in the number of people who could benefit from biobanks enabling such research; (2) larger collections increase the scientific value of biobanks; and (3) the range of applications of databanks is larger and this is true especially for genomics and population genomics databanks (ibid.).

Some DTC genetic-testing companies performing genome-wide testing are also conducting research with consumer data. Indeed, what has paved the way to make this possible is the fact that technologies have improved to the point where hundreds of thousands of SNPs can be relatively quickly and easily genotyped; companies offering only single gene/locus tests or a small number of SNP tests would not be able to build up the genotype information that would make such a databank as valuable for research. It should also be noted that although the amount of data generated by genome-wide testing is not equivalent to that generated by sequencing an entire genome (i.e. 3 billion nucleotides or data points), this process nonetheless provides a large amount of data, which, when studied with phenotypic information could, indeed, provide the material necessary to fuel a large number of studies in the future. Even if companies do not retain the saliva or physical DNA sample of consumers, they retain consumers' genotyping data and collect phenotypic data, and as such can be considered databanks (Howard, Knoppers and Borry, 2010). In this way, some DTC genetic-testing companies are creating a type of biobank for research like those traditionally found in the academic or commercial settings (ibid.). That being said, criticism and concerns regarding data obtained through online communities, especially regarding the self-reporting of phenotypes have been raised; these include selection bias, information bias, and confounding (Janssens and Kraft, 2012).

Using 23andme as an example, the company departs from the traditional model and practice of biobanks in at least two ways. First, the company, by default, returns genotyping results, since this is the product or service actually purchased by the consumer to begin with. Second, as well as using an explicit invitation to take part in research without having to purchase testing (www.23andme.com/pd), the company also uses an alternative recruitment method. Once a consumer has purchased DNA testing, the company sends them a request to fill out a questionnaire relating to phenotypes (i.e. diseases, health status, etc.) and invites them to be part of research. So for those in this group, one could say that they are, in an indirect way, paying to take part in research. As described in an original research article by 23andme reporting associations for common traits using consumer data, the authors describe the 23andme cohort as follows:

> Data for these studies was collected within a research framework wherein research participants, derived from the customer base of 23andMe, Inc., a direct-to-consumer genetic information company, consented to the use of their data for research and were provided with access to their personal genetic information ... They were then given the option of contributing phenotype data via a series of web-based surveys. The result is a single, continually expanding cohort, containing a self-selected set of individuals who participate in multiple studies in parallel.
> (Eriksson *et al.*, 2010)

We have summarized above the main characteristics of the DTC genetic testing phenomenon, described the basics of research biobanks, and given an example of a DTC GT company which undertakes research activities. We have also briefly discussed two ways in which DTC GT represents a convergence of activities at the individual level. First, the coming together of clinical tests offered in a commercial context blurs the line between consumer and patient. Second, the commercial offer of genetic tests and the research activities of companies blurs the line between consumer and research participant. Within the latter realm of convergence, we expand below on the issues of consent, transparency and trust specifically relating to the issue of commercialization of research results. Although we recognize how intertwined these issues are, for the sake of clarity we present consent under one heading and transparency and trust under another.

The issue of consent

The issue of consent in biomedical research is a topic regularly addressed in the literature when discussing the ethical, legal and social aspects. As stated by Hansson (2005), 'The requirement to obtain informed consent is the key principle of medical ethics and medical law. It represents respect for the moral authority of patients and research subjects' (ibid.: 415). Cambon-Thomsen specifies that 'Although it does not in itself protect an individual, informed consent allows individuals to exercise their fundamental right to decide whether and how their body, its parts and the associated data will be used in research' (Cambon-Thomsen, 2004: 869). Although the principle of informed consent is widely recognized 'its translation into practice encounters difficulties in the case of large-scale biobanks, long-term use of samples or data, or numerous exchanges' (ibid.). It is true that biobanks (even outside DTC GT companies) raise their share of ethical concerns over consent. The ongoing debate over the appropriateness of use of broad versus specific consent is a good example of issues that have yet to be resolved (Cambon-Thomsen, Rial-Sebbag and Knoppers, 2007). However, the positive aspect of this issue (even if unresolved) is the fact that it is being debated openly and among many stakeholders (albeit mainly academics). On the other hand, the issue of consent for research activities conducted by DTC GT companies has received relatively little attention, and this is, in part why we believe it merits particular attention here.

The first publication of original research results by 23andme using their 'consumer' biobank data in *PLOS Genetics* (Eriksson et al., 2010) did raise some ethical concerns. The journal itself published an editorial addressing the issues of institutional review, data access and consent in the same issue as the research article by 23andme (Gibson and Copenhaver, 2010). Regarding the consent process, the authors were concerned that the use of technical terms could lead to poor understanding by participants and participants potentially not fully understanding which data would be published. They also raised the question of whether the consent document met the standard legal requirements. They concluded that the consent document met the minimum legal criteria and that there was 'sufficient information for participants to realize they are participating in genetic research' (ibid.). They also stated that although the consent form contained ambiguities, they found no evidence that it was inadequate. The authors nonetheless concede the possibility for different views on their conclusions as they state that these may not 'sit well with some, perhaps many, readers' (ibid.). Around the same time as these articles appeared in *PLOS Genetics*, an article was published discussing the research activities conducted by companies selling DTC genetic testing (Howard, Knoppers and Borry, 2010). This article highlighted the blurring of the line between research subject and consumer and focused on the discussion of two questions: (1) are consumers aware that their data are being used for research? (2) Even if they are aware, is the informed consent adequate?

Based on the analysis of informed consent forms and privacy policies on the websites of five DTC genetic-testing companies that offered genome-wide testing, the authors suggested that some companies could be more transparent about the fact that they conduct research with consumer data (ibid.). Furthermore, contrary to the editorial in *PLOS Genetics* (Gibson and Copenhaver, 2010) based on a particular 'research edition' offered by 23andme at the time, the authors suggested that even when a company is being relatively up front about conducting research, there could be confusion for consumers about the research being conducted (Howard, Knoppers and Borry, 2010).

Moreover, the authors questioned whether, even if consumers are aware of companies' research activities, the consent obtained by companies was adequate when compared to that required by volunteers in similar genetic research in more traditional settings (i.e.: academic or public biobanks). Based on public views regarding their informational desires for the use of tissue or blood for purposes other than those planned at initial collection as well as the research guidelines from the Organisation for Economic Co-operation and

Development (OECD), Howard and colleagues concluded that there was little evidence that the consent process for consumers was fully informed (ibid.).

Tobin and colleagues (2012) also commented on the use by DTC GT companies of consumer data for research. In doing so they discussed four different companies, and highlighted issues relating to autonomy with respect to companies conducting possible human subject research (which was the case for three of the companies studied). They studied company policies to verify whether informed consent for research was explicitly requested. If companies requested this explicitly, the authors concluded that at the least, the principle of autonomy was being supported. According to the authors, this was not the case for one of the companies studied since their policy did not allow consumers to choose whether or not they would be part of research: 'customers cannot avoid authorizing the use of their genetic data for research' (ibid.: 834). The authors concluded that this company policy was 'eroding' the autonomy of customers and that with respect to informed consent, 'it is appropriate for these companies to take seriously the responsibility of educating their customers, not only about the interpretations of the genotyping data they are purchasing, but also about their dual status as customers and as research participants' (ibid.: 835).

More recently, Janssens and Kraft (2012) also raised apprehensions about the claims made by 23andme and other initiatives that recruit research participants through online communities. They are concerned that such initiatives may overstate claims regarding the value of research results obtained through this research model and that this 'may impinge on individual autonomy and informed consent'.

Moving beyond the general issue of consent for research by DTC GT companies, Sterckx and colleagues (2012) focused on the issue of patents and commercialization of research results by DTC GT companies. The authors point out that based on the reactions of some customers to the patent announcement for 'Polymorphisms associated with Parkinson's Disease' (PD) (US Patent No. 8187811), it would appear that the information given about this issue in the company's consent process is 'ethically inadequate' (2012: 385). The quotes left by some customers show that they were unaware that 23andme were planning these patents:

> I would not have talked my mother and others in my support group into participating if I had understood this was going to be a profit driven enterprise. I believe 23andMe has been disingenuous in gathering a free database.
> (http://blog.23andme.com/news/announcements/
> announcing-23andmes-first-patent)

> I had assumed that 23andMe was against patenting genes and felt in total cahoots all along with you guys. If I'd known you might go that route with my data, I'm not sure I would have answered any surveys.
> (http://blog.23andme.com/news/announcements/
> announcing-23andmes-first-patent)

Also related to consent (and transparency, discussed below), both Sterckx et al. (2012) and Allyse (2013) discuss the wording used by 23andme in documents such as the terms of service and the consent form. In both articles, the authors point out that the word patent is not used explicitly with respect to the results (Allyse, 2013). Sterckx and co-authors highlight that the word is only used with respect to the information presented to users. 'The wording by no means makes it clear that patents would be sought for the research results' (Sterckx et al., 2013: 384). The company does state that customers will 'acquire no rights in any research or commercial products that may be developed by 23andme' and that 'If 23andme develops intellectual property and/or commercializes products or services, directly or indirectly, based on the results of this study, you will not receive any compensation' (ibid.: 384). Hence, as stated by Allyse, the company does 'inform customers that the commercialization may occur' (2013: 68) but in agreement with the conclusions of Sterckx and colleagues 'based on the reaction of its community members, simple disclosure does not appear to relieve the burden' of obtaining fully informed consent (ibid.: 69).

Sterckx et al. go on to say that the reactions to the Parkinson's disease patent requested by and granted to 23andme, 'show the limitations of the use of a vague and unclear consent when there are potential commercial applications. We do not suggest that 23andMe has done the research without consent; rather the issue is whether the consent extended to cover the patenting of results' (2013: 385).This is to be considered also in the light of a European study on biobanks and the public's perceptions which states 'Even those who wanted to support biomedical research were reluctant to support research for commercial gain, or without societal benefit. People associate private interests with inequitable distribution of benefits, biased research aims and potential misuse of personal data' (Gaskell et al., 2012: 16).

Thus, the issue of consent has specific resonances in the realm of DTC GT derived biobanks and empirical studies of perceptions and opinions of customers of DTC GT companies who have also 'become' research participants should be conducted. Admittedly, it may not be so simple to predict or even obtain the (actual) attitudes of consumers who may integrate or blur both their satisfaction regarding the service and information provided to them as consumers with their considerations regarding their status as research participants.

Transparency and public trust

Another concern associated with the research activities and the consequences of DTC GT companies creating biobanks and conducting research with consumer data relates to transparency and trust; two issues which are also intimately linked to informed consent discussed above. Sterckx and co-authors (2013) have looked specifically at these two issues with respect to patents taken out by DTC GT companies. Using 23andme as a case study, the authors discuss the patent for 'polymorphisms associated with Parkinson's disease' which the company announced on its website the day before the patent was granted (ibid.: 382). The authors discuss how the announcement that the company applied for this patent sparked controversy with some of its consumers. As is evident from the quotes presented above, some customers were not fully aware that the company would apply for patents when they agreed to participate in research. The authors also address the issues of lack of transparency and the consequent potential loss of trust in such a situation, focusing primarily on the fact that the company was not fully transparent about the fact that they were applying for patents; part of this is intimately related to informed consent (discussed above). Another part of the transparency issue has more to do with the way in which the company has been inviting customers to take part in research, the company's rhetoric and the way they have of presenting themselves to the public, which in some ways may contradict some of the their research goals, namely applying for patents, and the consequent commercialization of research results.

Sterckx *et al.* highlight how the company only communicated information about the patent on their website the day before the patent was granted (in 2012) while the application for the patent was filed in 2009, and the research results on which the patent is based were published in 2011. They comment on this delay and its potential contradiction with what the company claims to value:

> The delay in drawing attention to the patent application seems odd, given that 23andMe even recently underlined that 'open dialogue about complicated issues like patents is important' and that it wanted to be 'as open as possible about our intentions, including letting people know about our patent and why we have filed it.
>
> (Sterckx *et al.*, 2013: 384)

Moreover, the authors highlight that these patent applications stand in contrast to 'the open, altruistic, science-driven, and common-good image that 23andMe has clearly been trying to create' (ibid.). As described by Tutton and Prainsack, 23andme has 'the explicit goal of "revolutionising" research by encouraging growing numbers of people to engage in it not only as participants but also as drivers of research and consumers of its findings' (2011: 1082). The 23andme research initiative is further described by Linda Avey, cofounder of 23andme, as a 'Do-it-yourself Revolution in Disease Research' (http://blog.23andme.com/tag/linda-avey). Indeed, 23andme has been inviting consumers to take part in research with rhetoric citing their research as different because it is a 'community' effort, in which participants would have some 'say' or input into the research conducted: 'This is research of, by and for the people, directed and advanced by you' (www.youtube.com/watch?v=WfI62N8pOkE).

Sterckx and co-authors go on to say that academic researchers, including those who use biobanks, also apply for patents, but this is not a problem per se. The authors explain that the problem with 23andme is that the company promised:

> to build something with communal resources, building it, and then claiming ownership, and (potentially) charging for access. The implied

suggestion that the result would be a community good was misleading. An analogy might help: a company in a village next to a river says: 'the village needs a bridge, give us the wood and we'll build it'; the wood is given; the bridge is built; but the company charges a toll. In both cases, the contributors (the research participants/villagers) did not realize that contribution did not guarantee public ownership. The fault lies not in 23andMe/the builder owning the result, but in the lack of transparency in the appeal for the necessary contributions. The contributors did not understand what was going on until after their contribution was made, and, had they understood, many might not have contributed. Having been misled, contributors may in future be less likely to contribute to the attainment of public goods, fearing that they might not be public after all, which, in turn, might lead to a more morally impoverished community.

(Sterckx *et al.*, 2013: 384)

Did some customers lose trust in the company after the patent announcement? Based on quotes like the following from some customers reacting to the patent announcement, it would appear so:

this is simply crowd-sourced greed. As a longtime 23andMe customer, this patent is extremely disappointing and alarming. Our family is done with your service.

(http://blog.23andme.com/news/announcements/
announcing-23andmes-first-patent)

Why is this loss of trust important? The trust among current and future participants, including patients, is 'essential for the success of biobank research' (Hansson, 2005: 415). For persons deciding whether or not to participate in research, trust in their doctor or the researcher or institution are major reasons to accept an invitation to participate in research (Gaskell *et al.*, 2012). A loss of trust in the research activities of a commercial genetic company could lead to less public participation (Bussey-Jones *et al.*, 2010) in research and consequently hamper genetic research in general. As Allyse states:

like the academic research community before them, commercial entities that fail to ensure honest and open communication with their customers about their true intentions and motivations may find it increasingly hard to build up biobanks with the number of samples needed to do genuinely useful research.

(2013: 69)

Thus, transparency and trust are major components of (future) biobanking and the specific balance to reach for DTC GT companies may not have been addressed yet in its full dimension but should be such that research participants' trust is not undermined.

Discussion and conclusion

We have addressed above some of the concerns related to the convergence of companies offering genetic testing directly to consumers and their research or biobanking activities, namely surrounding consent, transparency and trust. It would appear that the positioning of these companies' activities outside the traditional health care system yet offering tests related to health, and their dual role as biobankers/researchers has placed them in a type of 'no man's land', where stakeholders have been hesitant, or simply have not been able to agree on how to deal with these activities. Indeed, it has been previously mentioned that the offer of genetic testing DTC for variants related to health has created, to a certain extent, a double standard with regard to the criteria expected to be met for the offer of such testing in the traditional clinical setting. Specifically, this has been mentioned with respect to the lack of involvement of an HCP (Howard and Borry, 2012a, 2012b) as well as in the possibility of testing in minors (Howard, Avard and Borry, 2011). Could it also be said that such a double standard exists for research being conducted by DTC GT companies when compared to more traditional genetic or genomic biobank research? Research by DTC GT companies is not the only way traditional genetic research is changing; other fundamental changes are also happening with respect to where research takes place and who is conducting it. For example, participant- or patient-centric research initiatives like 23andwe, Genomera and DIYGenomics are becoming more popular. These initiatives put users or research participants in a position where they supposedly have a greater say over what happens in research projects. Although this has some positive aspects, ethical concerns also exist over consent and transparency in research. Hence, in the interest of protecting research participants and respecting their autonomy in these new research contexts, as well as trying to safeguard public trust in research, these questions and double standards should be addressed presently. With respect to the biobanking and research activities of DTC GT companies, the academies of science (European Academies of Science Advisory Council (EASAC)) and medicine (Federation of European Academies of Medicine (FEAM)) affirm that:

> While there is some evidence for a possible useful contribution by DTC testing in identifying novel gene–disease associations (e.g., in Parkinson's disease32), the provider–consumer relationship risks circumventing the normal regulatory controls for research and might undermine public confidence in clinical research more generally. It is imperative that a framework for good practice is developed by companies for the conduct of research in this setting. When desiring to use data for research, companies must seek proper, additional, consent, specifying the handling of samples and information derived, as discussed in the ESHG recommendations.
>
> (Fears and Ter Meulen, 2013: 705)

As with the academic research community, in order to recruit participants in an ethical manner, and merit and maintain participants' confidence and trust, DTC GT companies should strive to obtain ethically sound informed consent from participants and they should be transparent about their research activities and goals. This is not only the responsible approach with respect to consumers and research participants, but it could also help to distinguish the blurred boundaries created by the convergence of their commercial and research activities such that stakeholders will have a better idea of how to best consider these companies in the genetic testing and genetic research landscapes.

Acknowledgements

HCH is supported by an FP7 Marie Curie career development award IEF-GA-2010–276136. This work was also supported by the French Public Health Research Institute (IRESP) and the EU contracts BBMRI-LPC, 'BBMRI – Large Prospective Cohorts' Grant agreement no: 313010 and BioSHaRE-EU 'Biobank Standardisation and Harmonisation for Research Excellence in the European Union', grant agreement 261433. Part of this work was also supported by COST Action IS1303 and the FWO-project 11Q5714N (Research Foundation Flanders). We thank Dr Jane Miller for revising a draft of this chapter.

Note

1 On 22 November 2013, the Food and Drug Administration of the United States sent a letter to 23andme stating that the company had to stop the marketing of their health-related genetic testing services 'until such time as it receives FDA marketing authorization for the device'. As a result of this letter, 23andme stopped offering new consumers access to health-related genetic tests in December 2013. (23andme b)

References

Allyse, M. (2013) '23 and Me, We, and You: Direct-to-consumer genetics, intellectual property, and informed consent', *Trends Biotechnol* 31 (2): 68–9.

Anastasova, V. and E. Rial-Sebbag (2012) 'Les tests génétiques en accès libre: Quelle protection pour le consommateur européen?', *Revue de Droit Sanitaire et Social* 5: 817–27.

Berg, C. and K. Fryer-Edwards (2008) 'The ethical challenges of direct-to-consumer genetic testing', *Journal of Business Ethics* 77(1): 17–31.

Borry, P., H. C. Howard, K. Senecal and D. Avard (2009) 'Direct-to-consumer genome scanning services: Also for children?', *Nat Rev Genet* 10(1): 8.

——(2010) 'Health-related direct-to-consumer genetic testing: A review of companies' policies with regard to genetic testing in minors', *Familial Cancer* 9(1): 51–59.

Bussey-Jones, J., J. Garrett, G. Henderson, M. Moloney, C. Blumenthal and G. Corbie-Smith (2010) 'The role of race and trust in tissue/blood donation for genetic research', *Genet Med* 12(2): 116–21.

Cambon-Thomsen, A. (2004) 'The social and ethical issues of post-genomic human biobanks', *Nat Rev Genet* 5(11): 866–73.

——(2009) 'L'information génétique dans la société de l'information', *Revue politique et parlementaire* (1050): 111–21.

Cambon-Thomsen, A., E. Rial-Sebbag and B. M. Knoppers (2007) 'Trends in ethical and legal frameworks for the use of human biobanks', *Eur Respir J* 30: 373–82.

Chassang, G., E. Rial-Sebbag and A. Cambon-Thomsen (2011) 'Les aspects éthiques, légaux et sociaux des tests génétiques en accès libre', *Droits des patients, mobilité et accès aux soins, Les Etudes Hospitalières. Collection Séminaire d'actualité de droit médical*, pp. 197–208. Bordeaux.

Ducourneau, P., A. Gourreau, E. Rial-Sebbag, A. Cambon-Thomsen and A. Bulle (2013) 'Direct-to-consumer health genetic testing services: What commercial strategies for which socio-ethical issues?', *Health Sociology Review* 22(1): 75–87.

Eriksson, N., J. M. Macpherson, J. Y. Tung, L. S. Hon, B. Naughton, S. Saxonov, L. Avey, A. Wojcicki, I. Pe'er and J. Mountain (2010) 'Web-based, participant-driven studies yield novel genetic associations for common traits', *PLoS Genet* 6(6): e1000993.

Fears, R. and V. Ter Meulen (2013) 'The perspective from EASAC and FEAM on direct-to-consumer genetic testing for health-related purposes', *Eur J Hum Genet* 21(7): 703–7.

Foster, M. W. and R. R. Sharp (2008) 'The contractual genome: How direct-to-consumer genomic services may help patients take ownership of their DNA', *Personalized Medicine* 5(4): 399–404.

Francke, U., C. Dijamco, A. K. Kiefer, N. Eriksson, B. Moiseff, J. Y. Tung and J. L. Mountain (2013) 'Dealing with the unexpected: Consumer responses to direct-access BRCAmutation testing', *PeerJ* 1: e8.

Gaskell, G., H. Gottweis, J. Starkbaum, M. M. Gerber, J. Broerse, U. Gottweis, A. Hobbs, I. Helen, M. Paschou, K. Snell and A. Soulier (2012) 'Publics and biobanks: Pan-European diversity and the challenge of responsible innovation', *Eur J Hum Genet* 21(1): 14–20.

Genetics and Public Policy Center (2006, 2008) 'Direct-to-consumer genetic testing: Empowering or endangering the public?' *GPPC Issue Briefs*.

Gibson, G. and G. P. Copenhaver (2010) 'Consent and internet-enabled human genomics', *PLoS Genet* 6(6): e1000965.

Hansson, M. G. (2005) 'Building on relationships of trust in biobank research', *J Med Ethics* 31(7): 415–18.

Hogarth, S., G. Javitt and D. Melzer (2008) 'The current landscape for direct-to-consumer genetic testing: Legal, ethical, and policy issues', *Annu Rev Genomics Hum Genet* 9: 161–82.

Howard, H. C., D. Avard and P. Borry (2011) 'Are the kids really all right? Direct-to-consumer genetic testing in children: Are company policies clashing with professional norms?', *Eur J Hum Genet* 19(11): 1122–6.

Howard, H. C. and P. Borry (2009) 'Personal genome testing: Do you know what you are buying?', *Am J Bioeth* 9(6–7): 11–13.

——(2012a) 'Is there a doctor in the house? The presence of physicians in the direct-to-consumer genetic testing context', *Journal of Community Genetics* 3(2): 105–12.

——(2012b) 'To ban or not to ban? Clinical geneticists' views on the regulation of direct-to-consumer genetic testing', *EMBO Rep* 13(9): 791–94.

Howard, H. C., B. M. Knoppers and P. Borry (2010) 'Blurring lines: The research activities of direct-to-consumer genetic testing companies raise questions about consumers as research subjects', *EMBO Rep* 11(8): 579–82.

Hudson, K., G. Javitt, W. Burke and P. Byers (2007) 'ASHG statement on direct-to-consumer genetic testing in the United States', *Obstet Gynecol* 110(6): 1392–5.

Janssens, A. C. and P. Kraft (2012) 'Research conducted using data obtained through online communities: Ethical implications of methodological limitations', *PLoS Med* 9(10): e1001328.

Knoppers, B. M. (2010) 'Consent to "personal" genomics and privacy: Direct-to-consumer genetic tests and population genome research challenge traditional notions of privacy and consent', *EMBO Rep* 11(6): 416–19.

McGuire, A. L. and W. Burke (2008) 'An unwelcome side effect of direct-to-consumer personal genome testing: Raiding the medical commons', *JAMA* 300(22): 2669–71.

Sterckx, S., J. Cockbain, H. C. Howard, I. Huys and P. Borry (2013) '"Trust is not something you can reclaim easily": Patenting in the field of direct-to-consumer genetic testing', *Genet Med* 15(5): 382–7.

Tobin, S. L., M. K. Cho, S. S. Lee, D. C. Magnus, M. Allyse, K. E. Ormond and N. A. Garrison (2012) 'Customers or research participants? Guidance for research practices in commercialization of personal genomics', *Genet Med* 14(10): 833–35.

Tutton, R. and B. Prainsack (2011) 'Enterprising or altruistic selves? Making up research subjects in genetics research', *Sociology of Health & Illness* 33(7): 1081–95.

Vorhaus, D. (2012a) 'As deCODE Departs, 23andMe Reloads', *Genomics Law Report* (11 December).

——(2012b) 'DNA DTC: The return of direct to consumer whole genome sequencing', *Genomics Law Report* (29 November).

Wade, C. H. and B. S. Wilfond (2006) 'Ethical and clinical practice considerations for genetic counselors related to direct-to-consumer marketing of genetic tests', *Am J Med Genet C Semin Med Genet* 142C(4): 284–92, discussion 293.

Websites

23andme a: http://23andme.com/ [accessed 9 September 2013].

23andme b: http://blog.23andme.com/news/23andme-provides-an-update-regarding-fdas-review/ [accessed 9 September 2013].

23andme c: www.23andme.com/about/corporate/ [accessed 23 March 2014].

Food and Drug Administration letter to 23andme, www.fda.gov/iceci/enforcementactions/warningletters/2013/ucm376296.htm [accessed 23 March 2014].

Fast Company, Inside 23andme founder Anne Wojcicki's $99 DNA revolution, www.fastcompany.com/3018598/for-99-this-ceo-can-tell-you-what-might-kill-you-inside-23andme-founder-anne-wojcickis-dna-r [accessed 23 March 2014].

Genetics and Public Policy Center, Tables of Direct-to-Consumer Genetic Testing Companies and Conditions Tested – August 2011, www.dnapolicy.org/pub.reports.php?action=detail&report_id=28 [accessed 23 March 2014].

Part III
Governance

6 The messiness of convergence

Remarks on the roles of two visions of the future

Christopher Coenen

Introduction

In a workshop on convergence at Edinburgh University in September 2012, the editors of this volume drew attention to recent discourse on 'converging technologies' in which these technologies are expected to enable 'improving human performance' (Roco and Bainbridge, 2002) and, in epistemic terms, are characterized as 'enabling technologies and knowledge systems that enable each other in the pursuit of a common goal' (Nordmann, 2004: 14). They argued that various challenges exist regarding the analysis and governance of these technologies and that some of these are apparently caused by the concepts of convergence themselves. In this sense, any conceptual analysis of convergence can be understood as an element of the discursive governance of technoscience, and the editors have thus invited the contributors to this volume to approach existing interpretations of converging technologies with a view to developing a critical understanding of convergence and its governance. In their view, the host of rather broad research fields that are seen as constituents of converging technologies (such as nanotechnology, biotechnology, information technology and cognitive sciences, abbreviated 'NBIC' in discourse on converging technologies) are not well defined and are themselves constituted by a range of different epistemologies. The difficulties encountered when it comes to the analysis and governance of these fields of new and emerging technoscience are deemed by the editors to be elements of what they have called the 'messiness of convergence'.

This chapter sets out that, with regard to discourse on NBIC convergence, two visions of the future contribute to this messiness. Thus, the chapter is also an exercise in 'vision assessment' (see Grunwald, 2012), in the sense that it aims to analyse how specific visions of the future can have an impact on the governance of new and emerging technoscience. Due to the inclusion of the first vision, which is now usually termed 'transhumanist', discourse on converging technologies has taken on a strong ethical flavour, among other things. The second vision, that of a 'unity of science', appears to have enabled this discourse in the first place while at the same time (or even by) creating some of the epistemic problems pointed out by the editors of this volume. The arguably deliberate vagueness inherent to discourse on convergence is caused to a large extent by this vision and contributes to the hypertrophic character of the notion of converging technologies. Both visions have thus created distinct challenges for the analysis and governance of the NBIC fields.

Going back to Bernal, inevitably

As is often the case in current discourse on converging technologies and closely related discourse on 'human enhancement' – i.e. the improvement of human performance or betterment of humankind – we are well advised to go back to the writings of John Desmond Bernal (1901–71). In his seminal yet still underrated futuristic essay *The World, the Flesh and the Devil: An Enquiry into the Future of the Three Enemies of The Rational Soul* (1929), he not only sketched, as George Slusser has pointed out, 'the master plot' for the development of science fiction 'across the 20th century', but also 'located the two cultures gap as [the] culminating moment in the narrative of scientific advancement, placing it at the crux of transhuman promise' (Slusser, 2009: 96). It includes very far-ranging visions of the future of space research and colonization, material sciences, genetic engineering, neurotechnology and other fields, as well as the idea of a universal brain of the species, to be created by technological means. In Bernal's view, it will in any case be possible for the material conditions of civilization to reach a state of materialist utopia on earth. Some people, however – specifically the scientific elite and possible followers – will not be interested in living in such an earthly paradise. By gradually replacing parts of their body, including internal organs, they will transform themselves and reach out to the stars, secretly controlling a 'human zoo' on earth that is inhabited by the remnants of natural humanity (Bernal, 1929: 95). In outer space, the brains of the avant-garde will be isolated from their bodies and connected to advanced non-organic bodies. The man-machine hybrids will then form a kind of super-organism and control the universe. In using the words 'world', 'flesh' and 'devil' in the title, Bernal was metaphorically referring to the non-human physical world, to human biology and to the psyche or passions. The only thing he criticized retrospectively with regard to his essay was his reliance on Sigmund Freud's theories when discussing human passions, then advocating neuroscience instead (Bernal, 1970: 10). For all three realms, the world, the flesh and the devil, Bernal attempted to map out the utmost limits of technoscientific progress of which he could conceive, and found that there are almost no limits. Bernal's vision – which builds on the futuristic works of such authors as Winwood Reade, H. G. Wells and J. B. S. Haldane but adds technological imagination – is thus the blueprint for twentieth and twenty-first century transhumanism which, in turn, has strongly shaped discourse on NBIC convergence (see Coenen, 2010).

It is noteworthy, however, that Bernal was also a major modern proponent of the concept of 'unified science'. As Steve Fuller has written:

Bernal in his philosophical capacity believed that science was a vehicle for the self-realisation of the humanity, in which Abrahamic talk of 'spirit' was to be understood as a metaphorical rough draft for a project that would be brought to completion by dialectical materialism. In his own day, especially in the aftermath of the First World War, Bernal detected a fragmentation of scientific effort from this universalist aspiration that was largely driven by nationalist and capitalist concerns, the results of which increasingly destabilised the world order, measured in both military or financial terms. In this respect, Bernal regarded science as being in a 'fallen' state pitted against society, and both suffering as a result. This perspective led Bernal back to visions of unified science put forward by the likes of Friedrich Engels and ultimately Lamarck.

(2011: 680)

Since Bernal's pioneering role in creating the transhumanist vision of the future, which is crucial for current discourse and 'visioneering' with regard to a number of new and emerging technosciences (see Milburn, 2008; Coenen, 2010; McCray, 2012), has been analysed and fairly widely discussed in recent times (for publications in English, see, for example, Coenen, 2007; Slusser, 2009; Tirosh-Samuelson, 2012), we will focus below on his points of view about the 'unity of science', which are also more relevant to the topic of convergence than his early transhumanist vision.

In 1965, he wrote that the 'organic unity of all terrestrial life now may be considered as proved' and that this 'points again to the general convergence of all sciences in this century' (Bernal, 1969: 11–12). He stated that the 'connexion between microcosm and macrocosm has been transferred from the mystic imaginations of astrology to experimental, controllable facts' (ibid.: 12) and continued:

> Similar but not so dramatic discoveries have characterized the other boundary of biology, that which concerns itself with control and communications – the evolution of brain, of habit and consciousness of animals. This leads to consideration of the special social evolution of humanity itself, the noosphere of that imaginative thinker Teilhard de Chardin. For the first time in human history we can hope to trace precisely the whole field of knowledge from nebulae to politics.
>
> (ibid.)

In 1969 he elaborated on this view and suggested that:

> [o]ur new knowledge is not, however, in any sense absolute, quite the contrary. We know better now what we do not know. But that is not an expression of scepticism, it is a programme for action. The provisional nature of science was never more evident. We have to learn at the same time how to carry on intelligent action knowing that we do not know.

This demands the creation of what is effectively a new comprehensive branch of science, a real *science of science*, combining psychological, historical and material factors that lead to discovery and that will be needed in the planning of science. The planning of science is, indeed, one of the most important characteristics of this latest phase of the scientific-industrial revolution ... The effects of the convergence of scientific disciplines and their overlapping into the social and economic fields are tending to create a unified science ... This in turn is bound to affect the application of science, which will gradually spread over the whole of human activities'.

(ibid.: 12–13; italics in the original)

Compare these statements and Bernal's transhumanist vision with some of the most frequently quoted passages in the first report on NBIC convergence:

Formal education will be transformed by a unified but diverse curriculum based on a comprehensive, hierarchical intellectual paradigm for understanding the architecture of the physical world from the nanoscale through the cosmic scale. If we make the correct decisions and investments today, any of these visions could be achieved within twenty years' time. Moving forward simultaneously along many of these paths could achieve a golden age that would be a turning point for human productivity and quality of life ... The twenty-first century could end in world peace, universal prosperity, and evolution to a higher level of compassion and accomplishment. It is hard to find the right metaphor to see a century into the future, but it may be that humanity would become like a single, distributed and interconnected 'brain' based in new core pathways of society. This will be an enhancement to the productivity and independence of individuals, giving them greater opportunities to achieve personal goals.

(Roco and Bainbridge, 2002: 5–6)

As a socialist, Bernal of course placed more emphasis on the collective goal and endeavour, while the US National Science Foundation's Roco and Bainbridge, the latter an outspoken transhumanist, have at least paid lip-service to the sensibilities of current individualism – yet their visions of a humanity and world fundamentally changed by a unified technoscience are very similar.

In this context, we may recall a remark by Helga Nowotny, Peter Scott and Michael Gibbon (2001). They reminded us of how much our present discourse on science and technology, with its focus on public dialogue, up-stream engagement and so on, differs from the ideas of a 'small circle of young, mainly Marxist, scientists in Cambridge' (such as Bernal) who, in the interwar period, debated the future of science and society (Nowotny *et al.*, 2001: 231–2). Nowotny and her co-authors stressed, in our view quite rightly, that the visions of this circle were essentially scientistic and elitist, notwithstanding their adherence to political ideologies which emphatically endorsed egalitarian ideals. If visions, images and beliefs cannot be demarcated clearly from knowledge, and if knowing is inevitably rooted in some set of beliefs – which is also the view of Nowotny and her colleagues – then we should be attentive even to bold visions of the future and their relevance in discourse on new and emerging science and technology. It is, to quote Nowotny and colleagues, 'necessary to understand where ... visions of science [and technology] originate, how they are shaped and by whom' (ibid.: 232). While it may indeed – for state-of-the-art science and technology studies – be 'no longer possible to adopt a naïve "modernist" account of the efficacy of the sciences, of their origins, generations and outcomes', we also have to consider that such a view of science and technology still abounds in present discourse on new and emerging science and technology. What is more, we have witnessed that promoters of radical visions of technological convergence are not only in favour of public dialogue (see Roco *et al.*, 2013), but efficiently use science communication to promote their retro-modernist views. Briefly turning again to Bernal and his circle, we find that their scientistic elitism went hand in hand not only with an involvement in radical politics, but also with a forceful critique of the academic ivory-tower mentality, with an appraisal of the role of planned research and technology policies and, in many cases, with an enthusiastic embracing of educational measures for the masses aimed at the public understanding of science and technology (see, for example, Werskey, 1988).

Convergence and its discontents

In *Is It O.K. to Be a Luddite?* (1984), one of his rare non-fiction works, Thomas Pynchon has provided us with some remarkable reflections on Luddism, science fiction, technoscience and the tendencies of convergence. At the outset of the essay, he reminds us that 1984, its symbolically charged year of publication, was also the twenty-fifth anniversary of C. P. Snow's famous Rede Lecture *The Two Cultures and the Scientific Revolution* (1959). In this lecture, Snow had contrasted the scientific culture – the lifeworld, mind frame and political views of natural scientists – with the traditional culture of literary and other intellectuals. In his essay, Pynchon briefly discusses the obsolescence of the Two Cultures thesis and then turns to the question of what a Luddite is and if it is okay to be one. To this end, he first characterizes, quite rightly, the Snovian use of the word as clearly polemical, implying an irrational fear and hatred of science, technology, progress and the industrial revolution. Pynchon then turns to the outlook for Luddite sensibility in the 1980s, a time that was often perceived as the 'computer age'. Pointing out the usefulness and popularity of personal computers, he questions whether computer technology will attract relevant Luddite protests. Quite on the contrary:

> it may be that the deepest Luddite hope of miracle has now come to reside in the computer's ability to get the right data to those whom the data will do the most good. With the proper deployment of budget and

computer time, we will cure cancer, save ourselves from nuclear extinction, grow food for everybody, detoxify the results of industrial greed gone berserk – realize all the wistful pipe dreams of our days.

(Pynchon, 1984)

He also points to the new structures in technoscience:

> As well-known President and unintentional Luddite D. D. Eisenhower prophesied when he left office, there is now a permanent power establishment of admirals, generals and corporate CEO's, up against whom us average poor bastards are completely outclassed, although Ike didn't put it quite that way. We are all supposed to keep tranquil and allow it to go on, even though, because of the data revolution, it becomes every day less possible to fool any of the people any of the time.
>
> (ibid.)

On the other hand, Pynchon sees a new target of Luddite protest emerging, namely new processes of technoscientific convergence:

> If our world survives the next great challenge to watch out for will come – you heard it here first – when the curves of research and development in artificial intelligence, molecular biology and robotics all converge. Oboy. It will be amazing and unpredictable, and even the biggest of brass, let us devoutly hope, are going to be caught flat-footed. It is certainly something for all good Luddites to look forward to if, God willing, we should live so long.
>
> (ibid.)

About fifteen years later – when the world had in fact survived but had undergone some quite radical political changes – a new discourse emerged on converging technologies, the Two Cultures and the pros and cons of technoscience. In the mid 1990s, the literary agent John Brockman had already introduced the notion of the 'Third Culture', arguing that this culture consists of natural scientists:

> and other thinkers in the empirical world who, through their work and expository writing, are taking the place of the traditional intellectual in rendering visible the deeper meanings of our lives, redefining who and what we are.
>
> (1995: 17)

He characterized the ideas of these thinkers as 'speculative' and as representative of 'the frontiers of knowledge in the areas of evolutionary biology, genetics, computer science, neurophysiology, psychology, and physics' (ibid.: 20). In his view, the Third Culture gives rise to a 'new natural philosophy' (ibid.). Brockman and his network, including opinion leaders in other countries such as Germany (see, for example, Schirrmacher, 2001), polemically criticized the traditional intellectuals who in their view acted as pessimistic mandarins on the basis of outdated theories. The vision of convergence put forward by Brockman and those who followed him included social sciences to some degree but only in so far as they are fully compatible with the natural sciences.

The 1990s likewise saw the rise of a concept of convergence with regard to developments in the area of information and communication technologies. According to this conceptualization, economic sectors which were previously separated (such as broadcasting, information and telecommunications) are progressively merging, due to technological convergence (see, for example, Wirth, 2003, and the literature discussed in it). Soon after Brockman's proclamation of the Third Culture, however, a paradigm shift started when the renowned sociologist Manuel Castells introduced a notion of convergence which already included other technology fields, such as biotechnologies. Convergence went 'wet': Castells argued that the 'ongoing convergence between different technological fields in the information paradigm results from a shared logic of information generation' (1996: 63–4), citing the examples of bio-materials used in microelectronics and brain–machine interfaces. In his view, technological convergence 'increasingly extends to growing interdependence between the biological and microelectronics revolutions, both materially and methodologically' (ibid.: 63).

Various authors, influential science managers among them, argued in the late 1990s and 2000s that nano-bio-info-neuro convergence touches in the information paradigm on core features of the human condition and will massively change our societies. Far-reaching visions were articulated on the basis of this assumption, many of them drawing on the transhumanist tradition since Bernal, and strong and often deterministic claims concerning the future were made. In the second half of the 1990s, the idea that biotechnologies, information and communication technologies, neurotechnologies and nanotechnologies were converging had already been expressed in policy-oriented activities on nanotechnology in the United States by James Canton, a sociologist by training, who described himself on his website as a 'renowned global futurist, social scientist, keynote presenter, author, and visionary business advisor'. Acting as a 'public affairs consultant' and the only social scientist in a study of the Interagency Working Group on Nanoscience, Engineering and Technology of the US National Science and Technology Council Committee on Technology, he wrote in a report of this group:

> The convergence of nanotechnology with the other three power tools of the twenty-first century – computers, networks, and biotechnology – will provide powerful new choices never experienced in any society at any time in the history of humankind.
>
> (Canton, 1999: 179)

In his view, this will lead to a 'higher quality of existence' in the future, with the emergence of 'synthetic tissue and organs, genetic and biomolecular engineering, and "directed evolution", and "new choices" for the "augmentation of cognitive processes, and increase of physical and sensory performance"' (ibid.).

Canton was also one of the most active participants in the so-called 'NBIC initiative' which started with a workshop in 2001 and whose proceedings constitute the above-mentioned first report on NBIC convergence (Roco and Bainbridge, 2002). The year before in April 2000, the computer scientist and entrepreneur Bill Joy had published an essay in which he argued that '[o]ur most powerful 21st-century technologies – robotics, genetic engineering, and nanotech – are threatening to make humans an endangered species' (2000). The activities and ideas of the NBIC initiative attracted considerable attention in science policy circles and beyond. The transhumanist flavour of many of its ideas and its proximity to representatives of transhumanist organizations were among the major points of criticism expressed in the discourse on NBIC convergence. Although there is no need to summarize or continue these discussions here, it is important in our context to analyse the extent to which the two visions of the future – concerning human enhancement and the unity of science – and their critique have been and are still shaping discourse on NBIC convergence.

In the broader academic and public discourse on human enhancement that has flourished since the mid 2000s, the notion of NBIC convergence in general, and the NBIC initiative in particular, tend either to mark the visionary extreme of 'respected' discourse, beyond which exists only radical transhumanism that is usually not taken seriously, or to be referred to as evidence of the emergence of massive changes in the relationships between technoscience and humanity that may have potentially disruptive effects on our societies or indeed on the human condition. In any case, academic and policy-related discussions about human enhancement and transhumanism have been strongly influenced by NBIC discourse. A large number of papers, reports and books dealing with these topics and taking into account further-reaching visions of the future have been published in the 2000s and 2010s (for an overview, see Coenen, 2013). Early criticisms of the NBIC initiative often focused on their proximity to transhumanism and on the initiative's views (felt by many observers to be disturbingly enthusiastic) of a future convergence of humans and machines, in particular with regard to applications in the military domain. Several critics argued that the NBIC initiative's understanding of society and of what it means to be human is deeply flawed or even morally unacceptable.

The initiative, while far from having realized its goal to become a major official US policy activity (Coenen, 2010), has triggered various other, less visionary conceptualizations of 'convergence', such as an important report on 'converging technologies' written by a EU high-level expert group (Nordmann, 2004). Alfred Nordmann, the rapporteur of the group and main author of the report, later argued that it 'set out to clearly dissociate converging technologies from the program of improving the performance of individual humans. Charged with addressing a broadly accepted and socially relevant challenge, the project was thought to be sufficiently Europeanized to fully appropriate the original NBIC program' (2009: 294). According to Nordmann, this 'attempt to have it both ways proved to be a dead end, however', because the 'technical imagination remained fixated on nano, info, and cogno and thus on bringing cognitive processes into the realm of technical control' (ibid.). Nevertheless, the report prepared the ground for the idea that the European knowledge society can prove itself in 'collective experimentation' concerning new and emerging science and technology (Nordmann, 2009).

As regards the NBIC initiative's stance towards the future, Nordmann wrote in his influential critique of 'speculative nanoethics' that:

> there is nothing wrong with public debate of human enhancement technologies or molecular manufacturing where such visions provide a backdrop for society to reflect upon itself. However, if the point is to demonstrate foresight or to debate the ethics of technologies that converge at the nanoscale, claims about human enhancement are misleading and serve only to distract us from comparatively mundane, yet no less important and far more pressing issues.
>
> (2007: 43)

Further points of criticism included the following: a naïve or even dangerous utopianism; an 'unwarranted attribution of defectiveness' (ibid.: 45) to our bodies; an insouciance of the initiative's predictions and the confidence that the changes it endorses will make for a better world – which might on the contrary resemble 'the humanly diminished world' portrayed by Aldous Huxley in *Brave New World* (1932), 'whose technologically enhanced inhabitants live cheerfully, without disappointment or regret, enjoying flat, empty lives devoid of love and longing, filled with only trivial pursuits and shallow attachments' (PCBE, 2003: 7); the 'science-fictionizing of the world' (Milburn, 2008: 27); one-sided views of human nature and modern society (Nordmann, 2007; Saage, 2013); the introduction, under the guise of science, of irrational elements into science policy and societal discourse on science and technology (Coenen, 2009); and an unhesitating coupling of (US) political and military goals with somewhat dubious visions of a new 'social technology' (based on future social–cultural–neurotechnological–computational science) and lifestyle enhancements. These criticisms can be seen as reactions to the fact that the NBIC initiative's programme included the vision that 'the human body will be more durable, healthy, energetic, easier to repair, and resistant to many kinds of stress, biological threats, and aging processes', as well as a view of a massively transformed civilization looming on the horizon in which advances in NBIC convergence will enhance sensory and cognitive capabilities (also 'for defense purposes') and enable 'brain to brain interaction' (Roco and Bainbridge, 2002: 1, 5–6, 18–20). Many were also irritated by the ardour with which the key players of the NBIC initiative described the future, for example when they wrote that NBIC convergence will lead not only to 'wholly new ethical principles' that will govern 'areas of radical technological advance, such as the acceptance of brain implants, the role of robots in human society, and the ambiguity of death in an era of increasing experimentation with cloning', but also, hand in hand with 'human convergence', to a 'golden age' characterized by 'world peace, universal prosperity, and evolution to a higher level of compassion and accomplishment' (ibid.: 6). Further visions of the future put forward by the NBIC initiative and regarded by many of its critics as mere flights of fancy included the above-mentioned vision that humanity might then become something 'like a single, distributed and interconnected "brain" or a 'networked society of billions of human beings', possibly regulated with the aid of a 'predictive science of society', by applying 'advanced corrective actions, based on the convergence ideas of NBIC' (ibid.: 19) and an 'engineering' of culture. Some participants were even impressed by the long-term potential for uploading aspects of individual personality to computers and robots, thereby expanding the scope of human experience and longevity (ibid.: 86).

Suspicions that the NBIC initiative was pursuing a hidden transhumanist agenda were fuelled in the early and mid 2000s when one of its key players (Mihael Roco) denied on several occasions any affinities or connections with transhumanism, while another key player (William Sims Bainbridge) set out a clear and radical transhumanist agenda when giving key note speeches at transhumanist conferences. During the course of the 2000s, as transhumanism grew in terms of respectability and public prominence, such irritations faded, while visions of and ideas about human enhancement and transhumanism moved onto centre stage in certain publications released by the NBIC initiative and some of its key players (see, for example, Bainbridge and Roco, 2006).

Besides the above-mentioned features of the initiative and its visions of human enhancement, the vision of a unity of science, the concept of NIBC convergence and the use of speculations more generally (not only with regard to human enhancement) were also questioned. It was argued that the NBIC initiative claimed to do more than simply demonstrate future possibilities, evidenced for example by the frequent use of the 'constative future tense' in these visions (Grunwald, 2012: 255). The visions claim:

> to be anchored in today's scientific activity by being part of the current agenda and milestones to be attained, and, by going down this path, to lead to making the far-reaching visions come true.
>
> (ibid.)

Asserted with scientific authority, the claims of the NBIC initiative were attempts to bring about a self-fulfilling prophecy (Merton, 1948) and contributed to an overly speculative ethico-political discourse on converging technologies.

As regards the vision of a unity of science, criticisms were not limited to sceptical remarks about the ardent coupling of an extremely strong belief in technoscientific progress with visions of a new unity of humankind and 'human convergence', but also included doubts about the soundness of the initiative's approach with regard to certain problems of interdisciplinarity and the 'economy of attention' in the science system. Nordmann writes in 2008:

> Since everyone knows just how difficult one's own piece of work is one would like to imagine that that of the others is comparatively easy. This is necessary as to convince oneself that real progress towards achievement of the project goal is possible at all.
>
> (119)

What is more, the progress the NBIC initiative hopes to achieve is impeded by additional factors besides matters 'of ideology, different worldviews or paying lip-service to the perceived mindset and wishes of decision makers' or 'false assumptions about what prospective partners from other disciplines actually have achieved or will be able to achieve in the near future' (Rader, 2012: 15–17): they include a lack of experience of interdisciplinary work; a scarcity of incentives to dispel any myths concerning the potential of one's own research area; an absence of consensus between disciplines on concepts and terminology; the current organization of science and research policy which rarely reward or even truly acknowledge participation in interdisciplinary projects; and organizational aspects, particularly when interdisciplinary teams are:

> hastily assembled in response to funding opportunities provided by agencies that are aware of a need for interdisciplinary research to address pressing societal problems, but have not yet set up institutions or mechanisms adequate to decide which approaches are suitable and how work should be organized.
>
> (ibid.: 17)

Michael Rader (2012) has therefore argued, in our view quite rightly, that 'speculative interdisciplinarity' should be included in the list of topics to be dealt with in assessments of visions of the future, a field of analysis that has become increasingly important in recent years.

Conclusion: towards rational governance of visionary ideas?

Some of the above-mentioned criticisms have obviously been addressed to a certain degree in the most recent activities of the NBIC initiative, which appeared to lay dormant for a number of years but then organized a new series of workshops in 2011 and 2012 (Roco *et al.*, 2013: 401–2), culminating in a new report entitled *Convergence of Knowledge, Technology, and Society: Beyond Convergence of Nano-Bio-Info-Cognitive Technologies* (ibid.). The new report generally tones down enthusiasm concerning human enhancement and transhumanism but reaffirms that:

> it is realistic to believe that physical and cognitive potential can indeed be increased at the individual and collective levels to a significant extent ... this observation should not be mistaken for a fanciful dream but as [*sic*] a logical extension of advances in education, information and communication technologies, and cognitive science.
>
> (ibid.: 17)

However, the vision of a unity of science is indeed emphasized more strongly than in the older publications and is coupled with even bolder, albeit still vague visions of a qualitatively new unity of humankind:

> The most powerful creations of the human mind – science, technology, and ethical society – must become the engines of progress to transport the world away from suffering and conflict to prosperity and harmony. Today, because science and society are already changing so rapidly and irreversibly, the *fundamental principle for progress must be convergence*, the creative union of sciences, technologies, and peoples, focused on mutual benefit.
>
> (ibid: 8; italics in the original)

While the new report includes some reflections on the interplay of processes of convergence and divergence, the latter being seen as crucial for innovation (for a relevant analysis of the interplay of processes of convergence, divergence and emergence in the science system, see Bunge, 2003) and numerous, fairly detailed proposals being made as regards the institutional establishment of convergence research (including its embedding in society), it still breathes the spirit of the initiative's earlier publications, for example with regard to the frequent use of bold predictions.

What is most remarkable in our context, however, is the way the new report talks about the handling of visions of the future, particularly in light of the fact that it argues strongly in support of 'vision-inspired basic research'. The editors argue that 'there are multiple visions of both past and future, depending upon whether one sees converging technologies as a field of opportunities, or a quagmire of risks, or various points in between' (ibid.: 26). In their view, '[f]raming will be key to communicating with the public' and 'it will be important to get all visions on the table for discussion' and 'vital to consider our society's previous experience with earlier convergences and with current disturbance factors that are accompanied by major social change' (ibid.). The 'overarching challenge' is thus 'to support rational governance of visionary ideas that benefit from their positive possibilities, without being deceived by fads or abandoning those practices of the past that still function well' (ibid.). Such exercises in 'vision assessment' have for example been undertaken recently with regard to pharmacological cognitive enhancement (see, for example, Ferrari *et al.*, 2012; Racine *et al.*, 2014) and a wide range of emerging biotechnologies (see, for example, Nuffield Council on Bioethics, 2012).

In our view, such attempts to assess the scientific content, sociocultural aspects and strategic uses of visions of the future are much needed in our times of what is often exuberantly futuristic discourse on science and technology.

In the case of discourse on NBIC convergence, something else appears to be even more urgent, however: above all, the two guiding visions of the NBIC initiative, human enhancement and the unity of science, should be placed 'on the table' and discussed against the historical backdrop outlined above. With regard to visions of human enhancement and transhumanism, this would also need to address a wide variety of questions raised by the emergence of various bio-signal-based technologies (Böhle et al., 2013) – such as concerns about the loss of privacy, freedom and individual choices – and the rise of risky and somewhat disturbing cultural practices such as 'cyborgism' and 'do-it-yourself transhumanism' (see, for example, Lanxon, 2012). As far as the vision of a unity of science and its assumedly vital role for the future happiness of humankind are concerned, the first step would need to involve analysing how qualitatively new forms of interdisciplinary and transdisciplinary work can be realized in light of the considerable degree of departmentalization in our science systems and research policies. We should perhaps also ask whether – and, if so, to what extent – this vision is an expression of misplaced eschatological hopes with regard to the social function of technoscientific progress.

References

Bainbridge, W. S. and M. C. Roco (2006) *Managing Nano-Bio-Info-Cogno Innovations: Converging Technologies in Society.* Dordrecht: Springer.

Bernal, J. D. (1929) *The World, the Flesh and the Devil. An Enquiry into the Future of the Three Enemies of the Rational Soul.* London: Kegan Paul, Trench, Trubner & Co.

——(1969) 'Preface to the Third Edition', in *Science in History, vol. 1: The Emergence of Science.* London: C. A. Watts & Co., pp. 9–14.

——(1970) 'Foreword to the Second Edition', in *The World, the Flesh and the Devil: An Enquiry into the Future of the Three Enemies of the Rational Soul.* London: Jonathan Cape, pp. 9–10.

Böhle, K., C. Coenen, M. Decker and M. Rader (2013) 'Biocybernetic Adaptation and Privacy', *Innovation: The European Journal of Social Science Research* 26(1–2): 1–10.

Brockman, J. (1995) 'Introduction', in J. Brockman (ed.), *The Third Culture: Beyond the Scientific Revolution.* New York: Touchstone, pp. 17–31.

Bunge, M. (2003) *Emergence and Convergence: Qualitative Novelty and the Unity of Knowledge.* Toronto: University of Toronto Press.

Canton, J. (1999) 'The Social Impact of Nanotechnology: A Vision to the Future', in National Science and Technology Council Committee on Technology, Interagency Working Group on Nanoscience, Engineering and Technology (ed.), *Nanotechnology Research Directions: A Vision for Nanotechnology R& d in the Next Decade*, International Technology Research Institute, World Technology (WTEC) Division, pp. 178–80. Available at: www.wtec.org/loyola/nano/IWGN.Research.Directions/IWGN_rd.pdf [accessed 22 October 2013].

Castells, M. (1996) *The Rise of the Network Society (The Information Age: Economy, Society and Culture, vol. 1).* Malden, MA: Blackwell.

Coenen, C. (2007) 'Utopian Aspects of the Debate on Converging Technologies', in G. Banse, A. Grunwald, I. Hronszky and G. Nelson (eds), *Assessing Societal Implications of Converging Technological Development*. Berlin, edition sigma, pp. 141–72.

——(2009) 'Zauberwort Konvergenz', *Technikfolgenabschätzung – Theorie und Praxis* 18(2): 44–50. Available at: www.tatup-journal.de/downloads/2009/tatup092_coen09a. pdf [accessed 10 January 2014].

——(2010) 'Deliberating Visions: The Case of Human Enhancement in the Discourse on Nanotechnology and Convergence', in M. Kaiser M. Kurath S. Maasen, and C. Rehmann-Sutter (eds), *Governing future technologies. Nanotechnology and the rise of an assessment regime* (Sociology of the Sciences Yearbook 27). Dordrecht: Springer, pp. 73–87.

——(2013) 'Converging technologies', in G. Gramelsberger, P. Bexte and W. Kogge (eds), *Synthesis. Zur Konjunktur eines philosophischen Begriffs in Wissenschaft und Technik*. Bielefeld, transcript, pp. 209–30.

Ferrari, A., C. Coenen and A. Grunwald (2012) 'Visions and Ethics in Current Discourse on Human Enhancement', *NanoEthics* 6(3): 215–29.

Fuller, S. (2011) 'Science and Technology Studies and Social Epistemology: The Struggle for Normativity in Social Theories of Knowledge', in I. C. Jarvie and J. Zamora-Bonilla (eds), *The SAGE Handbook of the Philosophy of Social Sciences*. London, Sage, pp. 665–85.

Grunwald, A. (2012) *Responsible Nanobiotechnology. Philosophy and Ethics*. Singapore: Pan Stanford Publishing.

Joy, B. (2000) 'Why the future doesn't need us', *Wired*, 8 April. Available at: www. wired.com/wired/archive/8.04/joy.html [accessed 14 March 2014].

Lanxon, N. (2012) 'Practical transhumanism: Five living cyborgs', *Wired*, 4 September. Available at: www.wired.co.uk/news/archive/2012-09/04/cyborgs [accessed 14 March 2014].

McCray, W. P. (2012) *The Visioneers: How a Group of Elite Scientists Pursued Space Colonies, Nanotechnologies, and a Limitless Future*. Princeton, NJ: Princeton University Press.

Merton, K. (1948) 'The Self-Fulfilling Prophecy', *Antioch Review* 8(2): 193–210.

Milburn, C. (2008) *Nanovision: Engineering the Future*. Durham, NC: Duke University Press.

Nordmann, A. (2004) *Converging Technologies – Shaping the Future of European Societies* (A Report from the High Level Expert Group on 'Foresighting the New Technology Wave'). Luxembourg, Office for Official Publications of the European Communities.

——(2008) 'Ignorance at the Heart of Science? Incredible Narratives on Brain–Machine Interfaces', in J. S. Ach and B. Lüttenberg (eds), *Nanobiotechnology, Nanomedicine and Human Enhancement*. Berlin: LIT, pp. 113–32.

——(2009) 'European Experiments', *Osiris* 24(1): 278–302.

Nowotny, H., P. Scott and M. Gibbons (2001) *Re-Thinking Science: Knowledge and the Public in an Age of Uncertainty*. Oxford: Polity.

Nuffield Council on Bioethics (2012) *Emerging biotechnologies: Technology, choice and the public good, Nuffield Council on Bioethics*, London. Available at: www.nuf fieldbioethics.org/sites/default/files/Emerging_biotechnologies_full_report_web_0.pdf [accessed 12 January 2014].

US President's Council on Bioethics (PCBE) (2003) *Beyond Therapy*. Washington, DC: PCBE.

Pynchon, T. (1984) 'Is It O.K. to Be a Luddite?', *New York Times Book Review* 28(1): 40–1. Available at: www.nytimes.com/books/97/05/18/reviews/pynchon-luddite.html [accessed 20 November 2013].

Racine, E., T. Martin Rubio, J. Chandler, C. Forlini and J. Lucke (2014) 'The Value and Pitfalls of Speculation about Science and Technology in Bioethics: The Case of Cognitive Enhancement', *Medicine, Health Care and Philosophy* 17(3): 325–337.

Rader, M. (2012) 'The Jobs of Others: "Speculative Interdisciplinarity" as a Pitfall for Impact Analysis', *Journal of Information, Communication and Ethics in Society* 58(1): 4–18.

Roco, M. and W. S. Bainbridge (2002) *Converging Technologies for Improving Human Performance*. Dordrecht: Kluwer Academic. Available at: www.wtec.org/Converging Technologies/Report/NBIC_report.pdf [accessed 12 February 2014].

Roco, M., W. S. Bainbridge, B. Tonn and G. Whitesides (2013) *Convergence of Knowledge, Technology, and Society. Beyond Convergence of Nano-Bio-Info-Cognitive Technologies*. Dordrecht: Springer.

Saage, R. (2013) 'New Man in Utopian and Transhumanist Perspective', *European Journal of Futures Research* 1, article no. 14. Open access. Available at: http://link.springer.com/article/10.1007/s40309-013-0014-5/fulltext.html [accessed 12 January 2014].

Schirrmacher, F. (ed.) (2001) *Die Darwin AG*. Köln: Kiepenheuer & Witsch.

Slusser, G. (2009) 'Dimorphs and Doubles: J. D. Bernal's "Two Cultures" and the Transhuman Promise', in G. Westfahl and G. Slusser (eds), *Science Fiction and the Two Cultures: Essays on Bridging the Gap between the Sciences and the Humanities* (Critical Explorations in Science Fiction and Fantasy 16). Jefferson, NC: McFarland, pp. 96–130.

Snow, C. P. (1959) *The Two Cultures and the Scientific Revolution*. Cambridge: Cambridge University Press.

Tirosh-Samuelson, H. (2012) 'Science and the Betterment of Humanity: Three British Prophets of Transhumanism', in H. Tirosh-Samuelson and K. L. Mossman (eds), *Building Better Humans? Refocusing the Debate on Transhumanism*. Frankfurt am Main: Peter Lang, pp. 55–82.

Werskey, G. (1988) *The Visible College: A Collective Biography of British Scientists and Socialists of the 1930s*. London: Free Association Books.

Wirth, M. O. (2003) 'Editorial – The Future of Convergence', *JMM – The International Journal on Media Management* 5(1): 4–6.

7 Mapping the UK government's genome

Analysing convergence in UK policy one decade into the twenty-first century

Isabel Fletcher, Steven Yearley and Catherine Lyall

Introduction

Convergence is often presented as an attribute of technological knowledge or of technologies themselves. As knowledge and technological understanding grow, once-separate technical areas are able to link together and to give rise to novel kinds of products, capabilities and interventions. This notion of convergence is considered extensively in other chapters in this volume. The focus in this chapter is at a different level; it is on the way in which convergent techniques are governed or the manner in which the work of governance is affected by convergence. It is easy to see in principle the ways in which governance and convergence could be linked. Different technologies may be overseen by different regulatory agencies with the result that convergence between the technologies raises questions about the 'proper' regulatory authority or about the adequacy of regulation for the case in hand. Some examples of this kind or problem are addressed elsewhere in this volume where – for example – direct-to-consumer genetic information is simultaneously a question of data protection and the sale of medical services or information. But this chapter looks at the issue in a rather different way, examining how responsibility for genomic technologies and the use of genetic/genomic information in policy is distributed and allocated around UK government.

Based on a study of UK departments, ministries, and NDPBs[1] in 2012–13, this chapter documents how human and other genomes were used by government in the UK at that time. This study was not focused on the 'governance of the genome' per se (which is, in any case, often not the direct responsibility of national governments) but on governance 'by means of' genomic technologies although, inevitably, the two are often interwoven. We demonstrate how a surprisingly wide range of government and associated bodies in the UK have embraced – and appropriated – the concept of genomics. We contend that the notion of 'genomics' has become a powerful trope within UK government, where genomic information has been widely used to support and justify 'evidence-based' policies and the innovation agenda. Although we find that there has not been a 'genomicization' of government, we are documenting more than simply the dissemination and diversification of genomic technologies across disparate settings, and argue that the first decade of the twenty-first century has witnessed a unique case of convergence around a specific set of technologies that have attained an iconic status within the policy arena.

Even before the draft of the human genome was published in early 2001, it was anticipated that knowledge of the genome would change the way the UK (and other advanced, industrialized countries) was governed. This was most clearly expected to be the case in the parts of the government machinery that deal with health and well-being (see for example, BIA 2003; DoH 2003), though applications to education, the analysis of inequality and the understanding of criminality were anticipated too. In parallel, it was also expected that agriculture and possibly aspects of conservation and fisheries would be affected by broader genomics understanding as well. The UK's contribution to work on decoding the human genome was part funded by the Wellcome Trust (for a very vivid account of this, see Spufford, 2003) but, as in the USA, the UK government provided funds for the human genome and also for broader genomic studies. Famously, the idea of a human genome project was 'sold' to governments on the basis of the health benefits that would be (very) likely to arise (see Cook-Deegan, 1994).

Already, and dating from the mid 1980s, the possibilities of DNA 'finger-printing' in forensic and other forms of identification had given a vivid indication of the ways in which broadly genomic information could be used in governmental tasks: in new approaches to the handling of crime, of disasters and aspects of immigration and settlement. Subsequently, such finger-printing approaches have also been used in the governance of food quality (for example, the 2013 European horse-meat scandals), the protection of rhino horn in the nation's museums (see Fyall, 2012; also Conniff, 2011), and attempts to improve the policing and detection of wildlife crime.[2] This was an unanticipated form of convergence in governance techniques across previously unrelated areas. The barcoding of nature could be thought of as the next, related step in this emerging governance project, extending it into biodiversity policies, fisheries management and attempts to police the trade in endangered species (see Waterton *et al.*, 2013).

Over the last twenty years – the approximate period of the commitment to the Human Genome Project, its outputs and responses to it – there have been other changes which have also been critical to the UK government's handling of genomic information and techniques. Above all, there has been the adoption of what is commonly termed New Public Management (see Hood, 1991): the attempt to use targets and monitoring to discipline and increase the productivity and effectiveness of the public sector (Carter *et al.*, 1992). The effects of this have been strongly felt across government, from the Health Service to schools and universities, from the police and UK Border Agency to the Ministry of Defence. This emphasis on enhanced management was a strong feature of the 'New Labour' administrations from 1997 to 2010, and was exemplified in the establishment of the Prime Minister's Delivery Unit in PM Blair's second term (2001–05). The PMDU (see Barber, 2008) was headed by Michael

Barber and focused in close detail on the delivery of targets and reforms in key areas. After the decline of New Labour in the election of 2010, a coalition government was formed that was attracted to continuing the reforms but it was also committed to making reductions in government spending because of profound and pervasive economic problems. There was thus a constant pressure to limit and simplify what the government does as a way of cutting costs as well as continuing with reform-oriented initiatives such as the 'What Works' network of centres focused on the assessment of social policy options (Economic and Social Research Council, 2014). Given this recent context, the present analysis can only offer a 'snapshot'. There is no stable end point to which the UK government is heading in this regard and – in fact – some of the institutional responses to the genome have been affected by the coalition's attempts to cut public expenditure rather than by their view on genetics/genomics per se. None the less, this snapshot can identify new initiatives that have emerged to take advantage of novel forms of convergence around genomic knowledge or genomic techniques, and analyse the extent to which departments and NDPBs have 'converged' in their treatment of the genome and other forms of bio-information about people.

As has been discussed in detail elsewhere (see, for example, Barnes and Dupré, 2008: 3 ff.), there is no rigid divide between genetic and genomic approaches and, even within the life sciences, exact usage of the terms varies. Conventionally, genetics is defined as operating at the level of the analysis and/or manipulation of a single gene, whereas genomics analyses and/or manipulates the entire genetic material of an organism. However, in practical terms, the precise boundary between genetic and genomic technologies is unclear and beyond the scope of this kind of mapping research, so we have adopted the term genetic/genomic from Barnes and Dupré in much of the following discussion.

The remainder of this chapter will thus provide detailed insights into convergence, not so much at the level of the technologies themselves, but in relation to the institutions and arrangements that have been developed to manage and exploit genomic and related data for the purposes of governance.

The study: methods and descriptive observations

These results are derived from a series of searches of the websites of UK government departments performed between September 2012 and February 2013. One of us (I.F.) compiled a comprehensive list of departments using the List of Ministerial Responsibilities (including executive agencies and non-ministerial departments) published by the Cabinet Office in April 2012. Executive agencies, official bodies which carry out tasks for ministries (such as the Environment Agency), were also included in the list, with a note about the department to whose minister they are responsible.

The websites were searched using two different methods. First, a search was conducted page by page looking for relevant material, and second using a series of keyword searches. The terms we used most often were biodiversity, biotechnology, DNA, genetic and genomics, but in specific contexts use was made of alternatives such as genetically altered, GM, GMO, life sciences and PCR (polymerase chain reaction, a technique used to multiply sections of DNA to aid analysis). These two types of search technique gave overlapping results and we are confident that they identified a very large proportion of the relevant material available at this time.

When we consider an area of government activity to be relevant to this research it is because it relies – sometimes indirectly – on contemporary technologies of mapping and manipulating human, animal and plant genetic material. Using this criterion, we have excluded much of the promissory rhetoric around genetic/genomic technologies (such as, for example, its potential to revolutionize health care), but have included, for example, programmes to promote British biotechnology companies, the use of marker-assisted breeding in agricultural research, and policies to change the management of the national forensic DNA database. Commitments deriving from international agreements to preserve biodiversity are considered a borderline case, but we have included them because they ultimately depend on, and contribute to, the growing measurement of plant and animal genetic diversity.

The database[3] constructed for this study collates findings alphabetically within each government department (ministerial and then non-ministerial), followed by its sub-units such as executive and non-executive agencies and NDPBs. At the time of the research, a government-wide review of NDPBs had taken place with the aims of reducing their numbers significantly (the so called 'bonfire of the quangos', see Yearley, 2012), and the rapid changes associated with this process meant that for some departments it was difficult to locate basic information about these bodies and their activities. For example, the list of NDPBs attached to the Department of Health was unavailable when their website was first searched in the autumn of 2012, and throughout much of 2012 there was great uncertainty about the future of the Human Fertilisation and Embryology Authority. However, in the end, a decision was made in early 2013 to retain both it and the Human Tissue Authority (Sample, 2013).

Information in the database was reviewed by all three co-authors and further analysis then undertaken (by I.F. and S.Y.). Finally, in order to provide an easily searchable resource, each result was allocated to one of ten broad policy areas. These ten – defence & security, criminal justice, environment, health, food & farming, education & training, trade & industry, art & culture, science & innovation, family & relationships – were identified inductively from the kinds of label and classification used within the official sites and official publications.

This survey method does give rise to specific gaps in the data that are available to be gathered. The first of these gaps arises from the fact that genetic/genomic technologies in the UK are covered by several overlapping regulatory regimes – international, European, UK wide and national. The presence of these different levels of regulation influences what is discussed in legislation or policy documents. For example, if the EU definition of organic foods explicitly excludes GM ingredients, then after this has been defined, further references will be to the established definition and the topic will be 'black-boxed' within UK policy circles.

Other limitations of this research method include the fact that it is highly period sensitive due to its reliance on specific institutional arrangement of the coalition government, the high turnover of website content and the ongoing migration of the government department websites to one uniform website (at gov.uk). As noted above, the current UK coalition administration's attempts to reduce the number of NDPBs, by abolishing some and merging or moving others, made the collection of data more difficult than it might otherwise have been. Furthermore, it is important to remember that the public-facing nature of these websites may limit the information they contain, despite the statements of freedom of information and transparency that all government websites routinely display.

Overall, however, we believe we have offered a reasonably thorough exploratory analysis of the genome in the UK government and the searches performed demonstrated that the use of genetic/genomic technology is widely spread throughout ministries and associated bodies even if it is still a relatively small proportion of UK government activity. In some areas, such as plant-breeding research it is routinely used; it is employed also by the Food Standards Agency as the means for identifying GMOs in food imports. However, in other areas, such as the criminal justice or health-care system, it is one among several available technologies for analysing evidence or delivering treatments. Considering the entire range of government activities, it is still best described as an esoteric technology.

One striking feature is the pervasiveness of the approach. It is strongly represented in the activities of DEFRA and the Department of Health as one might expect but it is considered under several sub-sections by DECC (Department of Energy and Climate Change), the Department for Business, Innovation and Skills (BIS), the Department for Culture, Media and Sport, the Department for Communities and Local Government, the Foreign and Commonwealth Office (FCO), DFID (the Department for International Development), and the Ministry of Defence (MoD). It is also addressed extensively by the Ministry of Justice and the Home Office. Some of these numerous applications are straightforward and rather predictable: DFID is interested in projects using newly developed strains of rice to assist with adaptation to climate change in developing countries, and to supporting ventures with biofuels. The FCO is concerned with the potential proliferation of biological weapons and the ability to fabricate such materials in new and cheaper ways as a result of enhanced techniques of genome synthesis. BIS is concerned to promote innovation in the genomic life sciences sector, notably through the Technology Strategy Board.

On the other hand, there are more unexpected ways in which genetic/genomic approaches are tied to departmental concerns. The Department for

Communities and Local Government (DCLG), for example, is concerned with the possible increase in arson against stolen cars, thought to be motivated by a desire to destroy DNA evidence which may be left after car thefts and associated criminal enterprises. The relatively low-profile Department for Culture, Media and Sport (DCMS) has a surprisingly wide engagement with genomics broadly understood. First, it has an interest in using DNA-testing and other genomic approaches to human remains held in UK cultural collections, both for investigating and understanding these better and also in relation to potential claims on this material from relatives or ancestrally related groups, including those external to the UK. DCMS also has responsibility for aspects of horse-racing and gambling and is thus involved in looking into longitudinal studies of gambling behaviours to understand genetic and familial effects. It has responsibility for policies towards the historic environment and, now that claims for cultural value (for example in relation to winning internationally prestigious certifications such as UNESCO World Heritage designations) have to be made in more explicit and systematically evidenced ways, the availability of quantitative, scientific arguments about biodiversity value is potentially important. Finally, DCMS has responsibility in relation to sports and sporting participation and, in this regard, it commissions research on the role of genetic factors in the inclination to engage in sport and alludes to such research when taking direct measures designed at boosting public participation in sports and exercise. Thus, even within one relatively uncelebrated department there is a very wide engagement with evidence from, and the opportunities arising out of, genetics/genomics.

A similar degree of diversity can be detected in the case of the Home Office. The Home Office has responsibility for the Animal Procedures Committee[4] which 'oversees applications to use animals in research raising novel or contentious issues, or giving rise to serious societal concerns' (Animal Procedures Committee, 2009) (for example, applications involving the genetic modification of non-human primates or embryo aggregation chimaeras involving dissimilar species). This ministry also governs policy towards drugs and their misuse, and is thus concerned with understanding, for example, the role of genetic factors in possible relationships between psychiatric symptoms and cannabis use. Home Office staff also oversee policy concerning the maintenance and make-up of the National DNA Database which provides a repository for storing potential suspects' DNA samples and could, conceivably, become a database for research on ways to identify suspects' characteristics from their genomes. Genetic and genomic techniques are also used within the Home Office in relation to establishing the background and official nationality of people. In some cases these tests are employed to confirm (or indeed throw doubt on) claims about relatedness and thus the rights of relatives to join their parents or children who reside in the UK. There have also been attempts to use genomic material – for example from people's saliva – to work out their likely origin, in the Human Provenance Pilot Project (Tutton *et al.*, 2014). The suggestion was that genomic data might be useful in determining where people came from in cases where their origin or nationality is unknown, unacknowledged or contested. However, this scheme was extensively criticized, not least in technical terms, and subsequently dropped by the UK Border Agency (UKBA); in turn the UKBA was dissolved in 2013 with much of its work returning to the Home Office.

If we turn to DEFRA, its links to genetics/genomics are very numerous and diverse. It has responsibilities and commitments for food and farming, it is engaged in combating wildlife crime, it oversees animal health studies and veterinary laboratories, it is concerned with rural development, and all of this on top of its broad environmental remit. In all these areas it utilizes genetic and genomic approaches. In food and farming, for example, it is involved genomically in the regulation of innovations at the research forefront – perhaps best exemplified through concerns over the use of cloned farm animals for breeding programmes – but also in comparatively small-scale, niche concerns, for example over the identification and regulation of imported 'bush meat', a biodiversity and a public-health issue. DEFRA is one of the institutional homes of the Partnership against Wildlife Crime (PAW) and of the National Wildlife Crime Unit (NWCU). PAW has a Forensic Working Group while the NWCU has used DNA testing as evidence in prosecutions, for example to establish that remains of a poisoned wild bird show that it was a member of a protected species. A wildlife DNA forensic unit has been established. DEFRA commissions research and runs research entities such as FERA (the Food and Environment Research Agency) which – for example – includes the National Bee Unit that studies genetics and honey-bee diversity in the UK and investigates the genetics and pathology of bee disorders. DEFRA also works with the Forestry Commission and its research arm (Forest Research) on genomic studies of emerging tree diseases and pests, and uses genomic techniques in tree-infection identification. The Department also has responsibility for ensuring the genetic health of certain kinds of animals, notably those in conservation-oriented breeding programmes in zoos and also 'privately kept non-human primates'.

The details of other ministries' and departments' links to genetics and genomics are set out in the on-line report and spreadsheet, and need not be further described in detail here. However, the analytical point is that, just over ten years after the publication of the human genome, genetic and genomic techniques and knowledge are used across the great majority of departments. Moreover, the rise of the genome in government appears to be due to a variety of reasons:

1. There are opportunities to take executive action in new ways: for example to identify people and to establish their relatedness (and thus, for example, rights to reside or citizenship) in novel ways. At the same time, there arises a need for the regulation of uses of specific technologies either by the government or by other bodies e.g. the 1984 Police and Criminal Evidence Act, the Home Office Animal Procedures Committee, and the HFEA.

2. There are new kinds of research that can be undertaken. Ministries and departments have long commissioned research but there arise new types of research that may assist governmental work, whether on trends in gambling or assessments of the implications of cannabis use. In many parts of government, genomic and genetic approaches become routinely use by government researchers, for example within DEFRA's Food and Environmental Research Agency, Forest Research, the Health Protection Agency and NHS Blood and Transplant.
3. There is also an elective affinity between the availability of genetic and genomics information and the current calls for systematic evidence and the demand for policy with a sound evidence base. This connection holds true in a general sense, in that genomic information seems attractively quantitative and objective, and thus fits with the widespread contemporary appetite for evidence-backed policies. At the same time, the connection is also manifested in rather particular ways: there are some areas of governance – such as the assessment of aspects of cultural heritage – which have not previously been easy to assess in 'scientific' ways. Lately, it has been possible to deploy genomic data to try to provide objective-looking information in several of these cases. With intense international competition for awards and designations in cultural and ecological domains, these techniques have proved attractive to governments wanting to underline the strength of their bids.
4. Finally, it is noteworthy that certain forms of official engagement with genetics and genomics appear to be driven by the need to respond to others' actions. In many cases this arises from the government's wish to encourage innovative activity by commercial actors, for example through BIS's Office for Life Sciences or the Department of Health's Ministerial (Bio-pharmaceutical) Industry Strategy Group (MISG). But other kinds of actors are inventive in their own ways too, whether that is criminals' growing willingness to try to steal highly valuable rhino horn from public museums or moves by car thieves and other car-using offenders to set fire to those vehicles in the hope of destroying DNA evidence which they believe they are otherwise unable to eradicate. In such cases, governments turn to genomic approaches but less through their own innovative approaches than in response to the innovations of others.

Discussion and wider reflection on results

This chapter has had a primarily empirical and descriptive character, marking an attempt to 'map' the genome across the UK government at a particular time-point and to draw out some straightforward empirical generalizations. However, there are three broader themes about which we believe we can also say something based on the evidence presented here.

First, we observe that – though there is good evidence of a rapid spread of genomic and genetic techniques across Whitehall and the apparatus of government – there has not been a 'genomicization' of government. The fundamental ways of performing governance have not been greatly changed. If we compare the influence of the genomic 'revolution' with the impact of New Public Management then it seems that the innovation in management has had a much stronger impact on the practice and character of government than innovation in the life sciences. This is perhaps not an unexpected finding, but it does serve to remind us that there are important innovations in areas other than the sciences and that not all innovation stems from the worlds of science and technology. Indeed, as noted in this case, those other kinds of changes – for example the rationalization of public management and the demand for 'evidence-based' approaches – can be seen to condition the way that innovative forms of natural science are taken up and deployed for governance purposes.

Second, and relatedly, there is a sense that though the effect of genomics and genetics can be detected widely, there is not the transformative impact that was sometimes broadcast and maybe even expected. The economy has not become a bioeconomy, genomics has not transformed the health service into a personalized and prevention-focused activity, and the trends in some areas of initial rapid growth – such as the National DNA Database – have been reversed to a significant degree. In relation to the latter case, it came to be argued that certain social groups were unfairly over-represented on the database and that these groups faced a potential injustice since investigators had become tempted into an overreliance on the apparent certainties of genetic mapping. These results seems analogous to those that have already been analysed in other areas of contemporary biological and biomedical research. They match a pattern that social scientists have previously described (Brown and Michael, 2003) of a significant discrepancy between the promises made highlighting the significant social and economic benefits accruing from the development of such technologies, and the subsequent experience of a much more limited set of actual benefits. For example British PM Blair wrote the following in his 2003 foreword to a Department of Health report:

> The discovery in Britain of the structure of DNA 50 years ago – perhaps the biggest single scientific advance of the last century – marked the beginning of a golden age of bio-science in Britain which continues today. It is likely to have as big an impact on our lives in the coming century as the computer had for the last generation. The more we understand about the human genome, the greater will be the impact on our lives and on our health care. As an increasing number of diseases are linked to particular genes or gene sequences, we will be able to target and tailor treatment better to offset their impact and even to avoid the onset of ill-health many years in advance.
> (Tony Blair's foreword to the Department of Health's 2003 *Our Inheritance, Our Future: Realising the Potential of Genetics in the NHS*, p.1)

A pattern of 'hyper-expectations' followed by 'unfulfilled' promises corresponds well with the results of this study.

Finally – and this is in many ways the opposite side of the same coin – even if the uptake of genetics and genomics has not been transformative, it has been surprisingly pervasive. This is partly simply a question, as noted above, of how many government departments – for a variety of reasons – use genomic approaches. Governments are keen to deploy evidence; they commission vast amounts of research; and they look for new ways of carrying out their tasks more efficiently. All these tendencies provide opportunities for the uptake of genomics and genetics. But we also observe that the uptake has been driven by what other actors chose to do too: government embrace of genomics may be 'exogenously' motivated. And those other actors come from many backgrounds. They may be researchers and firms offering new techniques, lawyers or doctors putting forward new kinds of arguments and findings. But they also include police officers, criminals, gamekeepers, cultural agencies and agricultural advisers. Even if one wishes to assert that the UK government has become somewhat 'genomicized', it seems that it has been moved in this direction by others' choices as well as by its own decisions and preferences.

An earlier study by one of us (Lyall, 2003), which sought to identify key actors and policies relevant to genomics-related agriculture and food, health and pharmaceutical developments, highlighted the tensions between the different policy aspirations surrounding genomics at both the UK and European levels where, in many cases, government and other policy initiatives (*Foresight*, science policy, support for technology transfer, fiscal policy) were counteracted by policies operating at other points in the overall actor network (for example, the procurement policies of health services and policies for CAP reform in agriculture).

At the start of the twenty-first century, Europe did not have a unified policy for genomics 'but a patchwork of specific regulation, overlaid by many sectoral and horizontal policies at international, Community, Member State and local levels' (European Commission, 2002). In Europe, relevant responsibilities therefore fell across a broad range of policies and actors: the Commission lamented the absence of a shared vision, common objectives and effective coordination, and has since striven to ensure coherence across Community legislation and policies directly regulating, or indirectly impacting on, the development and application of life sciences and biotechnology.

The concept of genomics has thus become a powerful policy trope, symbolizing national, and supranational, conceptions of innovation and competitiveness. At the same time, the governance of genomics has continued to evolve into a much more multilevel phenomenon with new forms of polycentric governance resulting in power sharing and a variety of novel policy instruments and new institutions (e.g. Capano *et al.*, 2012). The totemic significance achieved by genomics in the first decade of the twenty-first century, as a marker of technological pre-eminence, may go some way to explaining why virtually every UK government department now vaunts its genomic credentials on its public-facing websites. But whether this evidence of convergence is actually an indication of coherence in the multilevel governance of the life sciences remains a much bigger question.

Nevertheless, one of the key factors that makes genomics so amenable to being enrolled into the work of government is the facility with which it can be used to generate discriminatory information about people, places and objects. This is especially powerful within a context where the agencies of governance are, in turn, converging around the use of knowledge made possible by current and emerging information technologies. As a recent report makes clear (National Academy of Sciences, 2014), convergence requires both improved coordination and a cultural shift for research organizations and, we would argue, government departments and policy makers. Synergies between various social and policy drivers (some of which we have illustrated in this chapter) and new and emergent technologies, challenge policy makers with a fundamental and genuinely convergent dynamic that, in turn, demands new ways of thinking about the role of the genome within government.

Acknowledgements

The authors would like to acknowledge support from the UK Economic and Social Research Council (ESRC grant RES 145–28–1005) and to express their appreciation for the contribution of two anonymous referees to this chapter.

The role of Professor Albert Weale – chair of the advisory board to the ESRC Genomics Policy and Research Forum throughout its life (2004–13) should be gratefully acknowledged here, since the original idea of mapping the genome in the UK government was actually his. We would also like to thank Dr Christine Knight at the University of Edinburgh who helped the Genomics Forum with the first stages of this project.

Notes

1 Non-departmental public bodies, which include such things as the Environment Agency and other entities which perform government's tasks but which are not directly 'owned' by departments or ministries.
2 Personal communication to Yearley at meeting of the Scottish Consortium for Rural Research at Royal Zoological Society of Scotland (RZSS) on Monday 21 January 2013 where such animal forensic DNA tests were described as part of the conservation work undertaken by RZSS.
3 The database constructed for this study is publicly available to enable readers to take our analysis further using our dataset as a starting point (https://public.sheet.zoho.com/public/mappingthegenome/mapping-the-genome-april2013-xls).
4 The Animal Procedures Committee was disbanded in 2012, and in 2013 the Animals in Science Committee took over its work.

References

Animal Procedures Committee (2009) *Guidance to Project Licence Applicants referred to the APC Applications sub-committee.* Available at: http://webarchive.nati

onalarchives.gov.uk/20120809104748/http://www.homeoffice.gov.uk/publications/age ncies-public-bodies/apc/guidance-proj-licence-applicants?view=Binary [accessed 14 May 2014].

Barber, M. (2008) *Instruction to Deliver: Fighting to Transform Britain's Public Services*. London: Methuen.

Barnes, B. and J. Dupré (2008) *Genomes and What to Make of Them*. Chicago, IL and London: University of Chicago Press.

Brown, N. and M. Michael (2003) 'A sociology of Expectations: Retrospecting Prospects and Prospecting Retrospects', *Technology Analysis and Strategic Management* 15(1): 3–18.

BIA (2003) *Improving National Health, Increasing National Wealth*. London: BioIndustry Association/Department of Trade and Industry/Department of Health.

Cabinet Office (2012) *List of Ministerial Responsibilities (including executive agencies and non-ministerial departments)*. London: Cabinet Office.

——(2013) *Efficiency and Reform Group: Public Bodies Reform*. Available at: www.gov.uk/public-bodies-reform [accessed 14 May 2013].

Capano, G., J. Rayner and A. R. Zito (2012), 'Governance from the Bottom up: Complexity and Divergence in Comparative Perspective', *Public Administration* 90(1): 56–73.

Carter, N., R. Klein and P. Day (1992) *How Organisations Measure Success: The Use of Performance Indicators in Government*. London and New York: Routledge.

Conniff, R. (2011) 'Defending the Rhino', *Smithsonian Magazine* [online]. Available at www.smithsonianmag.com/science-nature/Defending-the-Rhino.html [accessed 14 May 2014]

Cook-Deegan, R. (1994) *The Gene Wars: Science, Politics, and the Human Genome*. New York and London: W. W. Norton & Co.

DoH (2003) *Our Inheritance, Our Future: Realising the potential of genetics in the NHS*. London: Department of Health.

Economic and Social Research Council (2014) *What Works: evidence centres for social policy* [online]. Available at: www.esrc.ac.uk/collaboration/public-sector/what-works-evidence-centres.aspx [accessed 14 May 2014]

European Commission (2002) *Life sciences and biotechnology – A strategy for Europe*. Communication from the Commission to the European Parliament, the Council, the Economic and Social Committee and the Committee of the Regions COM (2002) 27.

Fyall, J. (2012) 'DNA trap for rhino horn raiders' *Scotland on Sunday Newspaper* [online]. Available at: www.scotsman.com/scotland-on-sunday/scotland/dna-trap-for-rhino-horn-raiders-1-2166006 [accessed 14 May 2014]

Hood, C. (1991) 'A Public Management for All Seasons', *Public Administration* 69 (spring): 3–19.

Lyall, C. (2003) 'Scoping study on the national and international policy environment for genomics', unpublished working paper.

National Academy of Sciences (2014) *Convergence: Facilitating Transdisciplinary Integration of Life Sciences, Physical Sciences, Engineering, and Beyond*. Washington, DC: National Academies Press.

Sample, I. (2013) 'Two health regulators spared axe but face efficiency review', *Guardian* [online]. Available at: www.theguardian.com/society/2013/jan/25/two-health-regulators-spared-axe [accessed 14 May 2014]

Spufford, F. (2003) *Backroom Boys: The Secret Return of the British Boffin*. London: Faber & Faber.

Tutton, R., C. Hauskeller and S. Sturdy (2014) 'Suspect technologies: forensic testing of asylum seekers at the UK border', *Ethnic and Racial Studies* 37(5): 738–52.

Waterton, C., R. Ellis and B. Wynne (2013) *Barcoding Nature: Shifting Cultures of Taxonomy in an Age of Biodiversity Loss*. Abingdon and New York: Routledge.

Yearley, S. (2012) *'Bonfire of the Quangos' Britain in 2013*. Swindon: Economic and Social Research Council, pp. 86–7.

8 Diagonal convergences

Genetic testing, governance, and globalization

Christine Hauskeller

Introduction

The actual and sometimes quite unexpected uses to which individuals put new technologies can undermine social norms. Beyond that, the notion of Converging Technologies (CT) represents government programmes that not only monitor and regulate a new technology but plan and steer the convergence of emerging technologies and their future potential uses. In the early 2000s the USA and Europe set up government programmes to induce and configure the convergence of the nano-, bio-, information- and cognitive sciences (NIBC) into technologies that will alter humanity's ways of being. CT is a form of meta-level governance that aims to control not only individual technological developments but also the ways in which scientific and technical innovations might intersect and cause social and economic change. This chapter treats CT as an especially ambitious and precarious instance of governance because it aims to predetermine future science, future technologies, their intersections and resulting societal changes. Drawing on examples of a convergence that is well under way, I aim to demonstrate some of the problems of such prospective policy-making and argue that it draws on an understanding of the power and means of national governments that is technologically already obsolete. National or local CT policies represent what Foucault called governmentality, an overreliance on manageability, regarding the formation of new platforms for decision-making that is happening alongside and irrespective of such government programmes. This situation demands new ways of policy-making if certain social values are to be protected.

This chapter begins with two critical approaches towards policy-making and its philosophical validation. One is by Alfred Nordmann, who, after years of studying CT programmes, reflected on the role of academics in such science and technology governance. I refer especially to two of his criticisms in his article 'Knots and Strands: An Argument for Productive Disillusionment' (2007). Nordmann's first criticism concerns the coalition of academic research and policy-making, the second the universality of claims inherent in the resulting policies which themselves are culturally markedly distinct. Following on from this second point, I step back from the CT controversy and refer to a feminist philosopher, Susan Sherwin. In *No Longer Patient* (1992), Sherwin proposes to overcome the divide between normative universalist claims and empirical cultural perspectivism through analysis of the power relations and participatory practices underlying the ethical judgments in policy-making.

There is an inherent contradiction in national policies for the mastery of converging technologies. This contradiction arises from the fact that the technologies with the greatest economic and social potential and uncertainty are those with global effect. National or regional politics are either locally restricted or need to adopt an imperialist approach if they want to govern global convergence for the local benefit. This point of friction between global and local values and how they play out will be illustrated in the following discussion of two case studies dealing with attempts to control technology and its uses. Both cases are about access to genetic tests; direct to consumer genetic tests sold online, and non-invasive prenatal genetic tests offered in the same way. Within a decade genetics has moved from being firmly in the hands of academic and state institutions. The convergence of information technologies and global marketing practices has taken it out of that controlled sphere. Converging Technology projects have partly reckoned with the change towards open access to genetic tests, but authorities have not found ways of restricting them and present only weak arguments why they ought to do so.

The genetic case studies illustrate four points: (a) a systematic misrepresentations of consumers' knowledge and interests; (b) a focus on the technologies instead of the cultural contexts of their application, which distorts the perception of ethical problems and prevents viable political responses to social concerns; (c) the cultural specificity of ethical imperatives with which new technologies are examined; and (d) that academics pursue an agenda of their own in their cooperation with regulators on genetic testing. The convergence of genetics, global information technologies and market infrastructures has created an environment in which genetic tests can no longer be controlled through the mediation of experts and prohibitions.

Following Sherwin's suggestion about examining power relations, I consider the present debate about direct-to-consumer genetic tests to be about privileges of power and knowledge in the guise of stewardship and patronage over citizens' DNA-derived information. This has often been framed by experts as concern with quality management in genetic testing. Yet, the quality of the tests could and possibly should be safeguarded generally through international standards and certificates. Local quality control is impossible to implement in an open global market. In the case of non-invasive prenatal genetic tests for sex selection, the conflict between consumers' interests and the long-term common good needs to be addressed at source, following Sherwin's arguments. Policy-making has to tackle the cultural values and practices that make it a rational choice for many to prefer a male to a female child. That would not only prevent sex-selective use of genetics but address sex discrimination in the relevant cultures on a much wider scale and enhance the welfare of the whole community, girls and women included.

Two philosophical approaches

Nordmann, who is one of the leading experts on the NIBC convergence in Europe and the USA, has published both policy reports and academic critiques of the involvement of academics in the governance of science and technology. In 'Knots and Strands: An Argument for Productive Disillusionment' (2007), a paper that reflects his experience in government-funded research projects for policies to manage convergence and its ecological, societal and ethical effects, he distinguishes two different approaches to CT. One justifies the direct steering of converging technologies with future national interests for economic prosperity. The other is explicitly motivated by ethical issues and aims to prevent societal risks of convergence beyond the risks that each science and technology alone is seen to carry. Nordmann aligns the first approach with the attitude taken in the US programmes on CT, where directing the convergence of nano-, bio-, information- and cognitive (NBIC) sciences and technologies is an important means to secure future economic revenue from technological advances. In contrast, in Europe:

> we find ourselves in a situation where various enabling technologies and many pressing societal issues (global warming, obesity, water and energy supply, etc.) challenge us to institute converging technologies as a means of gearing emerging capabilities towards common goals.
>
> (2007: 219)

The common goals are ethical and concern human welfare and social cohesion and inclusion:

> This comparison of U.S. and European definitions of 'converging technologies' leaves us in a paradoxical situation. On the one hand, it speaks very clearly to different cultural perspectives and thus to a kind of parochialism on both sides. On the other hand, neither perspective views itself as parochial but claims universality.
>
> (ibid.: 220)

The passages above summarize critically the political attitudes and perspectives in the programmes on NIBC to which Nordmann has directly contributed. He authored the European Commission Research Report *Converging Technologies – Shaping the Future of European Societies* (Nordmann, 2004), which sets out the challenges arising from the transformative potential of CT. This report begins with defining four problems of the NIBC convergence arising from the tension between potential economic and social benefits and 'threats to culture and tradition, to human integrity and autonomy, perhaps to political and economic stability' (ibid.: ii). The transformative potential of CT is described not in the language of profits but, rather, of an ethics of the human species. His four characteristics are: (a) embeddedness: the ubiquity of artificial environments that may transform human self-understanding; (b) unlimited reach: the potential that everything can be transformed into computable information and that everything molecular can be controlled. An attitude of technological quick-fix may come to reign supreme; (c) engineering the mind and the body: this entails the proposal that CT policies must have a humanitarian bias; (d) specificity: the conflict between the potential of personalized medicines and case-specific technology solutions, which may lead to social problems (ibid.: 3). These characteristics mirror the risk aspects that have been ascribed to genetics since the 1970s, strongly emphasizing concerns about injustice and the instrumentalization of human life. The European approach to CT stresses the need for ethical governance. The US mode pronounces economic advance as justification for policy-making. Nordmann refers to Sheila Jasanoff's distinction between hubris and humility in her paper on cultures of modernity in the USA and Europe. She identifies:

> hubris in attempts to politically manage potential resistance (Jasanoff, 2002). The opposing attitude of humility looks to ethics ... in order to buy time for reflection and to mobilize the cultural resources that will allow for local adaptations of technological agendas and avoidance of uniform global diffusion.
> (Nordmann, 2007: 221)

I would prefer to leave it an open question as to whether this USA–Europe difference is a general characteristic, or simply contingent and occasional, and possibly in part rhetorical and due to cultural codes of legitimacy for political governance. These value-laden characterizations cannot be readily applied to the policies concerning genetic testing. Humility as ethical attitude implies deference to established orders and values, and the case studies below show that with regard to direct-to-consumer genetic testing (DTCGT) such ethical aspects are important motivators in current US science and technology policy.

Following his involvement in the European Converging Technologies research programme, Nordmann reflects on the contribution of academics to policy-making. Through dedicated research funding, growing impact agendas and genuine overlap of interests, philosophers and social scientists are drawn into technology assessment and science governance. Academic experts are often called upon when government bodies and research or ethics institutions consider policies on new sciences and technologies. In the publication of their research findings, and more directly in reports to policy committees, bioethicists, social scientists and philosophers participate in the ideological and conceptual framings of the issues and thus share responsibility for the policies that emerge. Nordmann describes the entanglement of academics in framing the issues as a 'deadly embrace' into normative political agendas, an issue of being drawn into set definitions of ethical problems which can undermine academic rigour and independence frequently discussed in bioethics in recent years (Eckenwiler and Cohn, 2009). He suggests that academics engage in the 'disentangling' of normative, sociological and ontological concepts as an analytic method to keep a self-critical distance from the conceptual and normative alliances formed in the policy development process (Nordmann, 2007: 226–7). Yet he remains vague about how to do this in practice. The gist is a stepwise self-reflexive disentanglement of the concepts tied together in the technology assessment discourses and their normative agenda-setting. The tension between culturally specific normativities in the European-style CT programme and its inherent claim to universality when setting out ideas of human nature also troubles him. He does, however, not suggest an approach with which STS and bioethics might address this problem.

The tension between universalist claims and sociocultural parochialism is highly relevant for the credibility and potential success of nationally or geopolitically focused CT programmes. Feminist philosophers examining medical and bio-technologies in particular have analysed the problem of universalism, pluralism and cultural diversity in the context of ethical issues that are gender specific. One such author is Susan Sherwin. In *No Longer Patient* (Sherwin, 1992), she discusses the conflict between the universalism inherent in moral claims and the fact of culturally diverse perceptions of what is right and wrong. She proposes to look not at the values and norms that are contested, but rather at the procedures and power structures in force in how policies are made and decisions taken. Discussing abortion and female genital mutilation, Sherwin defends a feminist moral relativism that examines the participation procedures that carry an established moral system. The power and interpersonal relations of those engaged and subjected to normative expectations provide the clues about its fairness:

> it is necessary to consider how the system evolved, whose interests are served by it, and, most importantly, whose interests are sacrificed to it.
>
> (ibid.: 71)

She stresses the need for both tolerance and the contextualization of norms and practices on the one hand, and on the other hand, a strong and powerful critique of oppression, wherever it occurs, without false respect for cultural or national boundaries (ibid.: 73).

Sherwin argues that analysis of power relations and participatory practices opens up a space for critique beyond the verdict of Western moral imperialism. I will refer to this method when discussing the credibility and efficacy of current policies to control access to genetic testing. The social conditions following this convergence allow global citizens forms of self-determination that they seem to appreciate and which defy previous modes of regulatory prohibition and elitist restrictions of access to technology. The two case studies, DTCGT and its application in non-invasive prenatal testing for sex selection, are not commonly discussed under the label of convergence. Yet both are products of the recent manifest convergence of genetics with information technologies and social ideas and processes of globalization. Fast and cheap genetic testing methods, global knowledge exchange and worldwide operating markets for goods and services create conditions of open access. Disputes about these new developments characterize the regulatory agenda for life sciences under labels such as do-it-yourself biology and open markets for drugs and tests. Government agencies, and the medical professions especially, aim to reign in the public use of genetics. The presentation of the case studies highlights two important aspects regarding the governability of convergence: the presupposed relationship between governments and their experts towards the public, and the empowerment for individual citizens that poses new opportunities and new challenges for the social impact of genetics.

'Genetic exceptionalism', or the private management of personal data

Genetics has become the most extensively attended subject in bioethics because of its perceived risks in many ethical and political dimensions regarding human nature and human rights, concerns which reappear in the debate around the CT programme. Studies in and on genetics have been very well funded, and consequently bioethics has grown into an expert discipline that would inform policies and public attitudes. The multidisciplinary bioethics field that studies the ethical, social and legal aspects of genetics evolved into a major expert sub-discipline alongside the sciences that make sense of DNA and what genetic tests may indicate about a person's biological make-up. *Genethics* (Suzuki and Knudtson, 1989), as this field became known, investigates the regulations for genetics needed to protect individual rights and the social fabric at large. Important for my argument is that among scientists, regulators and the bioethics disciplines, genetics was perceived as so powerful that the control of its societal effects became a major political and societal issue. National and transnational legislations and moratoria are in place to restrict the use of genetic data,[1] and informed consent to testing was made a necessary prerequisite for many tests. Genes were seen as providing conclusive and unchanging information about a person's phenotype, heath and future health, personality traits, race and ancestry, biological relatedness, and more.

Around the year 2000 this simplistic image of genetics, and with it the exceptional status of DNA test findings, began to disintegrate. The Human Genome Project found that humans have far fewer 'genes' than their complex biology seemed to require. It had to be concluded that many biological properties are not simply written in the genes and that DNA tests do not tell us everything about biological traits. Consequently, genetics has matured from a position of imagined omnipotence to an increasingly refined set of specific applications. Most tests available today only provide approximate information about health risks or other traits. Science and technology studies and bioethics literature has changed along with genetics and adopts a more observant attitude to new knowledge and testing practices and how they influence specific social configurations of identity and self (Petersen, 2006).

However, the potential of people appropriating genetics in the same way as other tests and on their own account was not much considered. The genetics–information–technology–globalization (GIG) convergence that occurred was not well anticipated. The literature discusses the loss of the exceptionalist status of genetics and whether previously established prohibitions ought to be upheld. An example is price-setting in health insurance. Moratoria on the use of genetics for health insurance risk calculation are in force in Europe, the USA, and other locations. However, if genetic information is only somewhat indicative of a person's health, these moratoria may be superfluous. Richard Ashcroft and Soren Holm exchanged arguments on this question in the *British Medical Journal* (Ashcroft, 2007; Holm, 2007). Holm argues that if genetic tests are of a predictive quality similar to that of family history of disease, which insurers can use, why should they then not use genetic information? The moratorium is in place in Europe until 2017. The convergence that changes access and management of DNA tests may have bypassed the efficacy of such control strategies by then.

While not much may be written in the genes directly, global markets and global communication networks enable new ways of doing things with genetic tests that individual consumers have shown interest in, such as health status, bio-geographical origin, or race (Hauskeller *et al.*, 2013). Members of the public buy genetic tests although regulators and experts recommend that genetics should be conducted with close supervision by scientific and medical authorities. There is a widening opposition between regulatory agencies and the private businesses and their customers' wish for self-management. The GIG-convergence troubles established knowledge and power relations in which lay individuals were fully dependent on experts and regulators.

DTCGT: a regulatory conundrum

The industry offering DTCGT sells intelligence about biological relations, race, bio-geographic origins, health risks and personality traits to private customers. Tests can be bought easily and at a low cost. In November 2013 a paternity test cost £130 in the British pharmacy chain Boots, and a health and ancestry test from web-based provider 23andMe was £62. The transition of genetics from an expert-led to a lay-access technology has caused regulatory concern, not least because this shift undermines established safeguards against discriminatory uses.

Below I briefly summarize first the regulatory struggles to limit DTCGT and the related academic debates. I separate regulatory and academic discourses, although academics are involved in policy processes, in order to point out their alignment in content. The ethical and social science debates single out the same points that are raised in regulatory papers. This underlines Nordmann's notion of a non-obvious entanglement. In the direction of Sherwin's critique, this alignment signposts that expertise and power are closely entwined when the authority over new science and technology is at stake. Both DTCGT and prenatal sex selection are instances of a growing tension, if not in fact directly opposing interests between expert and government bodies on one side and consumers on the other.

For over thirty years it was generally accepted that genetics needs to be regulated for the good of the public. For many, DTCGT only increases this need and creates new ethical problems (Berg and Fryer-Edwards, 2008; Wasson et al., 2005). Calls for regulation have been published by government bodies and ethics committees in Australia, the USA, European, and Asian countries. The National Institute of Health (NIH) Task Force on Genetic Testing considered regulation as early as 1998[2] and published several recommendations in recent years. In 2009, the UK Human Genetics Commission (HGC) issued a 'Framework of Principles for direct-to-consumer Genetic Testing' ('Principles') which outlines criteria for acceptable practices with respect to informed consent, marketing, risk communication, availability of counselling, and data protection.[3] The Australian National Health and Medical Research Council's report for health professionals acknowledges problems with DTCGT, noting that marketing as such cannot be banned.[4] The shared assumption is that public users cannot make good sense of these tests and will burden health services with unnecessary expert visits. In the USA regulators have begun to proceed against testing companies. In March 2011, the advisory committee on molecular and clinical genetics of the US Food and Drug Administration (FDA) enforced NIH recommendations from 2000 concerning the advertising of DTCGT products as non-diagnostic.[5] This intervention followed the prohibition of some private genetic testing companies operating in California in 2009 and the FDA's inquiry into US-based companies in summer 2010.

The academic debate emphasizes the lack of quality of the privately offered tests and consumers' ability to make sense of the findings. Also, wider use may adversely affect health services and wider society (Hall and Gartner, 2009). Other concerns include effects on the medical professions and their expertise requirements (Annes et al., 2010; Edelman and Eng, 2009), because of a lack of professional training in genetics. Ethics committees and academics suggest new data protection and privacy laws (Hogarth et al., 2008; Javitt et al., 2004; Kaye, 2008) as well as comprehensive informed consent regulations (Bunnik et al., 2012). Genetics has put notions of informed consent under strain in several ways, not least because genes are shared among relatives (Corrigan, 2003; Hauskeller, 2004; Lunshof et al., 2008; Mascalzoni et al., 2008). Genetic and biobank research projects, such as the UK Biobank or the Iceland National Human Genome Project, operate with open unspecific consent to data use (Palsson and Rabinow, 1999) in order to reduce cost and widen the usability of collected information and body materials. However, open consent to public or private biobank enterprises implies that the participating public understands what goes on and must trust these institutions with their personal data. It is contradictory to invite the public to donate to biobanks with open consent, yet not trust it to be able to comprehend the vagueness of

DTCGT tests and use them sensibly. The academic critique of DTCGT concentrates on common complex disease and ancestry testing, and how difficult it is to understand and contextualize the information. Regulation is needed to prevent social harm (Kolor et al., 2009; Messner, 2011).[6]

The academic and regulatory literature on DTCGT portrays the consumer as emotion-ridden and without sufficient scientific understanding. This person is a potential threat to society because she will respond unreasonably and cause increases in the cost of health care and social services. Following previous requests for stricter DTCGT marketing strategies, the FDA issued an enforcement action against 23andMe in November 2013, stating that the:

> FDA is concerned about the public health consequences of inaccurate results from the PGS device; the main purpose of compliance with FDA's regulatory requirements is to ensure that the tests work ... 23andMe must immediately discontinue marketing the PGS until such time as it receives FDA marketing authorization for the device.

Among its motives to act, the FDA states that:

> [t]he risk of serious injury or death is known to be high when patients are either non-compliant or not properly dosed; combined with the risk that a direct-to consumer test result may be used by a patient to self-manage, serious concerns are raised if test results are not adequately understood by patients or if incorrect test results are reported.[7]

This restriction was still in place in January 2014. Note, however, that this does not constitute a general restriction to selling private genetic tests but is specific to a piece of equipment and health advertising. The FDA's intervention for the public good encountered hostile public response, especially on community forums and internet news sites. Consumers mostly defended 23andMe, criticizing the FDA as over-regulating and recently experts have expressed a similar view (Green and Farahany, 2014).

Citizens ask why they should be prevented from buying genetics tests if they want them, and why the management of their genetic data should rest in the hands of experts and large organizations. Given that the consumption of many harmful products burdens health care systems, a situation largely unregulated with regards to adult buyers, it seems that the argument for the allegedly exceptional harm deriving from DTCGT needs to be actively made rather than simply assumed on the basis of previous and now largely discarded beliefs in the determining power of DNA. Lifestyle is increasingly seen as a major causal factor for common diseases, and medical public health experts and government institutions increasingly demand that individuals self-govern with a view to maintaining their health. Experts and institutions offer lifestyle guidance, issue food labels, devise smoking bans, set age restrictions on sales of alcohol, and promote sports in schools, in order to influence citizens' behaviours. The DTCGT market could be seen as an instrument to increase health awareness and autonomy in lifestyle choices, if the tests possess decent validity, and ideally are clinically useful. Of course, this ability to encourage healthy lifestyles depends on the common public understanding of genetics to enable the sensible use of DTCGT results. Initial studies on the uses of DTCGT and its effects on the clinic indicate that this might be assumed (Giovanni et al., 2010). DTCGT consumers are on the whole aware of the complexity of genetic knowledge and that results are indicative not predictive for each individual testee (Hall et al., 2010). Larger studies about consumer behaviour and professional experience with genetic information are under way.

The DTCGT debates in North American, Australia, and European countries are similar in their arguments concerning risks for public health, the deficit of scientific understanding among consumers, and the lack of scientific quality of the tests on offer. This uniformity is remarkable given the different societal effects DTCGT has in the diverse provisions of health care, and the cultural differences in the public and political attitudes towards genetics in these countries. Yet regulators and academics predominantly agree that public access to genetic tests ought to be tightly supervised. I am concerned that this grand agreement arises from a potential in DTCGT rarely mentioned in the discourses above, namely that it threatens the authority of science, the medical professions, and bioethicists' special expertise. Some critics of bioethics as a profession (De Vries et al., 2009; Evans, 2012) have pointed out the dilemma inherent in the professionalization and status of ethicists as specialists, that the decrease in demand for their services puts at risk individual careers and expert disciplines. The same can be assumed for genetic counsellors and medical expert professions in the field. The enabling potential of quality-assured DTCGT as a self-determined health strategy may not be borne out because of diverse sets of conflicts challenging the multidisciplinary panels that advise regulatory organizations, as Nordmann (2007) points out with respect to the NIBC convergence.

The central first-level problem is that given the GIG convergence prohibitive regulation may save time but is not a long-term method of containment. National laws, moratoria, or weak instruments such as the 'Principles', suggesting standards for testing, cannot suppress the use of a product marketed worldwide via the internet if consumers are motivated to have it (Hogarth et al., 2008). Neither the legislation nor the policing institutions are in place to prevent online marketing, sale, and trade. I suggest elsewhere that international product standards and certification procedures are the only reliable means of securing test quality (Hauskeller, 2011). International quality certificates would not control all products available but would offer consumers the choice of investing in a high-quality product, a choice currently unavailable.

Standards can only address test quality and validity, not problems that arise from the diversity between cultural scenarios and value systems within which the same genetic test can take on very different roles and meanings. This problem is best illustrated with the case of non-invasive prenatal genetic testing and especially its use for sex determination. This example will also highlight how the authorities' neglect of moving towards a system of global technocratic quality assurance obstructs a sensible global debate about the culturally dependent and diverse effects of DTCGT.

Non-invasive prenatal diagnosis (NIPD)

NIPD is a special case of DTCGT because its utility and uses depend on cultural contexts and values. In that it is a challenge for the foresight expectations of CT programmes and agendas which assume that technological benefits can be nationally defined and at the same time subjected to universal ethical stewardship.

DNA from the embryo/foetus circulates freely in the pregnant woman's blood during pregnancy. Technologies that detect the embryo's or foetal DNA in a maternal blood sample, and ascertain its genetic condition on that basis, have been under development since 1997. The medical and ethical advantage is that the method is non-invasive and can be used early (from week 6) in pregnancy. Many Western medical and public health communities see NIPD as highly desirable because it avoids the medical risks and ethical problems of late abortions carried by the current invasive techniques to extract foetal DNA. In several countries advanced stages of clinical trials with NIPD are under way and the technology is envisaged as a future routine element in antenatal care and national screening programmes.[8] There is a fast growing literature on the topic from which I will cite a selection to set the scene for the reflection on the cross-cultural effects of converging technologies and the resulting problems for science and technology policy-making.

The push to introduce NIPD into clinical routines (Chitty *et al.*, 2008; de Jong *et al.*, 2010) has been criticized by medical ethicists (Newson, 2008) who emphasize problems with informed consent (Wright and Chitty, 2009; Hall *et al.*, 2010) and the threat it poses to the principle of reproductive autonomy. In an exchange in *Nature Reviews Genetics* Schmitz, Netzer, and Henn defend parental autonomy, emphasizing that routine NIPFD would undermine the right not to know (Schmitz *et al.*, 2009). Against this view Ravitsky (2009) argues that prospective parents ought to be encouraged to have NIPD as early as possible. Others have argued that NIPD is yet another step towards the commodification of pregnancy and the genetic normalization of children (Skotko, 2009). NIPD offers, like other prenatal genetic testing, no therapeutic choices except continuation or termination of the pregnancy. It provides information on the genetics of the embryo/foetus only, other anomalies remain undetected. Kelly and Farrimond present findings from a small-scale study on public perceptions of NIPD in the UK, with participants generally responding positively but expressing worries about the potential for eugenic discrimination of disability. The participants favoured limiting NIPD to severe disorders (Farrimond and Kelly, 2013) and ask that sustainable regimes of counselling and care are put in place (Kelly and Farrimond, 2011).

The discussion I sketched above about the advantages and problems of NIPD reflects the concerns raised in countries where the sex of a child as such is generally not seen as an important aspect of its desirability. The problems and the general ethical and political picture change dramatically when NIPD is discussed in cultural contexts in which raising a male child is deemed much more preferable than raising a female child. The existing literature on NIPD mentions sex determination of the embryo and sex selection (Daar, 2011; King, 2011; Wright and Chitty, 2009) and suggests restricting sex selection to medical conditions such as sex-linked diseases. Yet it is recognized that there is no clear boundary which can be drawn in clinical practice between sex selection for foetal medical health and family acceptance. The wish for a 'balanced family', denoting a family consisting of mother, father, a boy, and a girl, had alarmed ethicists when reproductive technologies were applied in the USA for sex selection of pre-implantation embryos and in selective abortions. If this choice for a balanced family is socio-politically acceptable and part of clinical regimes, how can doctors single out the wish to have a son first? Cultural and political biases that disadvantage those who raise girls have motivated the use of pre-pregnancy sperm selection and sex-selective abortion, and have led to infanticide or abandonment in many countries, as has been documented since the 1980s (George, 2006). Global cross-cultural migration disperses the different cultural ideals of a desirable child across regulatory realms and challenges the cultural homogeneity implicitly assumed in the values that recommend NIPD in the UK or USA as ethically and medically beneficial. In 2012 and 2013 the UK revisited the rules under which sex selection and abortion are practised following reports that some doctors abort female foetuses on request. Grounds to prosecute these doctors could not be established. Yet, during the debate the issue was raised as to whether the detrimental effects of the birth of a female child to the mother's well-being and health ought to be considered in clinical decision-making about an abortion request in the UK. There are no firm boundaries for medical indications, and in multicultural societies ethical advice and ideals that built on relative value homogeneity within particular countries are simply inadequate.

The availability of NIPD not only through medical services but also on DTCGT markets means that its effects on practices of sex selection cannot be tightly controlled. This worries authorities in India and China, for example, where the sex ratio of births is becoming skewed towards male birth, increasingly causing negative effects on social life. It is not possible to prevent the use of technologies that are commonly used in some countries in other countries, or to treat pregnant women differently within one country based on the presumed cultural values of their country of origin or ancestry. The convergence of technologies, information exchanges and multicultural society and lifestyles mean that laws and best medical practice guides cannot stop the uptake of NIPD at home. There are also no defensible grounds from which a subsequent demand for an abortion, which we may assume to be in the rational best interest of the pregnant woman, cannot be denied or simply disregarded. Cultural contexts in which it is rational to assume that sex selection is a long-term social problem can only counter sex selection through cultural re-evaluations and political interventions that change the status of girls and women. The arguments Susan Sherwin provides for considering the cultural aspects of abortion and female genital mutilation can readily be applied to prenatal sex selection.

Converging technologies, normativity, and sociocultural differences

The convergences that have transformed genetics from an expert-only high-risk science to a wide-ranging set of open access technologies can inform science and technology policies in at least two ways. First, the perceived nature of a science or technology can alter quickly and is difficult to predict. Second, in liberal–democratic societies the scope for effective national or local government control over knowledge and technologies is decreasing – its time may be over for all knowledge and technologies that can be distributed globally using new media.

The stark tension between government support for new science and business ventures on the one hand, and protective sentiments towards the social status quo in which authorities govern technologies on the other, is borne out in the DTCGT debates. Policy-makers adopt a paternalist attitude towards the public and portray an attitude of 'humility' concerning current sociocultural values when demanding control over DTCGT for the good of humanity. The major problem for regulators and authorities is the lack of control over the quality of the tests and over the uses people make of them. Both render unpredictable the wider social effects, not least for the authority of medicine and science itself.

The meaning of DTCGT and NIPD depends on individual, social, and political contexts. Some of the tensions over NIPD do not arise from the genetic eugenic technology as such but is grounded in misogynist socio-political conditions. Asking along with Sherwin who establishes these cultural rules and who benefits from them, as feminists in India and China have done, leads to insight into oppressive gender orders that are unjustified and directly harmful to women and subsequently the whole of society. Yet for each woman considered individually, having a female child may involve long-term damage to her, her family, her marriage, and her physical and mental health. Policies that try to manoeuvre through a morass of radically opposed public and individual interests are unsustainable. Sex-discriminatory practices can only be addressed by changes to the sociocultural fabric of values and the interests that sustain them.

Drawing on recent social science studies, I have tried to disentangle the web of values, concepts, and presuppositions in the DTCGT debate. Nordmann calls the mutual admiration of the scientific and STS communities a potentially 'deadly embrace' (2007: 226). I want to apply this metaphor for bioethics and

STS on convergence more generally. Geneticists, counselors, and many bioethicists owe their livelihood to their contribution to the governance of genetics, so that collusion might seem a life-saver – at least for the time being. Yet, in this 'deadly embrace' they are credited with responsibility for the effects of the resulting practices of governance, and negative social outcomes may undermine the critical function of academia in the medium term. Sherwin proposes that policies need to be assessed critically concerning the power structures that inform and perpetuate themselves within them. Social practices that in effect disregard or oppress parts of a society, be that women or migrants from diverse cultural backgrounds, are morally and ethically unjustifiable. The GIG convergence needs to be reflected upon regarding globalization in terms of both markets and cultural heterogeneity.

Globally responsible means of ethical and social governance may be needed. The development of international product standards can be an important step towards responsible online markets for genetic tests. Yet another step has to be taken alongside it. We need to develop new representational formats in which cultural diversity can be represented in the interests of communities affected by the way in which new technologies may be introduced or governed. Currently, governments and experts configure their relationship towards the public as if that public was homogeneous and homogeneously in need of guidance. Instead of enhancing the critical ability to manage scientific knowledge and technologies autonomously, restriction policies undermine the potential for individuals to engage. The perpetuation of the discrimination of girls and women through short-term solutions to pre- or post-natal sex selection, such as restricting access or criminalization, oppresses pregnant women and should alert democratic governments and ethicists to the urgency with which they need to realize the real challenges posed by scientific and technological convergence. It may be possible to slow down such development but black markets cannot be halted as long as individual consumers have strong motives to use the tests.

Diagonal convergence stands for the ways in which there is no homogeneous referent for moral values, ethical practice and social and economic interests in ongoing convergence phenomena that can be defined meaningfully. Responsible governance and regulation need transnational integration in order to address the issues of product safety, forms of use, and short- and long-term societal effects locally and globally.

Notes

1 Examples with legal force are the European Concordat and Moratorium on Genetics and Insurance, adopted in the UK in 2005 and extended until 2017. Details available at: www.dh.gov.uk/en/Publicationsandstatistics/Publications/PublicationsPolicyAndGuidance/DH_4105905 or the US Genetic Information Non-Discrimination Act, GINA, from 2008, at: www.genome.gov/24519851 which extends previous restrictions for insurance and workplace-related application (accessed November 2013).

2 National Institute of Health, Secretary's Advisory Committee on Genetic Testing: 2000. *Enhancing the Oversight of Genetic Tests: Recommendations of the SACGT* (NIH, Bethesda). Available at: http://oba.od.nih.gov/oba/sacgt/reports/oversight_report.pdf (accessed November 2013).
3 Human Genetics Commission, 2009. A common framework of principles for direct-to-consumer genetic testing services. Available at: www.cellmark.co.uk/pdfs/HGCprinciples.pdf (accessed November 2013).
4 Australian Government. 2010. National Health and Medical Research Council (NHMRC). Medical testing: information for health professionals (section 7.1). Available at: www.nhmrc.gov.au/_files_nhmrc/file/publications/synopses/e99.pdf (accessed November 2013).
5 United States Food and Drug Administration. 2011. Molecular and clinical genetics panel meeting minutes. Meeting 8 and 9 March 2011. Available at: www.fda.gov/AdvisoryCommittees/CommitteesMeetingMaterials/MedicalDevices/MedicalDevicesAdvisoryCommittee/MolecularandClinicalGeneticsPanel/ucm245447.htm (accessed November 2013).
6 United States Federal Trade Commission. At-home genetic tests: A healthy dose of skepticism may be the best prescription, 2006 www.ftc.gov/bcp/edu/pubs/consumer/health/hea02.shtm (accessed November 2013).
7 The FDA's warning letter of the enforcement action, dating 22/11/2013, can be accessed at: www.fda.gov/ICECI/EnforcementActions/WarningLetters/2013/ucm376296.htm (accessed November 2013).
8 The UK National Health Service has set up a website on its five-year NIPD research programme at www.rapid.nhs.uk. This site is kept up to date with links to the most recent scientific articles on NIPD. An expert working group in the UK analysed the medical, social, and ethical aspects of NIPD and its implementation into screening programmes. Its report is published through the Foundation for Genomics and Population Health at www.phgfoundation.org/download/ffdna/ffDNA_report.pdf.

References

Annes, J. P., M. A. Giovanni and M. F. Murray (2010) 'Risks of presymptomatic direct-to-consumer genetic testing', *N Engl J Med* 363: 1100–1.

Ashcroft, R. (2007) 'Head to head: Should genetic information be disclosed to insurers? No.', *BMJ* 334: 1197.

Berg, C. and K. Fryer-Edwards (2008) 'The ethical challenges of direct-to-consumer genetic testing', *Journal of Business Ethics* 77: 17–31.

Bunnik, E. M., A. Janssens and M. H. Schermer (2012) 'Informed consent in direct-to-consumer personal genome testing: The outline of a model between specific and generic consent', *Bioethics* 28(7):343–51.

Chitty, L. S., C. E. van der Schoot, S. Hahn, *et al.* (2008) 'SAFE – The special non-invasive advances in fetal and neonatal evaluation network: aims and achievements', *Prenatal Diagnosis* 28: 83–8.

Corrigan, O. (2003) 'Empty ethics: The problem with informed consent', *Sociol Health Illn* 25: 768–92.

Daar, J. (2011) 'One small step for genetics, one giant leap for genocide?', *Rutgers LJ* 42: 705–819.

de Jong, A., W. J. Dondorp, C. E. de Die-Smulders, *et al.* (2010) 'Non-invasive prenatal testing: ethical issues explored', *Eur J Hum Genet* 18: 272–7.

de Vries, R., R. Dingwall and K. Orfali (2009) 'The moral organization of the professions: Bioethics in the United States and France', *Curr Sociol* 57: 555–79.

Eckenwiler, L. A. and F. G. Cohn (2009) *The ethics of bioethics: Mapping the moral landscape*. Baltimore, MA: JHU Press.

Edelman, E. and C. Eng (2009) 'A practical guide to interpretation and clinical application of personal genomic screening', *BMJ* 339: b4253.

Evans, J. H. (2012) *The history and future of bioethics: A sociological view*. Oxford: Oxford University Press.

Farrimond, H. R. and S. E. Kelly (2013) 'Public viewpoints on new non-invasive prenatal genetic tests', *Public Underst Sci* 22: 730–44.

George, S. M. (2006) 'Millions of missing girls: from fetal sexing to high technology sex selection in India', *Prenat Diagn* 26: 604–9.

Giovanni, M. A., M. R. Fickie, L. S. Lehmann, et al. (2010) 'Health-care referrals from direct-to-consumer genetic testing', *Genet Test Mol Biomarkers* 14: 817–19.

Green, R. and N. Farahany (2014) 'Regulation: The FDA is overcautious on consumer genomics.' *Nature* 505: 286–7.

Hall, A., A. Bostanci and C. Wright (2010) 'Non-invasive prenatal diagnosis using cell-free fetal DNA technology: Applications and implications'. *Public Health Genomics* 13: 246–55.

Hall, W. and C. Gartner (2009) 'Direct-to-consumer genome-wide scans: astrologicogenomics or simple scams?', *The American Journal of Bioethics* 9: 54–56.

Hauskeller, C. (2004) 'Genes, genomes and identity. Projections on matter', *New Genet Soc* 23: 285–99.

——(2011) 'Direct to consumer genetic testing', *BMJ* 342: d2317.

Hauskeller, C., S. Sturdy and R. Tutton (2013) 'Genetics and the sociology of identity', *Sociology* 47: 875–86.

Hogarth, S., G. Javitt and D. Melzer (2008) 'The current landscape for direct-to-consumer genetic testing: Legal, ethical, and policy issues', *Annual Review of Genomics and Human Genetics* 9: 161–82.

Holm, S. (2007) 'Head to head: Should genetic information be disclosed to insurers? Yes', *BMJ* 334: 1196.

Jasanoff, S. (2002) 'Citizens at Risk: Cultures of Modernity in the US and EU', *Science as Culture* 11: 363–80.

Javitt, G. H., E. Stanley and K. Hudson (2004) 'Direct-to-consumer genetic tests, government oversight, and the First Amendment: What the government can (and can't) do to protect the public's health', *Okla. L. Rev.* 57: 251.

Kaye, J. (2008) 'The regulation of direct-to-consumer genetic tests', *Human molecular genetics* 17: R180-R183.

Kelly, S. and H. Farrimond (2011) 'Non-invasive prenatal genetic testing: A study of public attitudes', *Public Health Genomics* 15: 73–81.

King, J. S. (2011) 'And genetic testing for all … The coming revolution in non-invasive prenatal genetic testing', *Rutgers LJ* 42: 599–819.

Kolor, K., T. Liu, J. St Pierre, et al. (2009) 'Health care provider and consumer awareness, perceptions, and use of direct-to-consumer personal genomic tests, United States, 2008', *Genetics in Medicine* 11: 595.

Lunshof, J. E., R. Chadwick, D. B. Vorhaus, et al. (2008) 'From genetic privacy to open consent', *Nature Reviews Genetics* 9: 406–11.

Mascalzoni, D., A. Hicks, P. Pramstaller, et al. (2008) 'Informed consent in the genomics era', *PLoS Medicine* 5: e192.

Messner, D. A. (2011) 'Informed choice in direct-to-consumer genetic testing for Alzheimer and other diseases: Lessons from two cases', *New Genetics and Society* 30: 59–72.
Newson, A. J. (2008) 'Ethical aspects arising from non-invasive fetal diagnosis', *Seminars in Fetal and Neonatal Medicine*. Oxford: Elsevier, pp. 103–8.
Nordmann, A. (2004) 'Converging technologies – Shaping the future of European societies', *Interim report of the Scenarios Group, High Level Expert group*: 3.
——(2007) 'Knots and strands: An argument for productive disillusionment', *Journal of Medicine and Philosophy* 32: 217–36.
Palsson, G. and P. Rabinow (1999) 'Iceland: The case of a national human genome project', *Anthropology Today* 15: 14–18.
Petersen, A. (2006) 'The genetic conception of health: Is it as radical as claimed?', *Health* 10: 481–500.
Ravitsky, V. (2009) 'Non-invasive prenatal diagnosis: An ethical imperative', *Nature Reviews Genetics* 10: 733–733.
Schmitz, D., C. Netzer and W. Henn (2009) 'An offer you can't refuse? Ethical implications of non-invasive prenatal diagnosis', *Nature Reviews Genetics* 10: 515–515.
Sherwin, S. (1992) *No longer patient: Feminist ethics and health care*. Philadelphia, PA: Temple University Press.
Skotko, B. G. (2009) 'With new prenatal testing, will babies with Down syndrome slowly disappear?', *Archives of disease in childhood* 94: 823–26.
Suzuki, D. T. and P. Knudtson (1989) *Genethics: The clash between the new genetics and human values*. Cambridge, MA: Harvard University Press.
Wasson, K., E. D. Cook and K. Helzlsouer (2005) 'Direct-to-consumer online genetic testing and the four principles: An analysis of the ethical issues', *Ethics & medicine: a Christian perspective on issues in bioethics* 22: 83–91.
Wright, C. F. and L. S. Chitty (2009) 'Cell-free fetal DNA and RNA in maternal blood: Implications for safer antenatal testing', *BMJ* 339.

Part IV
Citizens, amateurs, and democratization

9 Do-it-yourself biology, garage biology, and kitchen science
A feminist analysis of bio-making narratives

Clare Jen

Introduction

An emerging do-it-yourself (DIY) biotechnology movement has gained media traction as a promising democratization project. Once costly laboratory equipment and methods are now increasingly available to populations outside of exclusive public–private research walls. As announced by Meredith Patterson (2010) – a widely cited spokesperson for the movement: 'We the biopunks are dedicated to putting the tools of scientific investigation into the *hands of anyone who wants them*' (emphasis added). This science-for-the-people ethos, in convergence with a commercialized *maker culture*, has propelled the DIY biotech movement from geeky fringe to hip populist technoscience. Its practices are dubbed *do-it-yourself biology, amateur biology, hobby biology*, and *outlaw biology*. Its more site-oriented terms include *non-institutional biology, garage biology, kitchen biology, backyard biology*, and *basement biology*. Additionally, its practitioners are called *biohackers, biopunks, citizen scientists*, and *makers*. Many of these terms have gendered inheritances that bear scrutiny in this chapter.

In using *-making* and *-maker*, I draw from Maker Media's *Make*, a quarterly magazine that 'brings the do-it-yourself mindset' to 'help you make the most of your technology at home and away from home' (Maker Media, 2013a). It is 'the first magazine devoted to DIY ... technology projects, and is leading the maker movement' (*Make*, 2013). Of its 300,000 total readership, 81 per cent is male, 97 per cent is college-educated, and 73 per cent own homes, with an average annual household income of $107,600 and an average age of 44 (ibid.). *Make* deploys a narrative of 'technological utopianism' (Sivek, 2011: 197). As such, makers *make* to save themselves and the world. The American public engages in creative science and technology projects at home as a way to solve problems toward a better future. By making, they reclaim an American spirit of self-reliance and innovation and, in turn, resist corporate oppression, rescue the economy, protect the environment, and save humanity (Sivek, 2011). Maker Media also produces Maker Faires – annual multi-city events that gather 'tech enthusiasts, crafters, educators, tinkerers, hobbyists, engineers, science clubs, authors, artists, students, and commercial exhibitors' (Maker Media, 2013b).

I use *bio-making* to foreground this movement as a flexible configuration of DIY technoscientific artefacts and biotech activities, sites of origin and practice, and social identities and subjectivities. By *sites of origin*, I borrow from medical terminology that refers to a primary location in the body where atypical cell growth begins. In this chapter, it refers to the narrativization of the movement's beginnings, including archetypal figures as parts of origin stories. *Sites of practice* pertain to locations where bio-making culture takes place. The bio-making movement merges sociocultural interests in biotechnology's promissory values, with the political economy of *maker culture*, mythologies of American exceptionalism, and gender stratification in science, technology, and biomedicine. The movement's status as a democratization project is difficult to determine without first considering who is designated a bio-maker in its dominant narratives, what practices are considered bio-making, and upon what these determinations are contingent. Making visible the ways dominant narratives gender sites of origin and practice is significant. It bears consequences with respect to the legitimization and exclusion of practitioners and practices. This chapter finds that current bio-making narratives gender its figures and sites of origin and practice. Additionally, ongoing scholarship and media depictions do not conduct explicit analyses of gender as a dimension of bio-making culture.

Gender – a dimension of social stratification – is a source of keen interest in science and technology studies, sociology of health, medical anthropology, and science education. Broadly speaking, feminist science studies is concerned with how technoscientific discourses shape gender, and how gendered knowledge-practices shape science, technology, and society. With respect to biology, women's and gender studies scholars critique the field's operationalization of sex, gender, and sexuality; they interrogate the ways social–cultural and biological discourses shape epistemologies, methodologies, and artefacts (as examples see Haraway, 1991; Spanier, 1995; Fausto-Sterling, 2000; Martin, 2001; Roughgarden, 2004; Jordan-Young, 2010). Nature and culture are approached less as binary oppositions – with culture seen as a neutral representation of nature – and more as 'naturecultures' with nature and culture as co-constitutive and inflected by power relations (see Haraway, 2003; Subramaniam, 2009). The material and discursive production of social identities and subjectivities – via medical diagnostics in stratified biomedicalization – is also a source of acute interest to feminist scholars (as examples see Clarke *et al.*, 2003; Mamo, 2007; Orr, 2006). Feminist research is additionally interested in the histories and sociocultural meanings of technologies – such as pelvic massagers, mathematical numbers, and reproductive devices (as examples see Maines, 1998; Takeshita, 2011; Weston, 2002). Feminist approaches consider gender and power analyses to be integral to studies of science, technology, health, and society.

If the bio-making movement considers itself a democratization project – self-described as a formidable David to Big Bio's Goliath (Carlson, 2010: 187; Kelty, 2010: 1) – then scholars and practitioners must consider bio-making's gendered dimensions: how do its narratives of promise gender its subjects and their practices? How is bio-making, which is discursively produced as a democratization project, contingent upon and constitutive of social identities and subjectivities? Who remains on the margins of the margins? What are its local particularities? Fully addressing these questions requires an interdisciplinary mixture of methods and methodologies, including multi-sited ethnography and interviews, close readings of representations, and policy analyses.

In this chapter, I conduct a close reading of bio-making narratives and draw from situational analysis as a method. My sources include government, academic, and popular science publications. As a feminist extension of constructivist grounded theory, situational analysis (SA) conceptually maps '*all* the actors and discourses in the situation regardless of their power in that situation' (Clarke, 2012: 398; emphasis in original). Clarke recommends using SA in feminist inquiries concerned with 'elucidating differences, making silences speak, and revealing contradictions within positions and within social groups' (ibid.: 304). Popular science and research publications provide descriptions, commentaries, profiles, and analyses of US-based and international bio-making culture and bio-makers (see Angrist, 2010; Carlson, 2010; Delfanti, 2013; Hitt, 2012; Kelty, 2010; Ledford, 2010; Mckenna, 2009; Maher, 2007; Patterson, 2010; Schmidt, 2008; Weise, 2011; Wohlsen, 2012; Wolinsky, 2009).

This chapter suggests an alternative narrativization for bio-making's sites of origin and practice. Historical struggles and experiences of women and girls in institutionalized science, along with gender equity pedagogical practices, and hacks devised by feminist activists, all enact new biotechnology knowledge-practices out of necessity. Why, then, are these practices, identities, and narratives not prominently featured in current depictions of bio-making? One possibility is that unlike most featured bio-makers in published ethnographies and interviews, these overlooked subjects lack the social and cultural capital required to achieve equitable access to education, professional status, and other resources. Popular science and scholarly works conduct ethnographies and interviews of key bio-makers who already possess high levels of education and professional training in science and engineering fields. Based on current configurations of bio-making culture, scholars should consider possible gendered and classed barriers to DIY participation, such as educational and professional pedigrees, discretionary funds to pay into community biolabs, surplus time apart from familial and caregiver responsibilities, and unwelcoming community lab environments. In approaching bio-making culture, I suggest future analyses consider overlooked feminist and gender equity-oriented histories, social identities, and discourses.

Promissory democratization narrative, or hype?

Technoscientific innovations are forward-looking enterprises and are highly regarded as drivers for national economies and societal development (Pustovrh, 2013). To promote buy-in and investment in innovations, interested parties deploy *promissory narratives*. These narratives generate future-oriented abstractions in the form of expectations, hopes, and promises (see Chapter 3 in this volume; Brown and Michael, 2003; Borup *et al.*, 2006; Sunder Rajan, 2006; Tutton, 2011; van Lente, 2012). Bio-making discourse deploys anticipatory narratives about biotech futures that are more democratic than the present. For example, *Make* (2103) describes itself: 'MAKE has a devoted audience of tech-savvy, DIY enthusiasts who are shaping the future with their innovative projects and ideas.' DIYbio.org states: 'Central to our mission is the belief that biotechnology and greater public understanding about it has the potential to benefit everyone.' Bio-making – as a science and technology innovation for the people – promises a more democratic future in which the public can interface with biotechnology in empowering ways. No longer will the public have to scale the tall walls of Big Bio.

Borrowing from Kelty's (2010) coinage of 'Big Bio', Delfanti (2013: 4) contours Big Bio's exclusionary characteristics: high costs of establishing and maintaining a laboratory; required levels of formal education and training for employment in university and corporate research labs; scientific and technological complexities of bioscience research; and legal bureaucracies related to bioinformation access. Physicist Rob Carlson (2005) – who is credited as having the 'first garage biology operation' (Church and Regis, 2012: 234) – famously declared in *Wired*: 'The era of garage biology is upon us. Want to participate?' In 2008, Jason Bobe and Mackenzie Cowell founded DIYbio.org to foster community and circulate knowledge-practices – such as how to hack ordinary household items into centrifuges and how to fund DIY biology collectives (DIYbio.org). Meyer (2012) considers 'citizen biotech-economies' as these DIY relations between objects, networks, and people. Bio-making lauds the hacking of mundane objects, values social networks that are mediated through artefacts, and promotes the open sharing of knowledge and resources. Since 2008, community biolabs – including Genspace and BioCurious – have opened in metropolitan areas across the USA.

The following section discusses two prominent threads in bio-making's democratization narrative: the bio-maker as American amateur, and the bio-maker as synthetic biology-oriented computer hacker. Both threads locate *garages* as sites of origin.

American amateurs and mythological garages

With article titles and headlines, such as 'Garage biology': 'Amateur scientists who experiment at home should be welcomed by professionals' (Campbell, 2010), it is clear that bio-making is associated with amateurism and at-home spaces. Journalist Jack Hitt (2012: 9) contextualizes bio-making as a legacy of an American amateurism that resides in the 'mythological garage'. Benjamin Franklin hobbied at home; Apple grew from Steve Jobs's Cupertino garage; amateur biologists tinker in homemade labs. While defining American amateurs as 'men or women, old or young', his framing – particularly his use of boyhood nostalgia – explicitly genders bio-making, its practitioners, and its siting as masculine (Hitt, 2012: 3).

He indulges in boyhood nostalgia, recounting experiences building secret forts and spray-painting government buildings. He compares his secret forts to his first visit to Cowell's 'secret meeting place where his crowd of local homebrew geneticists teach the basics of DNA extraction' (ibid.: 105). These experiences are considered boyishly playful and harmless in their risk-taking and indiscretions. His chapter's sub-heading (ibid.: 104), 'A Boy's Life, Recombinated', alludes to *Boys' Life* – a Boy Scouts of America publication (Boys' Life, 2013). Continued references include: 'How does one promote healthy Boy's Club fun for synbio[logy] at a time when Americans regularly hear about anthrax attacks' (Hitt, 2012: 110).

Additionally, Hitt interviews Jason Bobe, Mackenzie Cowell, and Meredith Patterson. His description of Patterson follows masculinist scripts. While he does not describe the physical appearances of Bobe and Cowell, he does at length for Patterson: 'She's Meredith Patterson, a thirty-something woman pushing five-foot-ten, who favors combat boots and butch leather jackets. She wears the kind of glasses slightly pinched at the tips like cats' eyes to finish off her look with a nice hint of 1950s girl nerd' (ibid.: 113). He directs the reader to assess Patterson's physical appearance using clear designations of masculinity and femininity. Emphasis on femininity and women's physical appearances is associated with levels of success in STEM fields (Pronin *et al.*, 2004), likeability in male-dominated tasks (Heilman and Okimoto, 2007), competence and trustworthiness (Etcoff *et al.*, 2011), salary (Nash *et al.*, 2006), and motivation in young girls to pursue STEM fields (Betz and Sekaquaptewa, 2012). Hitt's description reifies a double bind faced by women and girls. Second, while other amateur biologists practise in and around kitchens, only Patterson is invoked as a 'kitchen biologist' (ibid.: 116). The mythological garage is the assumed at-homing siting for amateur male-practised biology.

Computer hackers and mythological garages

In this second thread, the bio-maker is considered a computer hacker involved in synthetic biology (synbio). Emerging from convergences in engineering principles and living systems (Knowles, 2010: 38), synbio aims to make 'biology easier to engineer' (Zhang *et al.*, 2011: 3). It is commonly understood as 'the design and fabrication of biological components and systems that do not already exist in the natural world [and] the re-design and fabrication of existing biological systems' ('Synthetic Biology: FAQ'). Increased accessibility of lab equipment, such as DNA sequencers, and affordability of tasks, like protein synthesis through commercial services, have hastened the diffusion of synthetic biology outside Big Bio's fortress walls (National Research Council, 2011).

Biohackers usually have computer programming or engineering backgrounds, and they frame synthetic biology using metaphors of hardware, software, open source, and standardization. As an example, in a journal article, the application of engineering standardization principles is termed '*Pimp* my chassis', to describe the incorporation of bio-parts into a minimal genome (2008: 4). In the author's explanation, he alludes to *Pimp My Ride*, a MTV garage show about over-the-top car customizations (MTV). However, more importantly, mainstream cultural images that glamorize 'pimping' belie its real-life meaning as an economic system that sexually exploits women's bodies (Katz, 2006: 194). Consequently, the 'mythological garage' remains the masculine, perhaps unintentionally sexist, site of bio-making practice. After all, as science columnist Jason Golob (2007) explains: 'It took groups like the Homebrew Computer Club – *literally a bunch of unshaved guys in a garage* – to create the personal computer and really revolutionize the world' (emphasis in original). Additionally, the 'future Bill Gate of biotech could be developing a cure for cancer in the garage' (Wohlsen, 2008). Computer science is a male-dominated culture. Even in terms of education and training, computer science lags behind most other STEM fields with respect to US gender equity (Hill *et al.*, 2010). The computer-savvy bio-maker is a masculinized subject in a male-dominated realm.

Hype?

Bio-making practices of American amateurs and computer hackers are sited in literal and 'mythological garages'. The stressing of masculinized at-home sites – as opposed to feminized kitchens – is significant. Since the origins of modern experimental science, the siting of scientific knowledge production has been highly gendered, classed, and sexualized (Potter, 2001; Shapin, 1999). Bio-making also occurs in literal kitchens, so why not elevate the kitchen to mythological status? Why not consider feminized spaces as sites of origin and feminist subjects as archetypal figures? Is it because an alternative origin story – one that centres the historical and current struggles of women and girls as *kitchen scientists* – dampens bio-making's promissory democratization narrative?

When promissory narratives fail, they are often dismissed as hype. Borup *et al.* (2006: 290) explain: 'Expectations of technology are ... seen to foster a kind of historical amnesia – hype is about the future and the new – rarely about the past – so the disjunctive aspects of technological change are often emphasized and continuities with the past are erased from promissory memory.' If bio-making – as biotechnological innovation – ultimately fails to deliver on its promise to democratize science, then is its narrative more hype than promissory? Can bio-making's promissory narrative only stand on 'a kind of historical amnesia' that overlooks the relative educational and professional privileges of its leaders? Must it 'erase from [its] promissory memory' the populations that encounter structural barriers to science education and professions? It is clear that *garages* and *kitchens* are not interchangeable sites of practice in current bio-making narratives.

Reconfigured narratives: kitchen science 2.0, Ms. Science, and feminist biohealth hacker

Masculinized bio-making is predominantly framed as updated American amateur hobbyism and computer hacking. As an exception, Patterson's 'A Biopunk Manifesto' (2010) espouses an ethos that is explicitly political and implicitly feminist:

> Curiosity knows no ethnic, gender, age, or socioeconomic boundaries, but the opportunity to satisfy that curiosity all too often turns on economic opportunity, and we aim to break down that barrier. A thirteen-year-old kid in South Central Los Angeles has just as much of a right to investigate the world as does a university professor. If thermocyclers are too expensive to give one to every interested person, then we'll design cheaper ones and teach people how to build them ... Biopunks take responsibility for their research. We keep in mind that our subjects of interest are living organisms worthy of respect and good treatment, and we are acutely aware that our research has the potential to affect those around us ... we desire nothing more than to empower you to discover the answers to them yourselves.

Her biopunk principles build on the concept of 'hacktivism' – the use of computer technology as political activism (Magaudda, 2012). Mainstream coverage of hacker culture largely focuses on men and ignores women activist hackers and their feminist foundations (Muhammad, 2000/2001). Interestingly, Patterson's political and ethical concerns align with feminist activisms. Feminist interventions in scientific knowledge-practices also challenge barriers to scientific literacy (Hanson, 2009; Hill *et al.*, 2010) and emphasize sociocultural context as methodological concerns (Roy, 2004; Spanier, 1995). I argue that Patterson frames her biopunk vision as a form of feminist technoscience activism (Jen 2014). Extending her vision, I contend that biohacking thermocyclers is as akin to *kitchen science* as it is to *garage biology*. This expresses a rupture in current dominant bio-making discourse in which the 'mythological garage' precludes the *kitchen* as an equally legitimate origin site.

In this section, I pose a different configuration of bio-making that is not contingent on masculinized promissory narratives. First, I trace bio-making as kitchen science 2.0. This updated version is a legacy of household science. By doing so, I recast bio-making as science on the feminized periphery. Second, I bring into relief bio-making's relation to the US women's health movement. Out of necessity and often to save lives, feminists have had to hack biomedical devices and *make* alternative citizen biotech economies. This different assemblage recognizes the convergences of everyday biotechnology knowledge-practices with STEM equity struggles and feminist activisms.

Bio-making as kitchen science 2.0

In his ethnography of 'biohackers' around the world, Delfanti (2013: 115) finds that citizen biology evidences little of its media's portrayal as paradigm-shifting scientific innovation: 'in many cases citizen biology consists of very elementary scientific practices, and community labs are often poorly equipped and cannot be compared to corporate or academic labs ... DIYbio activities often consist of basic practices such as DNA extraction or bacteria isolation with household tools and products'. One survey finds that DNA extraction is the most frequently performed activity (Grushkin *et al.*, 2013: 11). If this is the current state, then masculine garage biology is actually very similar to the at-home biology practices of feminized kitchen science. The same DNA extraction method is described as an example of kitchen science activities funded by the National Science Foundation (NSF).

NSF (2003) provides grants to support localized efforts around the country aimed at proportionate representation of women and girls in STEM fields. In its report, NSF invokes 'kitchens' in two ways. Kitchens are mentioned in terms of 'kitchen science' and as kitchen objects that can double as laboratory equipment and materials. Second, the kitchen is mentioned as a literal place where women, who upon returning to school in STEM fields, may find themselves 'struggling alone with calculus ... on the kitchen table late at night' (ibid.: 174). In these ways, *kitchens* serve as sites of scientific education and practice for women and girls. Stated differently, kitchen science functions as an alternative citizen biotech economy that aims to democratize access to scientific investigation. Why, then, is *kitchen science* not elevated to the realm of masculine bio-making as part of the next industrial revolution? Why not canonize the *mythological kitchen*?

Other science pedagogy curriculums use kitchen science practices to support diversity in STEM fields. Kitchen Science Investigators couples hands-on cooking with lab activities to teach students how scientific reasoning can improve food preparation (Gardner and Clegg, 2009). This food science approach is not without controversy. Critics assert that the use of domestic frames to teach science to girls is actually more oppressive than empowering. It 'can limit what is recognized as scientific knowledge for girls. As with boys, girls need access to "big" science as well as "kitchen" science' (Cervoni and Ivinson, 2011: 471).

Exploring this discounting of kitchen science – and why current bio-making narratives follow masculine and avoid feminine scripts – requires understanding the historical marginalization of women in university science departments. Nerad (1999) provides a thorough case study of how home economics departments functioned as gender stratification mechanisms. During the Progressive Era, university presidents faced increased numbers of women students and feared that women would outcompete men. As a response, male educators supported the establishment of home economics departments to effect a sex segregation of the student body and, in turn, created an unequal separate

DIY biology, garage biology, kitchen science 133

sphere of women's work at the faculty level. Women scientists, who earned doctorates in male-dominated disciplines like organic chemistry and biochemistry, faced enormous difficulty securing faculty positions in their fields of training. However, they did find employment teaching household sciences in grossly underfunded and low-status home economics departments (ibid.: 78, 138). This did not mean they were not engaged in rigorous, innovative scientific research; women scientists published prolifically and advanced human nutrition into a prestigious and grant-worthy research area (ibid.: 124, 138).

Bio-making as kitchen science 2.0 is rooted in the overlooked feminist struggles and successes of twentieth-century women scientists. Current bio-making activities also align with the food science component of home economics. As an example, University of California, Los Angeles hosts 'Science and Food', a public lecture series associated with its life sciences course, 'The Physical and Molecular Origins of What We Eat'. It 'promote[s] the public understanding of science through food and food through science' (Keller, 2013). Its website features 'DIY Kitchen Science' – a collection of recipes coupled with their biochemical explanations (scienceandfood.org). Additionally, a direct connection between kitchen science and bio-making can be made in food science-based activities in Singapore and Indonesia. Singaporean bio-making, in a 'strange form of science activism', empowered citizens to hack rice cookers into *sous-vide* baths in protest against a government health campaign (Kera, 2012). An Indonesian biohacking project democratized fermentation methods by creating wine brewing kits for the public to challenge 'exploitative' alcohol taxes (ibid.).

The *garage* carries residues of privileged masculine exclusivity. An alternative narrative reclaims the *kitchen* as a metaphorical site of origin and practice. Even with its complicated history as a separate sphere for women's scientific practice and education, to frame bio-making as kitchen science 2.0 expands its promissory narrative to include overlooked histories and experiences. The following subsection considers a convergence between bio-making's patient advocacy narratives and feminist health politics.

Bio-making and US women's health movement

Popular science and scholarly writings spotlight many of the same individuals whose bio-making activities are driven by health-related necessities. In the following cases, these depictions present bio-makers as patient advocates. Kay Aull – who earned the first biological engineering degree from Massachusetts Institute of Technology – developed an inexpensive genetic test for hemochromatosis in her closet biolab. She wanted to determine whether she and her mother were carriers for the disorder (Angrist, 2010; Mckenna, 2009; Ricks, 2011; Wohlsen, 2012). One of Meredith Patterson's projects included developing an accessible tool for the developing world to test for melamine contamination in milk supplies (Wohlsen, 2012; Meyer, 2012). Prompted by a friend's death from cancer, Eri Gentry, who is a co-founder of BioCurious, and her friend John Schloendorn raised funds to start a biotech lab in Gentry's garage to conduct anti-cancer research (Church and Regis, 2012). Finally, physician Hugh Reinhoff is depicted as frustrated with current medical science's inability to diagnose his daughter's mysterious health condition; he works at home to identify gene variants in his daughter's sequence data (Angrist, 2010; Maher, 2007; Ricks, 2011).

Most existing literatures on bio-making do not connect this patient advocacy narrative to feminist activism. *Nature* editor Brendan Maher's (2007) and geneticist Misha Angrist's (2010) features on Reinhoff are close. Reinhoff is described as a 'social activist' who works to 'raise consciousness', 'empower others', and demystify science (Maher, 2007: 776). However, as Maher (ibid.) explains, his daughter's doctor was concerned that 'Rienhoff's example may lead some parents down the wrong path, searching for answers in genes and diverting resources from the important goal of making sure their children are receiving proper care.' Angrist (2010: 186) describes this sentiment as shocking 'paternalism'.

Maher (2007) and Angrist (2010) frame Reinhoff's bio-making as patient advocacy – social activism aimed at the empowerment of others, increased scientific transparency, and resistance against paternalistic biomedicine. This advocacy narrative echoes US women's health movement politics. As brief illustration, 1960s feminist health activism successfully brought about federal government requirements that contraceptive pill manufacturers include patient package inserts containing side-effect information. Before this requirement, women relied on physicians for safety information; however, many physicians withheld information out of paternalistic concerns that they would needlessly worry women. Feminists wanted women to have all available information necessary to ensure real informed consent (Watkins, 2012). This patient advocacy narrative – with Reinhoff as its star – has roots in women's health politics.

Ms. Science and feminist biohealth hacker

An analysis of bio-making's gendered dimensions prompts these queries: how do its narratives legitimize practitioners? For whom is bio-making a democratization process? Who remains on the margins of the margins? In his summary of bio-maker figures, Kelty (2010) poses three masculine archetypes: the 'outlaw' ('like Robin Hood'), the 'hacker', and the 'Victorian Gentleman Scientist'. I pose two additional figures: Ms. Science and the feminist biohealth hacker. Current narratives of bio-making exclude feminized and feminist knowledge-practices and, in turn, delegitimize them as bio-makers.

Ms. Science embodies bio-making as kitchen science 2.0. Wolinsky's (2009: 683) interview with Debra Katz, an amateur biologist, expresses this: 'Katz said that extracting her DNA "[…] was not hard at all. I was getting a kick out of trying to be *Ms Science*." She noted that although she had no interest in science during her high-school and college years, conducting this particular procedure herself connected her intellectually with her genetic-genealogy work and helped to make DNA more real for her' (emphasis added). Ms. Science delights in her scientific curiosity and finds empowerment in her at-home biolab. She challenges the hyper-masculinization of dominant bio-making narratives.

Feminist biohealth hackers embody a convergence of biotechnologies and feminist technoscience practices. Out of necessity, women have constructed alternative citizen-biotech economies to provide for women's needs in ways not adequately met in stratified biomedicalization. In the 1970s, women's self-help groups formed as US feminist consciousness-raising networks. They shared information about their medical establishment experiences, educated each other about their bodies, and disseminated alternative medical treatment information. Pelvic self-exams, using speculums and mirrors, gained practical and iconic significance as an empowerment tool and technology of resistance. From these groups grew women's health publications, including *Our Bodies, Ourselves*, and women-controlled, women-centred alternative clinics (Kapsalis, 1997: 161–2). Between 1986 and 1972, the Jane Collective – founded and ran by women college students who taught themselves termination procedures – provided over 12,000 safe, affordable, illegal abortions (Kirtz and Lundy, 1996). Contemporarily, women's health practitioners in developing countries biohack Pap smears. They use vinegar and carbon dioxide from tanks obtained from Coca-Cola bottling plants to visualize and freeze off possible cancerous cells (McNeil, 2011). Feminist biohealth hackers work to democratize technoscientific literacy and healthcare services for those most marginalized; they should be considered part of the bio-making movement. Like Aull, Patterson, Gentry, Scloendorn, and Reinhoff, they contribute to alternative citizen biotechnology economies aimed toward meeting population-level healthcare needs.

Dominant narratives showcase masculinized figures – amateur, outlaw, hacker, Victorian Gentlemen Scientist – and locate its origins and practices as garage biology. An alternative narrative recasts bio-making as kitchen science 2.0 and feminist health politics. It introduces additional figures – Ms. Science and feminist biohealth hacker – as integral to bio-making's promissory democratization vision.

Conclusion: feminist thoughts on a bio-making future

In 2011, Maker Media accepted a $10 million grant from the US Defense Advanced Research Projects Agency (Altman, 2012). This partnership with the US military prompted Mitch Altman, an esteemed hacker pioneer, to refuse further participation in its gatherings. His departure made waves in the Maker Faire community. Given that this highly visible fragment of bio-maker culture has partnered with the US military–industrial complex, are we at a crucial moment? Are we ushering in a *bio-making regime*? Is the lay public now subject to a new sphere of neo-liberal technoscientific governance?

As explained by Brown (2005: 42), neo-liberal governmentality 'normatively constructs and interpellates individuals as entrepreneurial actors in every sphere of life. It figures individuals as rational, calculating creatures whose moral autonomy is measured by their capacity for "self-care" – the ability to provide for their own needs and service their own ambitions.' This logic legitimizes decreased government responsibility for social provisions and exalts privatization and individual responsibility (Gill and Scharff, 2011: 5). Critics charge this mode of political–economic rationality as disparately impacting historically marginalized populations who experience diminished access to resources (Jen, 2013; Mariner *et al.*, 2005). Achieving status as a model neo-liberal subject is largely contingent upon consumption as an exercise of moral autonomy. Under Sunder Rajan's (2006: 3, 149) concept of *biocapitalism* – defined as a new phase of capitalism in which 'biotechnology is a new form of enterprise inextricable from contemporary capitalism' – the configuration of the Western neoliberal subject includes 'patients- and consumer[s]-in-*waiting*' (emphasis added). Under the logic of a bio-making regime, model neo-liberal subject status becomes contingent upon one's bio-making capacity. Bio-makers do not *wait* for biocapitalism to shape their already present subjectivities as patients-consumers. Bio-makers are now expected to employ scientific knowledge and technological knowhow as entrepreneurial actors; they bio-engineer their own technoscientific artefacts as solutions; they bio-make in the pursuit of self-care.

Dr Amy Baxter's 'Hacking Healthcare' (2013) talk at Maker Faire Bay Area illustrates a nascent bio-making regime. Triply situated as physician, mother, and inventor, she announces maker culture's potential to fix the nation's healthcare system:

> The $500 co-pay [for the removal of a splinter] is not the disease but a symptom of a healthcare system that has gotten so complicated and a legal system that has gotten so scary, that we feel we cannot act … If we are makers, we should be able to take this problem like we take any other; take it apart, figure it out, and come up with a solution … How we approach healthcare is the final hack … You take care of your healthcare everyday. It is your body every single day. We should be empowered to act … We're paying for this system. We need to own it.

She upholds her own medical device invention as a symbol for how the public needs to hack its way out of the healthcare system's inequalities. She adheres to Maker Media's technological utopian vision, while she challenges dominant masculine maker archetypes. However, caution against conflating Baxter's bio-maker subjectivity with feminist biohealth hacking is warranted. She poses a promissory narrative that problematically adheres to the logic of an emergent bio-making regime. She engages in the 'historical amnesia' required of failed promissory narratives. The lay public – who mostly do not share Baxter's level of social and cultural capital in the biosciences – is not equipped to succeed as newly configured bio-maker subjects. Additionally, this bio-making regime frames citizen-sourced biotechnological inventions as solutions to structural problems. This is not a bio-making future to hasten.

For this reason, researchers should pay attention to maker culture's appropriation of gender equity and feminist activisms as they converge with biotechnologies. With increased commercialization of bio-maker culture and tighter alliances with biocapitalism and the US military–industrial complex, a rising bio-making regime may reconfigure neo-liberal governance in ways that newly discipline subjects to assume bio-making as moral imperative. This would disparately impact marginalized populations who already encounter barriers to scientific literacy and skills.

This chapter argues that existing bio-making discourse deploys promissory narratives that are laden with gendered archetypes and symbols. Government, popular science, and research publications neither reflexively consider their uses of gendered languages, nor do they conduct explicit gendered analyses of bio-making discourse. Furthermore, though these texts lack uniformity in their delineation of bio-making's practices, purposes, and participants (and thus signal its liquid and shifting configurations), these texts overwhelmingly remain silent on biotechnology's convergences with STEM equity initiatives, women's historical struggles in US institutionalized science, and women's health activisms. This is especially surprising considering bio-making's promissory democratization narrative. For whom are bio-makers democratizing biotechnologies? This analysis suggests that future research priorities will likely include the following: incorporation of gender analyses of bio-making discourse; engagement in a methodological reflexivity that considers gendered dimensions of a bio-making regime; inclusion of women, girls, and feminists as informants; and attentiveness to maker culture's appropriation of gender equity and feminist activist discourses.

References

Altman, M. (2012) 'Hacking at the Crossroad: US Military Funding of Hackerspaces', *Journal of Peer Production* (2). Available at: http://peerproduction.net/issues/issue-2/invited-com ments/hacking-at-the-crossroad [accessed 15 June 2013].

Angrist, M. (2010) *Here Is a Human Being: At the Dawn of Personal Genomics*. New York: HarperCollins Publishers.

Baxter, A. (2013) 'Hacking Healthcare – How Makers Can Save Medicine, Maker Faire Bay Area'. Available at: http://fora.tv/2013/05/19/Amy_Baxter_Hack ing_Healthcare_How_ Makers_Can_Save_Medicine [accessed 16 June 2013].

Betz, D. E. and D. Sekaquaptewa (2012) 'My Fair Physicist? Feminist Math and Science Role Models Demotivate Young Girls', *Social Psychological and Personality Science* 3(6): 738–46.

Borup, M., N. Brown, K. Konrad and H. Van Lente (2006) 'The Sociology of Expectations in Science and Technology', *Technology Analysis and Strategic Management* 18(3/4): 285–98.

Boys' Life (2013) http://boyslife.org [accessed 19 December 2013].

Brown, N. and M. Michael (2003) 'A Sociology of Expectations: Retrospecting Prospects and Prospecting Retrospects', *Technology Analysis and Strategic Management* 15(1): 3–18.

Brown, W. (2005) 'Neoliberalism and the End of Liberal Democracy', in *Edgework: Critical Essays in Knowledge and Politics*. Princeton, NJ: Princeton University Press, pp. 37–59.

Campbell, P. (ed.) (2010) 'Garage biology', *Nature* 467(7316): 634.

Carlson, R. (2005) 'Splice it Yourself', *Wired* 13(5). Available at: www.wired.com/wired/archive/13.05/view.html?pg=2 [accessed 25 June 2013].

——(2010) *Biology is Technology: The Promise, Peril, and New Business of Engineering Life*. Cambridge, MA: Harvard University Press.

Cervoni, C. and G. Ivinson (2011) 'Girls in Primary School Science Classrooms: Theorising beyond Dominant Discourses of Gender', *Gender and Education* 23(4): 461–75.

Church, G. and E. Regis (2012) *Regenesis: How Synthetic Biology Will Reinvent Nature and Ourselves*. New York: Basic Books.

Clarke, A. E. (2012) 'Feminism, Grounded Theory, and Situational Analysis Revisited', in *The Handbook of Feminist Research: Theory and Praxis*. Los Angeles, CA: Sage. pp. 388–412.

——, et al. (2003) 'Biomedicalization: Technoscientific Transformations of Health, Illness, and U.S. Biomedicine', *American Sociological Review* 68: 161–94.

Delfanti, A. (2013) *Biohackers: The Politics of Open Science*. London: Pluto Press.

DIYbio.org (n.d.) 'An Institution for the Do-It-Yourself Biologist', *DIY BIO*. Available at: http://diybio.org [accessed 29 June 2013].

Etcoff, N. L., et al. (2011) 'Cosmetics as a Feature of the Extended Human Phenotype: Modulation of the Perception of Biologically Important Facial Signals', *PLoS ONE* 6(10): 1–9.

Fausto-Sterling, A. (2000) *Sexing the Body: Gender Politics and the Construction of Sexuality*. New York: Basic Books.

Gardner, C. and T. Clegg, (2009) *KSI Overview Handout*. http://home.cc.gatech.edu/ksi/uploads/10/KSI_Overview.pdf [accessed 20 June 2013].

Gill, R. and C. Scharff (2011) 'Introduction' in *New Femininities: Postfeminism, Neoliberalism and Subjectivity*. London: Palgrave Macmillan, pp. 1–17.

Golob, J. (2007) 'Homebrew Molecular Biology Club', *The Stranger*. Available at: http://slog.thestranger.com/2007/11/homebrew_molecular_biology_club [accessed 11 June 2013].

Grushkin, D., T. Kuiken and P. Millet (2013) *Seven Myths and Realities about Do-It-Yourself Biology*. Washington, DC: Wilson Center. Available at: http://bit.ly/I10Esr [accessed 19 November 2013].

Hanson, S. L. (2009) *Swimming Against the Tide: African American Girls and Science Education*. Philadelphia, PA: Temple University Press.

Haraway, D. (1991) *Simians, Cyborgs, and Women: The Reinvention of Nature*. New York: Routledge.

——*The Companion Species Manifesto: Dogs, People, and Significant Otherness*. Chicago, IL: Prickly Paradigm Press.

Heilman, M. E. and T. G. Okimoto (2007) 'Why Are Women Penalized for Success at Male Tasks? The Implied Communality Deficit', *Journal of Applied Psychology*, 92(1): 81–92.

Hill, C., C. Corbett and A. St. Rose (2010) *Why So Few: Women in Science, Technology, Engineering, and Mathematics*. Washington, DC: AAUW.

Hitt, J. (2012) *Bunch of Amateurs: A Search for the American Character*. New York: Crown Publishers.

Jen, C. (2013) 'How to Survive Contagion, Disease and Disaster: "Masked Asian/American Woman" as Low-Tech Specter of Emergency Preparedness', *Feminist Formations* 25(2): 107–28.

Jen, C. (2014) 'Feminist Techno Science Activism: A Double Stranded Reading of Dr. Boduar's Ig Nobel Striptease', *Rhizomes* 26. Available at: www.rhizomes.net/issue26/jen.htm/ [accessed 29 October 2014].

Jordan-Young, R. (2010) *Brain Storm: The Flaws in Science of Sex Differences*. Cambridge, MA: Harvard University Press.

Kapsalis, T. (1997) *Public Privates: Performing Gynecology From Both Ends of the Spectrum*. Durham, NC: Duke University Press.

Katz, J. (2006) *The Macho Paradox: Why Some Men Hurt Women and how All Men Can Help*. Naperville, IL: Sourcebooks.

Keller, C. (2013) 'UCLA's "Science and Food" 2013 Lecture Series Lineup Announced', *Los Angeles Times*. Available at: www.latimes.com/features/food/dailydish/la-dd-ucla-science-and-food-2013-lecture-series-lineup-announced-20130315,0,2449451.story [accessed 20 June 2013].

Kelty, C. M. (2010) 'Outlaw, Hackers, Victorian Amateurs: Diagnosing Public Participation in the Life Sciences Today', *Journal of Science Communication* 9(1). Available at: http://jcom.sissa.it/archive/09/01/Jcom0901%282010%29C01/Jcom0901%282010%29C03/Jcom0901%282010%29C03.pdf [accessed 12 June 2013].

Kera, D. (2012) 'Hackerspaces and DIYbio in Asia: connecting science and community with open data, kits and protocols', *Journal of Peer Production* (2). Available at: http://peerproduction.net/issues/issue-2/peer-reviewed-papers/diybio-in-asia/ [accessed 15 June 2013].

Kirtz, K. and N. Lundy (1996) *Jane: An Abortion Service*. Independent Television Service.

Knowles, L. P. (2010) 'Dual-Use Governance Measures', in *Double-Edged Innovations*. Ft. Belvoir, VA: Defense Threat Reduction Agency, pp. 38–63.

Ledford, H. (2010) 'Garage Biotech: Life Hackers', *Nature* 467(7316): 650–2.

Mckenna, P. (2009) 'Amateur Biologists play with DNA', *New Scientist* 200(2688): 20–1.

McNeil, Jr., D. G. (2011) 'Fighting Cervical Cancer with Vinegar and Ingenuity', *The New York Times*. Available at: www.nytimes.com/2011/09/27/health/27cancer.html?_r=0 [accessed 16 June 2013].

Magaudda, P. (2012) 'How to make a "Hackintosh": A Journey into the "Consumerization" of Hacking Practices and Culture', *Journal of Peer Production* (2). Available at: http://peerproduction.net/issues/issue-2/peer-reviewed-papers/how-to-make-a-hackintosh [accessed 16 June 2013].

Maher, B. (2007) 'His Daughter's DNA', *Nature* 449: 772–6.

Maines, R. (1998) *The Technology of Orgasm: 'Hysteria', The Vibrator, and Women's Sexual Satisfaction*. Baltimore, MD: Johns Hopkins University Press.

Make (n.d.) *Make 2013 Media Kit*. Available at: http://cdn.makezine.com/make/sales/2013-Media-Kit-Sales.pdf [accessed 29 August 2013].

Maker Media (2013a) 'Frequently Asked Questions', *Make*. Available at: https://reader services.makezine.com/mk/SubFAQ.aspx?PC=MK&pk=m25scho#faq001 [accessed 24 June 2013].

——(2013b) 'Maker Faire: A Bit of History', *Maker Faire*. Available at: http://makerfaire.com/makerfairehistory [accessed 24 June 2013].

Mamo, L. (2007) *Queering Reproduction: Achieving Pregnancy in the Age of Technoscience*. Durham, NC: Duke University Press.

Mariner, W., G. Annas and L. H. Glantz (2005) 'Jacobson v Massachusetts: It's Not your Great-Great-Grandfather's Public Health Law', *American Journal of Public Health* 95(4): 581–90.

Martin, E. (2001) *The Woman in the Body: A Cultural Analysis of Reproduction*. Boston, MA: Beacon Press.

Meyer, M. (2012) 'Build Your Own Lab: Do-It-Yourself Biology and the Rise of Citizen Biotech-Economies', *Journal of Peer Production* (2). Available at: http://peerproduction.net/issues/issue-2/invited-comments/build-your-own-lab/ [accessed 22 May 2013].

MTV (n.d.) 'About the Show', *Pimp My Ride*. Available at: www.mtv.com/shows/pimp_my_ride/season_5/series.jhtml#moreinfo [accessed 26 June 2013].

Muhammad, E. (2000) 'Hacktivism', *Ms* 11(1): 74–6.

Nash, R., *et al.* (2006) 'Cosmetics: They Influence More than Caucasian Female Facial Attractiveness', *Journal of Applied Social Psychology* 36: 493–504.

National Research Council (2011) *Life Sciences and Related Fields: Trends Relevant to the Biological Weapons Convention*. Washington, DC: National Academies Press.

National Science Foundation (2003) *New Formulas for America's Workforce: Girls in Science and Engineering*. Arlington, VA: National Science Foundation. Available at: www.nsf.gov/pubs/2003/nsf03207/nsf03207.pdf [accessed 22 May 2013].

Nerad, M. (1999) *The Academic Kitchen: A Social History of Gender Stratification at the University of California, Berkeley*. Albany, NY: State University of New York Press.

Orr, J. (2006) *Panic Diaries: A Genealogy of Panic Disorder*. Durham, NC: Duke University Press.

Patterson, M. L. (2010) *A Biopunk Manifesto*. Available at: http://maradydd.livejournal.com/496085.html [accessed May 31, 2013].

Potter, E. (2001) *Gender and Boyle's Law of Gases*. Bloomington, IN: Indiana University Press.

Pronin, E., C. M. Steele and L. Ross (2004) 'Identity bifurcation in response to stereotype threat: Women and mathematics', *Journal of Experimental Social Psychology* 40: 152–68.

Pustovrh, T. (2013) 'Socially Responsible Science and Innovation in Converging Technologies', in F. Adam and H. Westlund (eds), *Innovation in Socio-Cultural Context*. New York: Routledge, pp. 40–56.

Ricks, D. (2011) 'Bio Hackers', *Discover* 32(8): 58–70.

Roughgarden, J. (2004) *Evolution's Rainbow: Diversity, Gender, and Sexuality in Nature and People*. Berkeley: University of California Press.

Roy, D. (2004) 'Feminist Theory in Science: Working Toward a Practical Transformation', *Hypatia* 19(1): 255–79.

Schmidt, M. (2008) 'Diffusion of Synthetic Biology: A Challenge to Biosafety', *Systems and Synthetic Biology* 2:1–6.

scienceandfood.org (n.d.) *Science and Food: Promoting Knowledge of Science Through Food, and Food Through Science.* Available at: https://scienceandfooducla.wordpress.com [accessed 20 June 2013].

Shapin, S. (1999) 'The House of Experiment in Seventeenth Century England', in M. Biagioli (ed.), *The Science Studies Reader.* New York: Routledge.

Sivek, S. C. (2011) '"We Need a Showing of All Hands": Technological Utopianism in Make Magazine', *Journal of Communication Inquiry* 35(3): 187–209.

Spanier, B. (1995) *Im/partial Science: Gender Ideology in Molecular Biology.* Bloomington, IN: Indiana University Press.

Subramaniam, B. (2009) 'The Aliens Have Landed! Reflections on the Rhetoric of Biological Invasions', in M. Wyer, *et al.* (eds), *Women, Science, and Technology: A Reader in Feminist Science Studies.* New York: Routledge, pp. 133–42.

Sunder Rajan, K. (2006) *Biocapital: The Constitution of Postgenomic Life.* Durham, NC: Duke University Press.

'Synthetic Biology: FAQ'. *Synthetic Biology.* Available at: http://syntheticbiology.org [accessed 26 June 2013].

Takeshita, C. (2011) *The Global Biopolitics of the IUD: How Science Constructs Contraceptive Users and Women's Bodies.* Cambridge, MA: MIT Press.

Tutton, R. (2011) 'Promising Pessimism: Reading the Futures to Be Avoided', *Biotech*, 41(3): 411–29.

van Lente, H. (2012) 'Navigating Foresight in a Sea of Expectations: Lessons from the Sociology of Expectations', *Technology Analysis and Strategic Management* 24(8): 769–82.

Watkins, E. S. (2012) 'Informed Consent', in B. Seaman and L. Eldridge (eds), *Voices of the Women's Health Movement, Vol. 1.* New York: Seven Stories Press, pp. 142–55.

Weise, E. (2011) 'DIY "biopunks" want science in hands of people', *USA Today.* Available at: http://usatoday30.usatoday.com/tech/science/2011-06-01-science-biopunk-hacker_n.htm# [accessed 9 June 2013].

Weston, K. (2002) *Gender in Real Time: Power and Transience in a Visual Age.* New York: Routledge.

Wohlsen, M. (2008) 'Do It Yourself DNA: Amateurs are trying genetic engineering at home', *Huffington Post.* Available at: www.huffingtonpost.com/2008/12/25/do-it-yourself-dna-amateu_n_153489.html [accessed 26 June 2013].

——(2012) *Biopunk: Solving Biotech's Biggest Problems in Kitchens and Garages.* New York: Current.

Wolinsky, H. (2009) 'Kitchen biology', *European Molecular Biology Organization Reports* 10(7): 683–85.

Zhang, J. Y, C. Marris and N. Rose (2011) *The transnational governance of synthetic biology: scientific uncertainty, cross-borderness and the 'art' of governance.* London: BIOS, London School of Economics and Political Science. Available at: http://royalsociety.org/uploadedFiles/Royal_Society_Content/policy/publications/2011/4294977685.pdf [accessed 13 June 2013].

10 Amateurization and re-materialization in biology

Opening up scientific equipment

Morgan Meyer

Introduction

What kinds of equipment do amateur scientists use? In astronomy, telescopes are essential; for ornithologists it's a pair of binoculars; in the field of botany magnifying glasses are important; and entomologists need a couple of nets. Add to that some field guides, jars, and pencils, and most amateur scientists can in theory start to do fieldwork and collect data about stars, birds, plants or butterflies. The kinds of equipment that amateur scientists need usually share the same characteristics: they are rather cheap, easy to find, and they can be purchased from specialized providers. They are, in a sense, 'convivial tools' (Illich, 1973), tools that can be easily, flexibly and broadly used. Some of this equipment can be bought second-hand, while other equipment can be built by oneself or tinkered with.

While there is now a long tradition of amateurs in natural history and astronomy, what about fields like molecular biology and genetics? Will these fields also open up to amateur practitioners? Are there some tools and techniques that, like the binoculars and the nets that amateur naturalists use, will become easily available? Will we witness the creation of fields like 'amateur genetics' or 'amateur molecular biology'? In order to provide a possible answer to these questions, this chapter focuses on the emergence of a new movement called 'do-it-yourself biology' (the term 'biohacking' is also alternatively used to describe the movement).[1] While the term do-it-yourself (DIY) biology emerged around 2006/2007 in the US, two networks of DIY biology have since been established: one in 2008 in the US, and one in 2012 in Europe. Estimations concerning the number of practitioners vary between several hundred to several thousand. They have various motivations (learning, experimenting, having fun, interacting with others, contributing to science, doing artistically oriented projects) and they do a range of activities: hacking scientific equipment, analysing one's own genome, producing biosensors to detect pollutants, re-engineering yoghurt bacteria, creating 'bio-art', and so on (see Wolinski, 2009; Ledford, 2010; Delfanti, 2013). It has been argued that through these practices, biology 'thus becomes a tool for the manufacturing of communal subjectivities' (Tocchetti, 2012), i.e. for creating communities and collective identities, and that there is a 'close connection between prototype testing and community building' (Kera, 2012a). More than just concerned with the scientific and technological facets of biology, DIY biology also tackles the politics and the sociability (the openness and communality) of biology.

In this chapter I examine the ways in which scientific equipment is tinkered with and redesigned by and for practitioners of DIY biology. Like software codes, which have been examined together with their circulation and distribution (MacKenzie, 2005) and as entanglements of materialities and identities (MacKenzie, 2006), I will analyse both the material culture and the social facets of DIY biology practices. The process that I will explore in more detail is how equipment is 'amaterialized'. I argue that we witness an *amateurization* of equipment to widen its usability beyond professional users. The list of DIY equipment and techniques is rapidly growing: alternative versions of microscopes, electrophoresis gels, PCR machines, magnetic stirrers and centrifuges have, for instance, been built. At the same time, we also see a *de-* and *re-materialization* of equipment, when tools and techniques are opened up, redesigned and made available in multiple versions: alternative versions, smaller versions, textual instructions to build them. Amaterialization is thus conceived as the combination between amateurization and re-materialization of scientific equipment. I use the term amaterialization for it allows me to capture, in a single term, a threefold process: the social process of making equipment available to amateurs; the technical work performed to transform equipment; and the co-construction of material versions and 'amaterial' versions of equipment (i.e. textual, digital or informational).

This chapter thus contributes to – but also departs from – several threads of academic work. Rather than focusing on 'civic epistemologies' (Jasanoff, 2005; Miller, 2005) and the links between people's knowledge claims, decision-making and politics, I am more interested in 'civic technologies' (Bennett, 2005; Marres, 2008) and the links between technological artefacts and social worlds (see also Clarke and Fujimura, 1992). Rather than trying to outline a 'democratization' of science, which would need an analysis of the discursive, procedural, cultural and/ or institutional facets of such processes,[2] I am interested in the concrete, local, material and tangible processes of transforming and building equipment – the ontology of amaterialization. I want to explore the work 'on' material objects, and how people 'tinker' with equipment (see Nutch, 1996). We will see below how DIY biologists produce alternative equipment through what Lévi-Strauss (1966) called 'bricolage': how people 'make do' by combining and reusing available material (see also Baker and Nelson, 2005).[3] Recent work in digital anthropology (Kelty, 2008; Coleman, 2010; Horst and Miller, 2012) will further allow me to situate this bricolage in digitally mediated worlds.

Amateur biology and open source

In order to understand DIY biology historically, sociologically and technically, we need to briefly come back to two issues: the place of amateurs in science and the open source movement (the idea to promote the redistribution and accessibility of the designs, blueprints and codes of products in order to make them more usable and modifiable).

The involvement of amateurs in science is not a recent phenomenon. Already in the sixteenth and seventeenth centuries, professional and amateur systems of knowledge could and did coexist (Findlen, 1994: 10). However, towards the end of the nineteenth century, the contrast between 'amateur' and 'professional' was reinforced (Drouin and Bensaude-Vincent, 1996: 418–19). Mathematization and the growing complexity of practical laboratory work were two key factors of the disappearance of the amateur from certain sciences (O'Connor and Meadows, 1976: 78). '[P]rofessionalization, involving as it did increasing stress on credentials, research apprenticeship, and sophisticated instrumentation, pushed even the wealthy amateur toward the sidelines' (Lankford, 1981: 289). In a number of countries, during the first decades of the twentieth century, professional biologists sought international credibility by distinguishing themselves from amateurs, establishing advanced degrees as credentials, and establishing specialized journals for publication (Star and Griesemer, 1989: 393). Yet, despite the increase of laboratory science, amateurs continued to collaborate with laboratory-based biologists.

Amateurs and laypeople are today active in a number of fields: in 'popular epidemiology', in AIDS treatments, in natural history (including botany, zoology, entomology, ornithology) and in astronomy. Amateur and professional scientists come together in various places to meet, discuss and share their data and experiences: pubs, coffeehouses, museums, the field, botanical gardens, learned societies (see Livingstone, 2003). However, while academic work has varyingly examined the histories, motivations, spaces, politics and cultures of amateur scientists, less effort has been devoted to specifically examine the scientific equipment that amateurs use. This chapter therefore concentrates on 'amateurs of scientific equipment', rather than science amateurs per se.

There are, of course, many popular books dedicated to amateur equipment,[4] but an academic analysis of the uses of these books, and the way they render scientific instrumentation and experimentation more accessible to amateur practices, is still lacking. Often, such equipment is only briefly mentioned. For instance, in his social history of naturalists in Britain, Allen (1994: 4) explains how field equipment – like geologists' hammers, botanists' collecting tins and entomologists' butterfly nets – were beginning to appear and be used around 1700 and how these tools also became emblems and played a role in giving a sense of collective identity. Yet a thorough engagement with the material practices and constructions of equipment is usually hard to come by. A notable exception is Larsen's study of equipment in natural history which, she argues, enabled people to pursue activities with 'minimal financial investment' (1996: 363). Another analysis is provided by Kohler, (2002) who studied fieldwork and instruments such as 'quadrants' that are, as he puts it, simple, flexible, precise and cheap. Reference also needs to be made to von Hippel's (1976) study of innovation in scientific instruments, which showed that users are more innovative than manufactures (the latter are usually concerned with product engineering only, i.e. reliability and manufacturability). Callon and Rabeharisoa (2003) have offered a contemporary example of the use of equipment in their study of patient organizations' involvement in research. They use the term 'proto-instruments' to talk about cameras, camcorders, written accounts, letters, etc. that enable their users to create 'formal, transportable, cumulative, and debatable knowledge' (Callon and Rabeharisoa, 2003: 197). The term protoinstrument seems to stand for a particular quality of an instrument: it points to rather archetypal and (proto)typical instruments, which are arguably less complex and costly than professional instruments. Yet, as we will see below, DIY biology aims to rematerialize objects and to produce alternative versions of instruments, in other words, to foster *post*-instruments.[5]

The most theoretical engagement with the equipment that amateurs use is most likely Star and Griesemer's (1989) seminal article on amateurs and professionals in a museum of vertebrate zoology. In this article, they define 'boundary objects' as 'those scientific objects which both inhabit several intersecting social worlds ... *and* satisfy the informational requirements of each of them' and state that they are 'plastic enough to adapt to local needs' and 'robust enough to maintain a common identity across sites'. 'They are weakly structured in common use, and become strongly structured in individualist use. These objects may be abstract or concrete' (Star and Griesemer, 1989: 393). The authors use the term boundary object to conceptualize field notes, maps of particular territories, methods of common communication, vague but adaptable objects such as species, diagrams, and atlases as well as repositories (ordered 'piles' of objects such as museums or libraries) (Star and Griesemer, 1989: 408–11). While this concept is fertile when studying the equipment of amateur scientists, there are several shortcomings. First, the concept is used to describe objects that already exist and that are ready to be used; their construction and emergence are not problematized. Second, due to its historical perspective, the paper does not address a feature that is essential for fields such as DIY biology and the open source movement more generally: the relationships between objects and information, and the transformations and translations between materiality and digitality.

The production, transformation and circulation of amateur equipment, especially with the rise of information and communication technologies (ICT), is therefore an important element to consider. 'Increasingly, groups possessing various levels of technical expertise are able to *simultaneously make and share both things ('material') and knowledge ('immaterial')* through newly conceived digitally mediated practices', Ratto and Ree (2012) write. With the rise of ICT, 'digitization raises the mobility of what we have customarily thought of as not mobile' and '[a]t its most extreme, this liquifying de-materializes its object' (Sassen, 2002: 369). Yet, despite this potential to de-materialize objects, we must not forget that even digital entities have to be materially produced (Sassen, 2002). The worlds, ethics and practices of hackers, for instance, are not only produced digitally. They combine both face-to-face interactions and digital interactivity, which leads Coleman (2010: 66) to ask whether 'the circulation of discourse can captivate so strongly and across time and space because of the rare but socially profound and ritualistic occasions, such as conferences, when members of some publics meet and interact'. Authors like Sassen and Coleman caution us from arguing that almost everything nowadays can be digitalized and dematerialized. Rather, the links between the digital and the material do (still) matter and deserve academic scrutiny.

The boundaries between objects and information are key here. Of course, information differs from objects in terms of its usability, circulability and diffusability (see Hope 2008). It is usually argued that the more a technology has been transformed into information (or 'codified') the more easily and quickly this information can travel. This is, in essence, what an 'open biology' promises to do: to render more mobile and accessible information, equipment and data. But – and this is important to keep in mind – the *relationships and translations* between information and materiality is one of the key motors of movements like DIY biology.

There are a number of parallels/convergences between the open source movement and DIY biology: both are based on the movement of goods/information, both represent a particular mode of circulation (free circulation and distribution) and both authorize and even encourage changes to the goods being circulated. Practitioners in both the open source movement and DIY biology are encouraged to 'freely reveal' (von Hippel, 2005: 77–91) their innovations. In addition, the *modifiability* of the objects and information being circulated is crucially important. Kelty (2008: 11) defines this modifiability as 'the ability not only to access ... but to transform [something] for use in new contexts, to different ends, or in order to participate directly in its improvement and to redistribute or recirculate those improvements within the same infrastructures while securing the same rights for everyone else'.

Yet, despite these parallels between open source and DIY biology, there are several key differences between a potentially 'open biotechnology' and open source: a source code is in itself both descriptive (it explains) and functional (it is the technology), which is not the case for the tools used for biotechnology; and there are differences in terms of the level of skill, capital and commitment needed, which is arguably higher for biotechnology than for software development (Hope, 2008: 171–2). It thus remains to be seen whether, in the future, tinkering with scientific equipment by DIY biologists will become as easy and widespread as the 'refactoring' of computer codes or the 'remixing' of songs.[6] Convergences between these various kinds of technologies – and the ways to open them up, both materially and culturally – can be expected.

Reassembling and circumventing scientific equipment

At the time of writing, there are around 40 DIY biology laboratories around the world. Most of them are community laboratories located in the Western world, in major European cities (i.e. London, Paris, Amsterdam, Prague, Vienna) and US cities (i.e. New York, Boston, Los Angeles, San Francisco). Further labs have been established in Canada, in India, and in several Asian countries such as Singapore, Japan and Indonesia (see Kera, 2012a). DIY biology usually takes place in industrialized and (sub)urban spaces. Labs are often co-located in hackerspaces – as is the case for Biologigaragen in Copenhagen and the London Biohackspace, for example. Several 'home' laboratories have also become rather prominent in the recent past: those of Kay Aull, Meredith Patterson and Rob Carlson, all three in the US, and that of Cathal Garvey in Ireland.

The kinds of activities that take place within these labs are diverse. For instance, at the kick-off meeting of the European network of DIY biology, four collaborative projects emerged and will be developed over the coming years: a DIYbio starter kit with the basic means for producing the consumables needed for genetic experimentation; a common platform for environmental biology quests; the production of bio-plastics that can be used in 3D printers; and a DNA-based communication network (Seyfried *et al.*, 2012). One activity that is widespread among DIY biology practitioners is what they call the 'hacking' of yoghurt: the genetic re-engineering of yoghurt to make it taste differently, or produce new substances like fluorescent proteins, vitamin C or Prozac. Out of the long and heterogeneous list of activities and projects, let us further mention: the DNA barcoding of plants, the production of bioreactors (i.e. to produce biofuels), the development of safe home-brewing kits for the public, genetic testing using one's own DNA, bio-art projects (i.e. using bio-luminescence), molecular gastronomy, the production of biosensors to detect pollutants in food (i.e. melamine) and in the environment, and various other outreach activities and workshops. The living organisms used for these projects include bacteria, yeast, algae, human cells and various plants.

In order to perform these activities a range of alternative and transformed equipment is used: converting a webcam into a microscope (by removing the lens and putting it back on backwards); using the DremelFuge instead of a conventional centrifuge; putting test tubes in one's own armpits to incubate them; using a pressure cooker instead of an autoclave; purifying DNA with a mixture of non-iodized table salt, meat tenderizer and shampoo. In other words, DIY biology favours creative workarounds, that is, inventive ways to work without conventional and expensive material. People use creative workarounds *around objects* when transforming and combining them and using them in unusual ways; and they perform workarounds *around institutions*, when trying to circumvent conventional relationships between industry and the university (i.e. via donations or imitations of equipment).[7] We see here a convergence between several domains: the DIY movement; the ethics of hacking and open source; and molecular and synthetic biology. This raises the question of whether there will be an open source movement in molecular biology comparable to that in the ICT field (see Hope, 2008). Regarding the links between the hacker movement and DIY biology, various proximities can already be observed: a physical proximity, as hackerspaces and DIY biology laboratories are often shared; a semantic convergence with the formation of new hybrid terms such as 'biohacker' or 'biopunk'; and the adoption of the ethics and practices of hackers – i.e. accessibility, sharing and collaboration – by DIY biology. For instance, one of the founders of DIYbio.org explicitly developed DIY biology following hacker practices (Roosth, 2010: 130).

Let us turn to two examples of equipment that have recently been developed: the Open Gel Box and the Open PCR. Both pieces of equipment have been fabricated by Tito Jankowski and Josh Perfetto, who describe their endeavour as 'hard work' (Jankowski, personal communication, 2013). The Open Gel Box is an alternative method to doing a gel electrophoresis, a method commonly used in molecular biology and biochemistry for separating and analysing nuclear acids (DNA or RNA) or proteins, based on their size. Open Gel Box is described as follows:

> Gel electrophoresis is one of the most basic and commonly used tools for molecular biology. However, the gel electrophoresis chambers available on the market often lack essential features that would make this daily routine more pleasant. We aim to create a professional grade open and extensible electrophoresis gel box, available as design documents, unassembled, and assembled kits for researchers to obtain and improve upon.
> (Open Gel Box 2.0 description on OpenWetWare, 2009)

The Open Gel Box is licensed under a Creative Commons Attribution-Share Alike 3.0 License, a copyright licensing system that holds that other users are free to copy and distribute the work and to 'remix' and adapt it. However, users must attribute the work in the manner specified by the author/licensor and if the work is altered or transformed, the resulting work can only be distributed under the same (or a compatible) licence.

The Open Gel Box was designed to be 'simple', 'minimalist' and 'inexpensive, using off the shelf parts'. While the project to build the device started in 2009, a company called Pearl Biotech was soon established (in San Francisco). The company sells its gel box for US$299 (conventional electrophoresis sets cost between US$500 and 1,500) and has to date sold almost 100 of them. The creation of Pearl Biotech initially raised some criticisms from other members of the DIYbio community, because of missing blueprints and because it was not seen to be an open endeavour. Jankowski reacted and said that they wanted to:

> make better biotech hardware available to 2 groups: those who love building their equipment from scratch and those who want to just plug it in and go. The Open Gel Box project began as an RFC [Request For Comments], available on Openwetware … Creating this RFC was step 1. Step 2 involves turning that RFC into a real, working device – and making that device available to the community. Talking with community members, some DIYbiololgists love to work from blueprints – and others

want to buy a gel box and start using it immediately. In the coming weeks, full design documents will be available, free to use and hack. Kits and pre-built boxes will be made available at the same time.

(post in a discussion forum, 4 December 2009)

The Open Gel Box and the Blue Transilluminator (developed by Pearl Biotech) are not the only DIY versions of gel electrophoresis. A similar tool called DIY Gel electrophoresis kit has been developed during workshops in Ljubljana, Zurich and Zagreb – a tool that crosses the 'conventional barriers between home appliances (IKEA Tupperware), food available from the local store (Agar Agar, food colours, salt), pharmacy product (stainless steel syringe needles), etc.' (Kera, 2012b).

Another example is the Open PCR Machine. A PCR machine, for Polymerase Chain Reaction, is essential in molecular biology to amplify DNA and RNA sequences; it relies on the method of 'thermal cycling', that is, cycles of repeated heating and cooling for the melting and enzymatic replication of DNA. In order to develop the Open PCR Machine, a call for funding was made via Kickstarter, an online system to fund creative projects via a threshold pledge system. Here is an extract of the project description:

> Do you want to explore your own genome, hack together DNA code, build your own biofuel, or prove that the trees in your backyard really are Truffula trees? You'll need a PCR machine, one of the cornerstones of molecular biology, which costs $4,000 up to $10,000. How are the Steve Jobs, Bill Gates, or Andy Warhol of biotech going to get their start if the simplest biotech tools cost so much? ... We want to make an OpenPCR machine capable of copying DNA. We plan to make open source designs and kits so anyone can do PCR at their desktop, garage, hackerspace, or community lab for $400 or less ... We will release the open source design documents, software, parts list, kits, and instructions for you to make your own OpenPCR ... We believe in making tools for biotechnology more accessible.
>
> (Open PCR project description on Kickstarter, 2010)

The project eventually managed to raise US$12,000 during June and July 2010 and the Open PCR can today be ordered online for US$600 in the form of a kit (about 300 Open PCR machines have been sold to date). I asked the developers whether they saw a tension between DIYbio/open source and the fact that the Open PCR machine is being sold; their answer was:

> I don't see any tension between DIYbio/open source and selling machines. We provide the open source design for free, which was the original goal of our project. But because the project ended up using a lot of custom components like CNC milled metal parts, it made it very expensive for people to build based solely on the design. So to make it

easier for people to build, we did bulk purchases of components and resell it, to make it easier/cheaper for people to build the machine.

(Perfetto, personal communication, 2013)

After having ordered the machine, one must then assemble the different parts, and installation takes between three and five hours (see Figure 10.1). The tools that are required for the assembly are a standard screwdriver and pliers. On the website of Open PCR, instructions for building the machine are available in a 74-page document, which explains the process in a detailed way, with numerous drawings and pictures (a bit like the instructions for IKEA products). A number of elements can be downloaded from the website: an Open PCR application to run on a computer, the assembly instructions, the open source code, the CAD, and the circuits. All these files are licensed under the GNU General Public License (GPLv3), a 'copy-left' licence intended to guarantee the freedom to share and change all versions of a program and to make sure it remains free software for all its users. As in the case of the gel box, other alternative PCR machines have recently been constructed. There is, for instance, a project directly based on Open PCR called Wild Open PCR. The developer of Wild Open PCR is openly grateful to the Open PCR machine, saying that: its designers did 'a great job', the machine is 'well constructed' and one person from the 'OpenPCR team responded to all my emails and helped with open and precise answers' (Wild Open PCR description on Hackteria, 2013). Yet, the machine has been developed without the kit and

Figure 10.1 The Open PCR machine being assembled during a workshop
Source: Medical Museion, Copenhagen.

Amateurization and re-materialization in biology 151

Figure 10.2 Part of the instructions to hack the 'peltier' element for a PCR machine. The device can be found in electric fridges: 'Unscrew the blower and the cooler and you will find the peltier element'
Source: Wild Open PCR.

any of the supplied parts of the Open PCR but just from the descriptions available on its website. Given that some parts and software used for the Open PCR are not (yet) available as open source, Wild Open PCR is an attempt to build an even more open, modifiable, and accessible PCR machine (see Figure 10.2).

Equipment like the Open Gel Box and the Open PCR are just two examples of equipment specifically designed for DIY practices. Landrain *et al.* (2013) present a list of 25 alternative equipment including, apart from the examples just mentioned, pressure cookers (instead of autoclaves) and DIY magnetic stirrers. Information and internet platforms, where these kinds of equipment are available or discussed, have proliferated over the past few years. There are now a number of dedicated sites – i.e. openwetware.org, protocol-online.org, instructables.com, and diybio.org – on which there is information about where and how to purchase, build or transform equipment and how to find and build alternative tools. At several Maker Faires the tools of DIY biologists have been presented (Tocchetti, 2012). In addition, DIY biologists buy used equipment via eBay, Amazon or Craigslist, and they post video instructions to build and use equipment on websites such as YouTube. All these websites and platforms are a key element in the 'citizen biotech-economies' (Meyer, 2012) of scientific equipment that are currently emerging – economies which are portrayed as open, collective and decentralized and which aim at fostering a material redistribution, a democratization and an alternative to established science.

The innovations fostered in DIY biology do not develop outside of market logics. There are already a number of companies linked to DIY biology: Pearl Biotech, LavaAmp (a small, portable PCR machine) and Ginkgo Bioworks, a company that sells kits that contain DNA bio-bricks. There is thus a multifarious relationship – and potential tension – between DIY biology and corporate science. There is a relationship of dependency concerning cheap, second-hand or specialized products for amateurs. To be able to do their experiments, DIY practitioners rely on inexpensive material that they usually buy in supermarkets, specialized stores or via commercial websites. Also, there is a potential and entrepreneurial drive to transform hacked equipment into commercial equipment. Just as there is nowadays a noteworthy market for amateur telescopes, we can expect the development of a comparable market for amateur biology equipment.

The way in which the ethics of openness and sharing will react to – and coexist with – business ventures (with their patents and licenses) will be an interesting site for further empirical work. Will there be a tension between the politics against the monopolization of access and a politics seeking to secure and maintain privileged/economic access? As in the case of the Czech wireless community, there can be a contradiction between the will to produce innovations for users outside of market logics, and the reliance on global markets of existing devices and donations in order to develop these innovations (Söderberg, 2010: 255). I suggest that these issues merit further analyses. Several trajectories of DIY biology labs can already be imagined for the near future: their growing resistance to market logics; their splitting into several fractions or sub-groups; companies swallowing them; an in-house creation of start-ups and spin-offs; a ban of members with commercial interests; a transformation of some of its members from 'hobbyists' into entrepreneurs; a formulation and clarification of codes of ethics regarding commercial ventures; a differentiation of small and 'good' businesses versus big and 'bad' businesses (i.e. Big Pharma); a rather peaceful coexistence between communal and commercial projects.

Discussion: the politics of convivial equipment

We have seen in this chapter some examples of the ways in which scientific equipment is opened up, redesigned, reinvented and reassembled to make it more usable for amateur scientists. I call this process 'amaterialization'. Scientific equipment is amaterialized to produce other versions of equipment or, to be more precise, to produce a similar functionality with another kind of equipment. The amaterialization of equipment is, in fact, a manyfold process.

We see equipment being redistributed across social worlds, being technically transformed and redesigned, and, alongside material artefacts, we see a proliferation and an increasing circulation of non-material entities (texts, information, videos, etc.). These processes force us to reconceptualize convergence. Convergence is not only a process whereby distinct cultural fields somehow become similar; there seems to be an important prerequisite: the *conversion* of material tools and equipment.

As I alluded to at the beginning of this text, such equipment is redesigned, to serve as 'convivial tools': tools that can be more easily, more broadly and more flexibly used. In his classic essay on convivial tools, Illich writes that 'technology and science do not demand that tools not be convivial' and that such convivial tools are to 'be easily used, by anybody, as often or as seldom as desired, for the accomplishment of a purpose chosen by the user. The use of such tools by one person does not restrain another from using them equally. They do not require previous certification of the user' (1973: 22). In contrast to non-convivial tools – which are centralized, differentially distributed, and elitist – convivial tools are to be decentralized, egalitarian and open (see Pfaffenberger, 1992: 305). They can further contribute to 'de-institutionalize' science – and the convergence between such processes of de-institutionalization and concepts such as lifelong learning or citizen science thus merit further analysis.

DIY biology produces and encourages its own set of convivial tools: equipment that is much less expensive than the equipment that professional scientists use, and that is more easily accessible, more mobile and often smaller. This equipment cannot be untangled from its 'immaterial' aspects. Open source ethics, internet websites, DIY communities are part and parcel of the constitution of these objects – of their conception, production and circulation. Even more so, their 'conviviality' is not only fostered by making them 'open', but also by allowing them to be modified and improved. 'DIYbio combines a sort of individual craftiness and self-determination *to do* things with a praxis in which things are left open, waiting for the next realization', writes Delgado (2013: 67).

These instruments resemble Star and Griesemer's 'boundary objects' in that they are plastic and/or robust, abstract and/or concrete, and weakly structured and/or strongly structured depending on their use and meanings in different 'social worlds'. In addition to this, their boundary nature is amplified by translations between several additional registers: material and non-material, physical and digital, original and alternative, construction and description, buying and hacking. Even more so, their temporal trajectories become important as well since DIY practices allow and encourage extensions and proliferations of objects. As we see, the amateurization of scientific equipment works by related processes: by redistributing objects; by multiplying (the versions of) these objects; and by closely entangling their construction, description and publicization.

This brings me to my final suggestion: that these new kinds of equipment – like the DremelFuge or the Open PCR – do not only enable scientific work, but that they also perform socio-political work. They are quickly becoming the emblems of the DIY biology movement (they are mentioned in media articles, presented in exhibitions, discussed on websites).[8] In so doing, they come to act as promissory equipment: equipment presented and circulated as success stories, equipment that promises future innovations and serves to demonstrate the potential of DIY biology to be realized. This equipment can act as a material link between, on the one hand, the actual experimentation in laboratories and, on the other, more general arguments about the 'democratization' and 'opening up' of biology. Hence, their value does not only derive from the fact that they can serve as boundary objects between amateurs and professionals. Their value also stems from their evocative power, a power that arises from a convergence between material practices and moral visions, between the redesign of scientific objects and the articulation of political objectives.

Acknowledgements

Thanks to Johan Söderberg, Romain Badouard, Liliana Doganova, Florian Charvolin, Tito Jankowski, Josh Perfetto and two anonymous referees for their comments. This chapter was presented – and has greatly benefited from discussions – at a workshop at the University of Edinburgh and a seminar at the Centre for the Sociology of Innovation (Mines ParisTech).

Notes

1 Despite the fact that DIY biology and biohacking are often used as synonyms by academics and practitioners, it is worth pointing to some differences: DIY refers to an older movement (related to home-improvement, fashion) and has rather positive connotations; hacking refers to a more recent movement and has both positive connotations (innovation, cleverness, playfulness) and negative connotations (security, criminality).
2 Such an analysis would require an unpacking and problematization of 'democratization' as a process that occurs *spatially*, by building new or reconfiguring spaces; *technically and materially*, by redesigning and opening up equipment; *economically* by rendering tools and experimentation cheaper; and *socially*, by opening up science to various sociocultural backgrounds (see Meyer, 2014).
3 Lévi-Strauss writes: 'The bricoleur is adept at performing a large number of diverse tasks; but, in contrast to the engineer, he does not subordinate each one of them to the acquisition of raw materials and tools conceived and procured for the project: his universe of tools is closed, and the rule of his game is to always make do with "what's available"' (1962: 31).
4 For instance books such as: *Astronomical Equipment for Amateurs* (1998), *The Plant Observer's Guidebook: A Field Botany Manual for the Amateur Naturalist* (1984), *From Field to Lab: 200 Life Science Experiments for the Amateur Biologist* (1993), *Illustrated Guide to Home Biology Experiments: All Lab, No Lecture* (2012).
5 The key differences are: rather than originals, alternative versions are used; rather than being standard and available, they are non-standardized and yet-to-be-made

available; rather than being used *before* – and in order to do – scientific research, they are developed *with* and *after* tinkering with science and technology.
6 The 'refactoring' of software code has been defined as the 'process of changing a software system in such a way that it does not alter the external behavior of the code yet improves its internal structure' (Fowler, 1999: xxi).
7 Akrich (1998) distinguishes four ways through which users can innovate: displacement, adaptation, extension and *détournement*. Using a pressure cooker instead of an autoclave can, for instance, be seen as a 'displacement' of a technology. However, the practice of 'workaround' ('*contournement*') appears as the key process in the cases reported in this paper.
8 We might add that the *properties* of materials are thereby narrated and rendered explicit – see Ingold's plea to redirect our focus from materiality to the properties of materials; the description of these properties means 'to tell their stories of what happens to them as they flow, mix and mutate' (2007: 14).

References

Akrich, M. (1998) 'Les utilisateurs, acteurs de l'innovation', *Education permanente*, 'L'innovation en Question' 1 (134): 79–90.
Allen, D. E. (1994) *The Naturalist in Britain: A Social History*. Princeton, NJ: Princeton University Press.
Baker, T. and R. E. Nelson (2005) 'Creating something from nothing: Resource construction through entrepreneurial bricolage', *Administrative Science Quarterly* 50: 329–66.
Bennett, T. (2005) 'Civic laboratories: museums, cultural objecthood and the governance of the social', *Cultural Studies* 19(5): 521–47.
Callon, M. and V. Rabeharisoa. (2003) 'Research "in the wild" and the shaping of new social identities', *Technology in Society* 25(2): 193–204.
Clarke, A. and J. Fujimura (eds) (1992) *The Right Tools for the Job*. Princeton, NJ: Princeton University Press.
Coleman, G. (2010) 'The hacker conference: a ritual condensation and celebration of a lifeworld', *Anthropological Quarterly* 83(1): 47–72.
Delfanti, A. (2013) *Biohackers: The Politics of Open Science*. London: Pluto Books.
Delgado, A. (2013) 'DIYbio: Making things and making futures', *Futures* 48: 65–73.
Drouin, J. M. and B. Bensaude-Vincent (1996) 'Nature for the people', in N. Jardine, J. A. Secord and E. C. Spary (eds), *Cultures of Natural History*. Cambridge: Cambridge University Press, pp. 408–25.
Findlen, P. (1994) *Possessing Nature: Museums, Collecting, and Scientific Culture in Early Modern Italy*. Berkeley and London: University of California Press.
Fowler, M. (1999) *Refactoring: Improving the Design of Existing Code*. London: Addison-Wesley.
Hope, J. (2008) *Biobazaar: The Open Source Revolution and Biotechnology*. Cambridge, MA: Harvard University Press.
Horst, H. and D. Miller (eds) (2012) *The Digital and the Human: A Prospectus for Digital Anthropology*. London: Berg.
Illich, I. (1973) *Tools for Conviviality*. New York: Harper and Row.
Ingold, T. (2007) 'Materials against materiality', *Archaeological Dialogues* 14(1): 1–16.
Jasanoff, S. (2005) *Designs on Nature: Science and Democracy in Europe and the United States*. Princeton, NJ: Princeton University Press.

Kelty, C. (2008) *Two Bits: The Cultural Significance of Free Software and the Internet.* Durham, NC: Duke University Press.

Kera, D. (2012a) 'Hackerspaces and DIYbio in Asia: Connecting science and community with open data, kits and protocols', *Journal of Peer Production* 2.

——(2012b) 'NanoŠmano Lab in Ljubljana: disruptive prototypes and experimental governance of nanotechnologies in the hackerspaces', *JCOM* 11(4).

Kohler, R. (2002) *Landscapes and Labscapes, Exploring the Lab-Field Border in Biology.* Chicago, IL: Chicago University Press.

Landrain, T., M. Meyer, A. M. Perez and R. Sussan (2013) 'Do-it-yourself biology: Challenges and promises for an open science and technology movement', *Systems and Synthetic Biology* 7(3): 115–26.

Lankford, J. (1981) 'Amateurs and astrophysics: A neglected aspect in the development of a scientific specialty', *Social Studies of Science* 11(3): 275–303.

Larsen, A. (1996) 'Equipment for the field', in N. Jardine, J. A. Secord, and E.C. Spary (eds), *Cultures of Natural History.* Cambridge: Cambridge University Press, pp. 358–77.

Ledford, H. (2010) 'Life hackers', *Nature* 467: 650–2.

Lévi-Strauss, J. (1962) *La Pensée sauvage* (trans: The Savage Mind, 1966, University of Chicago Press). Paris: Plon.

Livingstone, D. N. (2003) *Putting Science in Its Place: Geographies of Scientific Knowledge.* Chicago, IL: University of Chicago Press.

Mackenzie, A. (2005) 'The performativity of code software and cultures of circulation', *Theory, Culture & Society* 22(1): 71–92.

——(2006) *Cutting Code: Software and Sociality.* New York: Peter Lang.

Marres, N. (2008) 'The making of climate publics: Eco-homes as material devices of publicity', *Distinktion: Scandinavian Journal of Social Theory* 9(1): 27–45.

Meyer, M. (2012) 'Build your own lab: Do-it-yourself biology and the rise of citizen biotech-economies', *Journal of Peer Production* 2.

——(2014) 'Hacking life? The politics and poetics of DIY biology', in A. Bureaud, R. F. Malina and L. Whitelay (eds), *META-LIFE Biotechnologies, Synthetic Biology, ALife and the Arts.* Cambridge, MA: Leonardo and MIT Press.

Miller, C. A. (2005) 'New civic epistemologies of quantification: making sense of indicators of local and global sustainability', *Science, Technology & Human Values* 30(3): 403–32.

Nutch, F. (1996) 'Gadgets, gizmos, and instruments: science for the tinkering', *Science, Technology & Human Values* 21(2): 214–28.

O'Connor, J. G. and A. J. Meadows (1976) 'Specialization and professionalization in British geology', *Social Studies of Science* 6(1): 77–89.

Pfaffenberger, B. (1992) 'Technological dramas', *Science Technology & Human Values* 17(3): 282–312.

Ratto, M. and R. Ree (2012) 'Materializing information: 3D printing and social change', *First Monday* 17(7).

Roosth, S. (2010) 'Crafting life: A sensory ethnography of fabricated biologies'. Ph.D. thesis, MIT.

Sassen, S. (2002) 'Towards a sociology of information technology', *Current Sociology* 50(3): 365–88.

Seyfried, G., P. van Boheemen and T. Landrain (2012) *First DIYbio-Europe meetup sprouts 4 promising DIYbio projects.* Available at: www.diybio.eu [accessed 12 July 2013].

Söderberg, J. (2010) 'Reconstructivism versus critical theory of technology: Alternative perspectives on activism and entrepreneurship in the Czech wireless community', *Social Epistemology* 24(4): 241–64.

Star, S. L. and J. R. Griesemer (1989) 'Institutional ecology, "translations" and boundary objects: Amateurs and professionals in Berkeley's museum of vertebrate zoology, 1907–39', *Social Studies of Science* 19(3): 387–420.

Tocchetti, S. (2012) 'DIYbiologists as "makers" of personal biologies: how MAKE Magazine and Maker Faires contribute in constituting biology as a personal technology', *Journal of Peer Production* 2.

von Hippel, E. (2005) *Democratizing Innovation*. Cambridge, MA: MIT Press.

——(1976) 'The dominant role of users in the scientific instrument innovation process', *Research Policy* 5(3): 212–39.

Wolinsky, H. (2009) 'Kitchen biology', *EMBO Reports* 10(7): 683–5.

11 Converging technologies and critical social movements
An exploration

Franz Seifert

Introduction

In this chapter we investigate whether and to what extent converging technologies have become an object of organized criticism such as is typically articulated by social movements (Della Porta and Diani, 2006). Since the 1960s, critical social movements have constituted a significant social force and have left their imprint on many policy fields, e.g., civil, women's and minority rights, the environment, energy and new technologies. Social movements are mostly progressive forces (ibid.) though there are notable exceptions in nationalistic, religious and outspokenly reactionary movements. Critical movements are said to articulate grievances in the public sphere and push subjects onto the agenda which otherwise would remain under the controlling grip of interest groups, corporate or state power (Melucci, 1989). They widen the range of political viewpoints on a given problem and often influence the course of decision-making processes. While critical social movements' normative meaning for democracy depends on how one construes the idea of democracy, they have undeniably become part and parcel of Western liberal–democratic culture.

This chapter deals with the question of whether a critical social movement has formed around the issue of converging technologies and converging technological practices respectively. It is worth exploring this question since, while technological change is a key social force, the specific shape it assumes might still become subject of public and, in turn, political debate (Seifert, 2013a). Specifically, we focus on nanotechnology and synthetic biology (SynBio), and the newly emerging technological practice of do-it-yourself biotechnology (DIYbio). These three fields represent trend-setting developments that point towards changes in the making and content of techno-scientific innovation. Yet, we propose that very distinct socio-technological dynamics underlie nanotechnology and SynBio on the one side, and DIYbio on the other. We scrutinize these fields from a movement perspective for a number of reasons: first, by exploring the impact of social movements on the mentioned fields and processes, we seek to provide conceptual clarifications pertaining to the relationship between social movements, techno-scientific innovation and socio-technological dynamics which might be helpful in future research; second, the selection mirrors the agenda of the workshop this collection is based on. In particular, we take the opportunity to explore the questions that it raised through its unorthodox use of the convergence theme: going beyond an exclusive focus on technological convergence, it also addressed social and discursive forms of convergence which, too, contribute to science and technology in society; and third, the exploration is meant to suggest new questions for the analysis of socio-technological change. We begin with terminological clarifications.

Converging technologies

The term 'converging technologies' is conventionally used to describe technological advances that merge various branches of technology and let them evolve towards shared goals, applications, products or practices. Convergence encapsulates a great variety of trends and developments. The most popular conceptualisation envisions a major convergence of nanotechnology, biotechnology, information technology and cognitive science (Roco and Bainbridge, 2004). While our general approach draws on a wider understanding of convergence that also includes social and discursive dynamics, in the following we exemplarily focus on two technology fields that are conventionally categorized as 'converging technologies': nanotechnology and, as an emerging subfield of biotechnology, SynBio.

As we deal with these terms a conceptual caveat is indicated. We suggest conceptualizing 'converging technologies' as a discursive product rather than an assemblage of existing processes or products. The term conveys a vision or a projection into a possible future, grants it a tag or label, and denotes a discourse in media and the policy sphere. Policy analysis often deals with this kind of undefined socio-political issues by analysing the field as 'narrative', as a storytelling exercise permeating policy and public discourse. According to Gottweis 'policy making' has to be understood as:

> an attempt to manage a field of discursivity, to organize the overflow and disparity of meanings. This is typically done through the creation of narratives. By defining problems, actors, and strategies, narratives create order and stability.
>
> (1996: 103)

For the purposes of this exploratory analysis, a distinction is drawn between policy and public narratives. A policy narrative organizes the formation of a policy field by bestowing meaning on it, i.e., selecting, defining and explaining the problem the policy addresses and how it should be coped with. Public narratives, by contrast, are encountered in the public sphere, in the accounts given regarding specific issues, as exercises in making sense of disparate information by creating story structures. Public narratives exist in far greater diversity than policy narratives. Many public narratives might coexist in the public sphere allowing for a greater variety of voices and values. A public narrative does not necessarily influence political decision patterns but, one day, might do so by supporting or contesting a policy narrative or even evolving into one. Many of the issues discussed under the heading of 'converging technologies' still have the status of public narrative as they have hardly become subject of regulatory or political decision-making. As potential candidates for future policy narratives, they are worth exploratory inspection at an early stage.

Critical social movements

A critical social movement is defined by the following three characteristics: first, a movement is involved in conflict relationships with identifiable opponents; second, actors within movements are interlinked via informal networks, through which they coordinate their actions flexibly (movements are not to be confused with organizations, they rather consist of loose networks of organisations); and, third, movements share a distinct collective identity (Della Porta and Diani, 2006: 20).

For the purposes of this chapter, it is important to stress the first characteristic, a critical movement's conflictual, oppositional nature. This feature will become particularly important when we present the movement-like features of a critical movement forming around emerging technologies, on the one hand, and of the DIYbio field, on the other. It is important to note that there are other types of movements, too. For example, cultural movements may trigger changes in common values and social practices, but they do not necessarily have a network structure or a common adversary. Examples can be drawn from the wide range of alternative lifestyle movements such as, for example, veganism; polyamory; alternative medicine; or the 'slow' and 'simple living' movements. Many movements might mobilize on solidarity issues but, again, these 'consensus movements' lack the criterion of confronting a common adversary (ibid.: 22–3). We thus note that critical, or protest movements are distinguished from other types of movements precisely on grounds of their conflictual nature and their purpose of bringing about socio-political change.

Furthermore, in their quest to influence policy making, critical movements invariably make use of a crucial social mechanism: they seek to mobilize public support for their cause in order to gain leverage over governments or other actors who depend on public reputation. A key aspect of a movement's development, therefore, is the mastery of public narratives or – as it is termed in the literature – the development of 'collective action frames':

> an interpretive schemata that simplifies and condenses the 'world out there' by selectively punctuating and encoding objects, situations, events, experiences, and sequences of action within one's present and past environment.
> (Snow and Benford, 1992: 137)

In the following exploration of a movement engaging with converging technologies the concept of the 'collective action frame' will be applied.

A third movement characteristic is related to their evolution in time. Movement activity stretches over long periods of time, but degrees of intensity vary: for extended periods, movements remain submerged and inconspicuous. On rare occasions, however, periods of mobilisation follow, in which movements might rise into major forces in the public arena. It is important to recognize the long periods over which movement activities continue, in particular the long incubation periods during which these activities go unnoticed. Using the example of the anti-biotechnology movement in the 1970s and 1980s, Schurman and Munro (2006) show that, contrary to the impression that a movement remains inactive during these inconspicuous phases, certain key actors perform activities that are vital for their formation and potential later mobilization: they engage in preparatory work such as building up network connections, developing collective action frames and collecting expertise. We suggest that the rudimentary movements which will be dealt with in the following section, particularly those that engage with nanotechnology and SynBio, fall into this category.

Critical social movements also learn and borrow from each other. Ideas, symbols, action frames, strategies and protest methods diffuse freely among them. In fact, no movement stands on its own. For instance, non-violent civil disobedience which, for the first time, was systematically employed by Ghandi's decolonisation movement in the 1930s, later served to provide a backbone to other social movements, such as the US civic rights movements in the 1960s, the anti-nuclear movement in the 1970s and the multitude of protest movements of our days (McAdam and Rucht, 1993: 57–8). Hence, movements might prompt subsequent movements. McAdam, for example, distinguishes:

> between two broad classes of movements whose origins reflect very different social processes. The first category consists of those rare, but exceedingly important, initiator movements that signal or otherwise set in motion an identifiable protest cycle. Historical examples of such movements would include Solidarity in Poland and the American civil rights movement. The second and more 'populous' category of movements includes those spin-off movements that, in varying degrees, draw their impetus and inspiration from the original initiator movement.
>
> (1995: 219)

We will apply the concepts of 'initiator' and 'spin-off' movements in the following analysis.

Converging technologies and social movements

Can we identify a social movement that critically engages with converging technologies? The following sections will explore this question in relation to two selected technologies where convergence is thought to be occurring – nanotechnology and SynBio – and to the newly emerging technological practice of DIY biotechnology. We ask this question for good reasons. We mentioned earlier that, in the past, key technologies have become targets of movement activism. Particularly the case of biotechnology in Europe illustrates the potential impact of such a movement. In the mid-1990s, activists succeeded in sensitizing the European public to the alleged dangers of unlabelled GM food. The ensuing controversies led a number of state governments to impose a moratorium on EU approvals of GM products; made European retail chains ban GM products from their shelves; pressured EU authorities to issue a highly restrictive regulatory framework; and provoked a WTO conflict between the EU and GM-food-producing countries (Ansell et al., 2006; Seifert, 2009). In short, movements can influence a technology's career. Will they do so in the following technology fields?

Nanotechnology

Once again, analysis of the issues around nanotechnology refers to public policy and discourse rather than existing products or technologies, which are yet to be generated and currently very scarce and unspectacular. The tag nanotechnology, in essence, denotes funding policies for a great variety of research and development activities at the miniature scale of atoms, molecules and cells. The UK and Japan had dedicated nanotechnology funding already in the 1990s, however, major funding campaigns began in virtually the entire industrial world in the early 2000s in the wake of the US National Nanotech Initiative (NNI). These policies are based on policy narratives that revolve around nanotechnology's revolutionary potential which nations must not ignore lest they fall behind in the global technology race. Nanotechnology policy narratives also relate to public opinion, oscillating between conceptualizing nanotechnology as a challenge for democratic participation and presenting hostile public opinion as a possible obstacle to technological progress. Policies therefore employ a wide range of procedures to survey, educate and interact with the public (Seifert, 2013b: 69–71).

SynBio

The term 'SynBio' is used to describe a technology through which living organisms are assembled wholesale from non-living parts (Carlson, 2010). This is often seen as the next step of biotechnology, which operates by isolating genes from the genome of living organisms and transferring them into the genome of other living organisms (and has given rise to an entire industry formed around the life sciences). SynBio could make it possible in the future to build completely new organisms from scratch by creating artificial genomes, artificial cells and media through which they may replicate. However, even more than nanotechnology, SynBio is a very young technology field which has yet to develop fully. Therefore, for the time being, debate around this field exceeds actual development by far. In this case we are dealing with a public narrative rather than an actual policy.

DIY biology

Finally, another field we will address in this analysis is DIYbio (Delfanti, 2013: 111–29). The coinage refers to a shift in the relationship between knowledge producers and the means of scientific knowledge production: a rising number of people engage in biological research and development on their own account. Such activity used to be reserved to large-scale projects and formal academic organizations. DIY biologists who are rarely involved in institutional academia and usually operate at the margins of academic or industrial scientific research, set up their own private laboratories and become inventors or researchers in laboratory science, such as molecular biology, human genetics or drug discovery. While in the past such ventures would not have been possible, the availability of cheap laboratory equipment makes it possible for more and more people to set up their own working environments (see Chapter 10 in this volume).

DIYbio, however, is currently a nascent socio-technological trend that is being discussed in advanced industrial countries, primarily the USA and Western Europe. DIYbio has produced some results that have made it into peer-reviewed scientific journals (e.g. Yavuz *et al.*, 2009), but the field has yet to instigate a significant breakthrough, which might temper expectations as to its potential for knowledge production. Nevertheless, the new trend has received considerable attention from the media, which – as discussed later on – is arguably due to the multiple connections that can be established with various other current discourses on socio-technological development.

The nano- and SynBio-watch movements

Is there a social movement critically engaging with nanotechnology? One needs to keep in mind that to meet the definition of critical social movement one needs to examine whether its nature is political, whether it is structured as a network of ideas, actors and strategies, and whether it entails a confrontational element, challenging the established way of framing, sponsoring and regulating the technology. When it comes to nanotechnology all the above characteristics are in fact present, albeit in rudiments. To be able to empirically pin down this movement, we investigate the activities of various movement actors or critical NGOs respectively, who take issue with nanotechnology (Seifert, 2013b: 73–8). While a movement that is able to mobilize a broad public is not observed, a number of movement actors who, over several years, critically engage with nanotechnology are indeed identified. We call this social assemblage the 'nano-watch movement'. We furthermore observe that the actors involved in this movement are also prominently engaged in the much more prominent anti-biotech debate, which leads us to conclude that the nano-watch movement is a 'spin-off' from the preceding, highly visible movement against agro-food biotechnology (Seifert and Plows, 2014).

The first and most identifiable actor critical of nanotechnology over several years is the ETC Group (Action Group on Erosion, Technology and

Concentration; hereafter: ETC). ETC is a small group of concerned individuals that specialises in cutting-edge critique of the downsides of technological innovation in developing countries, and has already become known in the past as initiator and lead actor in the anti-biotech movement. ETC was the first international technology watchdog group to highlight nanotechnology as a key development with potentially ambiguous consequences for society. Since 2001, ETC has released a series of reports critically dealing with different aspects of nanotechnology (e.g., ETC, 2003, 2004, 2010), has been highly visible at international policy events, and has initiated various international petitions calling for greater precaution in dealing with nanotechnology. The NGO's critical analysis of nanotechnology is inspired by the collective action frame that was elaborated in the preceding controversy over agro-food biotechnology; it highlights nanotechnology's entanglement with state and corporate power and warns of the technology's unknown risks, not only regarding health and the environment, but also for those segments of society that are negatively affected by technology's advance. According to this criticism, the global South and the poor are likely to suffer further marginalization from nanotechnology's rise as ownership and control over the technology expands corporate power; innovations replace jobs; nano-pharmaceutical development strategies direct resources to affluent markets and away from the pressing health needs in the global South; and efforts to 'enhance' humans create a gap between the rich (who can afford to pay for the enhancements) and the poor.

Groups of the Friends of the Earth (FoE) network are also active in the field of nanotechnology. When ETC's peak activity on nanotechnology receded after 2006, FoE picked up where ETC had left off. Just like ETC, FoE are no strangers to similar controversies, in particular, the controversy around agro-food biotechnology where the FoE network played a key role. Within the FoE network, the Australian sub-organization is the strongest voice on nanotechnology. With support from this group, the German affiliate BUND and FoE USA, the network organization has published a number of critical reports that mostly focus on environmental and health risks (e.g., FoE 2006, 2008, 2010).

While these nano-watch actors operate in the international sphere, mainly addressing the elites of policy makers and educated critical publics, specific groupings can also be encountered in various countries. Movement strategies and activity patterns vary. In Germany, for example, the Bund für Umwelt und Naturschutz Deutschland (Alliance for Environment and Conservation Germany, BUND) is the key watchdog group (Seifert, 2013b: 74–5). This influential NGO is tightly interwoven with the German Nano-Commission which constitutes the centrepiece of Germany's nanotechnology policy of orchestrating social partners and stakeholders. Accordingly, BUND's action repertoire aims at attaining effects within the elite policy discourse; it is based on expertise and participation (albeit limited) in the policy process rather than strategies of mass mobilization or confrontational action.

A quite different picture presents itself in France where a radical group figures centrally in the national nanotech debate (Seifert, 2013b: 75–8). *Pièces et main d'oeuvre* ('Parts & Labour', PMO) is an activist group located in Grenoble, committed to the radical critique of industrial society and high technology, which they consider to be an inherent part of totalitarian power. PMO's campaign against nanotechnology was far more radical and confrontational than in any other country and managed to generate a greater amount of public interest than elsewhere. Crucial to this campaign was the boycotting of the '*Débat publique*' (nationwide public debate) on nanotechnology. The debate took place from October 2009 until February 2010 in the form of internet-supported panel discussions in 17 French cities. It ended in failure, mostly due to the obstruction techniques used by the activists: discussion was rendered impossible by endless oral contributions, chanting, heckling, use of stink bombs, etc., from the first event onwards. PMO's campaign was a success, in the sense that it generated more than enough public attention and confronted the French public with a critical framing of nanotechnology.

In conclusion of this section, with respect to what we term the 'nano-watch movement' we can confirm that a form of movement, albeit rudimentary, has assembled around the issue of nanotechnology. The movement, or rather rudiment of a movement, can largely be considered a 'spin-off' from the previous anti-biotechnology movement, as most of its actors are essentially the same as those once engaged in this controversy (Seifert and Plows, 2014). Its key actors are mainly professional or semi-professional NGOs who operate at the international and elite level and mostly count on the generation of critical expertise and direct involvement in the policy discourse, but it is active in national arenas too. In contrast to the powerful anti-biotech movement, however, no mass mobilization occurred against nanotechnology. Only in France has a radical protest group rallied a somewhat broader following of sympathizers and activists, thus attaining national media coverage. Arguably, one major reason for the failure to mobilize is that in this field critical movement actors respond to future-oriented public or policy narratives rather than to tangible problems. With no 'real-life experiments' going on such as, for example, contentious mass-produced food products on the market, there are no triggers to cause public concern. For example, an online database currently identifies 105 nano-products that are related to food. Most of them, however, are specialized food supplements or materials used in food handling (www.nanotechproject.org/inventories/consumer, accessed 17 June 2013). The only incident that, so far, could have turned into a potential trigger event for a broader mobilization was the case of the sealant spray 'Magic Nano' which, in April 2006, was reported to cause respiratory problems and immediately withdrawn from the German market. Media attention receded after an inquiry into the causes of the incident, conducted by the German Federal Institute for Risk Assessment (BfR), revealed that nanotechnology could not be to blame as the spray did not even contain nano-particles. To date, no comparable event has recurred.

Moving on to the topic of SynBio, we need to emphasize that this particular field has not yet emerged as a policy field. However, the issue is already generating a great deal of debate, or public narratives, and a fair amount of attention in academic and policy circles. The Royal Academy of Engineering in the UK, for example, published a report on SynBio (2009), and in 2010, the Presidential Commission for the Study of Bioethical Issues in the US deliberated on the issue, asking whether regulations would be necessary (Presidential Commission, 2010).

If merely rudimentary movement activity targeting nanotechnology was previously detected, even less activity can be observed in the field of SynBio. Furthermore, the low levels of movement activity that we are able to identify in this field generally involve the very same key players we observed in the nano-field, namely, the ETC group, and some members of the FoE network. ETC, for example, issued a critical report on SynBio in 2007 (ETC, 2007). As the report's title 'Extreme Genetic Engineering' implies, ETC portrays SynBio as a further aggravation of biotechnology's downsides, thus applying the collective action frame previously applied to both biotechnology and nanotechnology. Other 'familiar faces' from both the anti-biotech and nano-watch movements, such as FoE (USA) and the International Center for Technology Assessment have also been active in the SynBio field. Therefore, while we are even less entitled to speak of a 'movement' in the SynBio field, we do observe some incipient activity of movement actors, who are also established actors in similar preceding movements. Thus, again, we observe a 'spin-off', originating from these movements.

DIYbio as ambiguous discursive field

In contrast to the technological fields that have been discussed so far, DIYbio denotes a change in society's dealings with science and technology involving a great diversity of scientific and technological practices rather than a definable technological field. By obtaining the required machinery, laboratory equipment and information technology, and rendered possible by a culture of technical and social improvisation or 'creative workarounds' (Meyer, 2013: 126–8), an increasing number of people who often do not belong to established research institutions, are enabled to pursue individual research projects.

DIYbio has made the news in a number of articles, books and TV reports covering the trend while tangible technological advances due to DIYbio are incremental at best. DIYbio constitutes an ambiguous discursive field, i.e., it is the issue of a number of 'public narratives' which envision fairly different, and in many ways contradicting futures and meanings of DIYbio (Kelty, 2010). For instance, on the one hand, the DIY trend is hyped as a new stage in the history of garage entrepreneurship, recalling the commercial breakthroughs of information and communication technologies (ICT) and, once more, narrating the tale of high-tech capitalism's self-renewing vitality (Delfanti, 2013: 50–5). On the other hand, DIY is seen as fostering technology's democratization. One might expect, for example, that as more and more laypeople become experts, academia's epistemic monopoly would give way to a diversity of more egalitarian forms of knowledge production. More equal access to the means of knowledge production might also empower those who are directly affected by a techno-scientific problem such as a hereditary disease or a nearby toxic waste site to conduct research directly, thus bypassing major organizations whose interests may or may not coincide with their own. In a more critical vein, 'Biopunk' celebrates a more subversive type of heroism, envisioning landslide changes of science through the self-appropriation of the means of knowledge production and provocative taboo breaking. Another, comparatively idyllic counter-vision to today's corporate control over science, evoked by DIYbio, is the envisioned renaissance of the nineteenth-century gentleman scholar who pursues knowledge by his own means and for its own ends. Yet another narrative considers the real needs of developing countries that could be met by DIY biologists, as the bulk of corporate innovation caters to the markets of the developed world. Another analogy is drawn between DIYbio and DIY ICT, i.e., the manifold productive forms or self-organized non-profit IT services and user collectivities such as LINUX, Wikipedia etc.: 'open source biology' might signal a similarly revolutionary step in biology (Delfanti, 2013; but also see the critical view on the trope of 'open biology' in Chapter 10 in this volume). Nevertheless, the issue of 'bioterrorism' is the flipside of the very same process: biotechnologically proficient terrorists might create highly potent bio-weapons.

Discussion: divergences and convergences

The preceding section outlined a conceptual approach to the relationship between social movements and the multifaceted field of emerging technologies and we now proceed to explore trends of convergence and divergence that appear on the horizon within this field.

Divergence: DIYbio, critical movements and the use of techno-science

The case of DIYbio turned out to be multifaceted, touching upon diverse understandings and potentials for development. Does DIYbio constitute a critical social movement? Not in the sense we define it here. For one thing, the field is the subject of too many diverging narratives to accommodate key elements of the definition. For another, there are clear differences between a critical social movement and DIYbio: critical social movements, above all, seek to act as brakes on particular techno-scientific advances which they oppose for social, safety or ecological reasons. DIYbio, by contrast, ushers in a new, more egalitarian way of *advancing* the techno-sciences. This central divergence specifically shows in the different ways techno-critical movements and the DIYbio mobilizations relate to science and technology: DIYbio suggests that science and technology, for good or ill, can and should be appropriated by anybody (compare with Chapter 9 in this volume). A wide range of laypersons, from patient groups, to bioterrorists, to biohackers, to garage entrepreneurs, artists, biopunks and provocateurs have become DIY biologists. Both necessary equipment and information are relatively readily available. Like a puzzle, new knowledge may be assembled from the pieces available (e.g. Delfanti, 2013; Meyer, 2013).

For social movements that critically take issue with new technologies, be it nanotechnology, SynBio, biotechnology or nuclear power, science is an important factor, too. Here, however, the primary focus is on the element of risk. Techno-critical movements make strategic use of scientific knowledge in order to emphasize the perils of a specific technology rather than to assist in its advance. The regulatory restriction of new technologies within a liberal legal context typically hinges on risks to health and the environment, which is why the conflict around these technologies puts a premium on scientific expertise concerning these risks. From predictive models of climate change to the out-crossing risks of genetically modified organisms, actors seeking to influence the policy process mobilize scientific expertise. Hence, a major difference between critical social movements and the DIYbio field is that technology-watch movements use scientific knowledge to prevent the spread of a specific technology rather than to advance it, while DIYbio appropriates the tools of science and technology to 'tinker' with them, to indulge in a technological bricolage for a multitude of individual ends.

Convergences I: critical movements and DIYbio

What can be safely stated, however, is that there are some accounts of DIYbio that resemble a critical social movement. This is the case, for example, when DIY actors share some values and organizational features. 'Biohackers', for example, are organized in 'communities' i.e., in informal networks, and may also share a distinctive collective identity. Some biohacker meetings have been conducted in the past years, and a much noticed 'Biopunk Manifesto' constitutes a first attempt to programmatically define a collective identity (Patterson, 2010). 'Biopunk' and 'biohacker' communities and techno-critical movements also have a worldview in common, based on deep-seated anti-establishment, anti-corporate values. Another point of convergence of critical movements and DIYbio is their shared enthusiasm for 'open source' and the free circulation of information. However, although these aspects may make DIYbio actors appear as though they operate within a nascent critical social movement, the characteristics of the DIYbio field at large are too fragmentary to meet the definition. In particular, these actors are not involved in a conflict-based relationship against a clearly identifiable opponent. More to the point, we may concede that we are dealing with an emerging counterculture rather than a critical movement.

Convergences II: critical movements and policy discourse

Our exploration hints at another type of convergence that is worth highlighting: the convergence of movement criticism and policy discourses surrounding emerging technologies. It has been mentioned that the promissory narratives that go along with technology funding campaigns increasingly blend with discourses which recognize the fact that technological change does not take place without ambiguities or controversy and, therefore, emphasize public participation, ethics and precaution. It has been observed that these distinctive features of the policies in question mirror a learning process that has been prompted by earlier critical movements, particularly the movement against agricultural biotechnology (Rip, 2006; Kaufman et al., 2009; Seifert, 2013b). To some extent, technology policies can be said to have internalized movement criticism: today, policy discourses attribute more importance to the perceived drawbacks of technological innovation and that 'something has to be done' in order to avoid failure. To be sure, it remains to be determined how deeply this learning process goes; no doubt, national competitiveness remains the central policy objective, which is a major point of movement criticism. But at least at a rhetorical level there is clearly a trend towards convergence.

This convergence, in turn, shows at the actor level: the reflexive sidelines of the promissory policy discourse materialize in reports and programmes assessing ethical, legal and social aspects, stakeholder committees and in countless exercises in public participation and dialogue. The protagonists of this reflexive discourse are bureaucracies, technology assessment institutions, journalists, academics, think tanks and corporations who stress their commitment to ethics and 'open dialogue'. The small group of movement actors who critically engage in the field of emerging technologies operate amidst these policy-oriented actors as one among many other 'critical voices'. This also leads to a convergence of the methods they employ: as emerging technologies have never risen high on the public agenda, movement actors are unable to mobilize a critical public. Instead, they make use of the opportunities provided by these 'reflexive' policies. With their role evolving from challengers to invited critics of the policy process, with which they are ever more tightly interwoven, movement actors adapt their action repertoires to the new challenges, focusing on critical expertise and scrutiny of the regulatory process rather than activism and protest. Movement actors professionalize and become mainstream.

Summary and suggestions for further research

None of the three fields analysed above can be considered to be a clearly identifiable social movement. Yet, nanotechnology and, to an even lesser degree, SynBio discourses do show traces of a movement in the form of a network of movement actors and collective action frames. There is evidence that this network emerged as a 'spin-off' from the previous, influential movement against agro-food biotechnology. For lack of public responsiveness, however, this network never came close to a true protest movement.

Even so, the analysis of these rudimentary movements reveal noteworthy trends towards particular forms of di- and convergence. DIYbio constitutes an area in which both con- and divergences with critical social movements occur. To be sure, DIYbio is not a technology field but a socio-technological trend that cuts across a variety of science and technology fields. As there is no identifiable opponent, DIYbio fits the definition of a socio-technological subculture rather than that of a critical social movement. However, there are con- and divergences with critical social movements: on the one hand, some narratives about DIYbio bear a resemblance to a social movement as is the case with the egalitarian, even subversive qualities of some of DIYbio's manifestations; on the other, DIYbio diverges from critical social movements, for example, in taking a constructive rather than a critical approach to the techno-sciences.

Another convergence occurs in the nano- and SynBio fields in which movement criticism and increasingly precautionary and participatory policy discourses converge, even if only at the rhetorical level. As a consequence of this convergence movement actors increasingly operate within the policy process rather than outside of it; they professionalize and adapt to its specific opportunities by focusing on future projections, critical expertise and close scrutiny of the policy process. This indicates a parallel convergence between movement actors and other 'critical voices' from academia, technology assessment and journalism.

After having explored the emerging technology fields as discussed above, and drawn the necessary distinctions, we can go further and ask how techno-critical movements and DIYbio subcultures may interact in the future. Assuming the material conditions of the DIYbio trend – the broadening access to the means of knowledge production, dissemination and technological innovation – persist or even widen, DIYbio can be expected to further bloom. How will techno-critical actors react to this development? DIYbio has been presented as an emerging, polysemic field, inviting a variety of – often diverging – narratives and giving way to a number of diverging developmental pathways.

Accordingly, it can be hypothesized that techno-critical movements which may take issue with DIYbio will do so in ways that respond to either specific problems or opportunities created by the new development. For example, as unregulated, under-equipped freelancers or even 'bioterrorists' tinker with the 'tools of life', such as viruses and strands of DNA, DIYbio brings up considerable safety challenges (Bennett et al., 2009). Since catastrophic technical risks constitute a key motive of techno-critical movements, movement actors can be expected to highlight these dangers and press for tight regulation. Then again, movements' 'usual opponents' – pro-industry governments, big science and big corporations – are absent from such a scenario. Since denouncing or re-framing a technology's physical risks is often part of an unspoken struggle over the socio-economic structures and power relations underlying a given technology, movements might also remain low-key on the risks generated by DIYbio.

However, as has been emphasized before, DIYbio is enacted in and through techno-socio-economic convergences. Social movements and some

DIYbio subcultures do not only share certain beliefs, but may also provide examples for alternative socio-technological pathways: where corporations are reluctant to develop needed but unprofitable products and services, DIYbio might help to find solutions which are cheap, ecologically sustainable and tailored to the needs of the affected populations. Techno-critical movements, who generally focus on the denial of techno-scientific projects, could thus point towards constructive alternatives to the established pathways of techno-scientific innovation. Whether and how such positive or negative interactions will occur, however, is an empirical question to be tackled in future research.

Acknowledgements

Research and writing was financially supported by the Austrian Science Fund, FWF (P 21812-G17). A first version of this chapter was discussed at the workshop Direct-To-Consumer and Do-It-Yourself Biotechnologies. Challenges to Researching, Engaging and Governing the Messiness of Convergence, Edinburgh 27 to 28 September 2012. Many thanks to Matthias Wienroth, Eugénia Rodrigues and two anonymous reviewers for stimulating comments.

References

Ansell, C., R. Maxwell and D. Sicurelli (2006) 'Protesting food: NGOs and political mobilization in Europe', in C. Ansell and D. Vogel (eds), *What's the Beef? The Contested Governance of European Food Safety*. Cambridge, MA: MIT Press, pp. 97–122.

Bennett, G., N. Gilman, A. Stavrianakis and P. Rabinow (2009) 'Commentary: From synthetic biology to biohacking: are we prepared?', *Nature Biotechnology* 27(12): 1109–11.

Carlson, R. H. (2010) *Biology Is Technology. The promise, peril, and new business of engineering life*. Cambridge, MA: Harvard University Press.

Delfanti, A. (2013) *Biohackers: The Politics of Open Science*. London: Pluto Press.

Della Porta, D. and M. Diani (2006) *Social movements: An introduction* (2nd edn). Malden, MA: Blackwell.

ETC (2003) *The Big Down: Atomtech – Technologies Converging at the Atomic Scale*. Available at: www.etcgroup.org/sites/www.etcgroup.org/files/thebigdown.pdf [accessed 23 June 2013].

——(2004) *Down on the Farm: The Impact of Nano-scale Technologies on Food and Agriculture*. Available at: www.etcgroup.org/sites/www.etcgroup.org/files/publication/80/02/etc_dotfarm2004.pdf [accessed 23 June 2013].

——(2010) *The Big Downturn? Nanogeopolitics. A New Report from ETC Group*. Available at: www.etcgroup.org/sites/www.etcgroup.org/files/publication/pdf_file/nano_big4web.pdf [accessed 23 June 2013].

ETC Group (2007) *Extreme genetic engineering. An Introduction to Synthetic Biology*. Available at: www.etcgroup.org/sites/www.etcgroup.org/files/publication/602/01/synbioreportweb.pdf [accessed 23 June 2013].

FoE (2006) *Nanomaterials, sunscreens and cosmetics*. Available at: http://nano.foe.org.au/node/100 [accessed 23 June 2013].

—— (2008) *Out of the Laboratory and on to our Plates. Nanotechnology in food and agriculture.* Available at: www.foeeurope.org/activities/nanotechnology/Documents/Nano_food_report.pdf [accessed 23 June 2013].

—— (2010) *Nanotechnology, climate and energy: over-heated promises and hot air?* Available at: www.foe.co.uk/resource/reports/nanotechnology_climate.pdf [accessed 24 June 2013].

Gottweis, H. (1996) *Governing Molecules.* Cambridge, MA: MIT Press.

Kaufmann, A., C. Joseph, C. El-Bez and M. Audétat (2009) 'Why enroll citizens in the governance of nanotechnology?', in S. Maasen, M. Kaiser, M. Kurath and C. Rehmann-Sutter (eds), *Governing Future Technologies: Nanotechnology and the Rise of an Assessment Regime.* Heidelberg: Springer, pp. 201–15.

Kelty, C. M. (2010) 'Outlaw, hackers, Victorian amateurs: diagnosing public participation in the life sciences today', *Journal of Science Communication* 9(1): 1–8.

McAdam, D (1995) '"Initiator" and "spin-off" movements: diffusion processes in protest cycles', in M. Traugott (ed.), *Repertoires and Cycles of Collective Action.* Durham, NC: Duke University Press, pp. 217–39.

McAdam, D. and D. Rucht (1993) 'The cross-national diffusion of movement ideas', *Annals of the American Academy of Political and Social Science* 528: 56–74.

Melucci, A. (1989) *Nomads of the Present.* London: Hutchinson Radius.

Meyer, M. (2013) 'Domesticating and democratizing science: a geography of do-it-yourself biology', *Journal of Material Culture* 18(2): 117–34.

Patterson, M. L. (2010) *A Biopunk Manifesto.* Presentation delivered at the UCLA Center for Society and Genetics' symposium, 'Outlaw Biology? Public Participation in the Age of Big Bio', 1. January 2010. Available at: http://maradydd.livejournal.com/496085.html [accessed 23 June 2013].

Presidential Commission for the Study of Bioethical Issues (2010) *New Directions: Ethics of Synthetic Biology and Emerging Technologies.* Available at: http://bioethics.gov/sites/default/files/PCSBI-Synthetic-Biology-Report-12.16.10_0.pdf [accessed 24 June 2013].

Rip, A. (2006) 'Folk theories of nanotechnologists', *Science as Culture* 15(4): 349–65.

Roco, M. C. and W. S. Bainbridge (eds) (2004) *Converging Technologies for Improving Human Performance.* Dordrecht: Springer.

Royal Academy of Engineering (2009) *Synthetic Biology: Scope, Applications and Implications.* London. Available at: www.cbd.int/doc/emerging-issues/UK-submission-2011-13-Synthetic_biology-en.pdf [accessed 24 June 2013].

Schurman, R. and W. Munro (2006) 'Ideas, thinkers, and social networks: The process of grievance construction in the anti-genetic engineering movement', *Theory and Society* 35(1): 1–28.

Seifert, F. (2009) 'Consensual NIMBYs, contentious NIABYs: Explaining contrasting forms of farmers' GMO opposition in Austria and France', *Sociologica Ruralis* 49(1): 20–40.

—— (2013a) 'Antitechnology movements: Technological versus social innovation', in *Encyclopedia of Creativity, Invention, Innovation, and Entrepreneurship.* Dordrecht: Springer, pp. 67–73.

—— (2013b) 'Diffusion and policy learning in the nanotechnology field: Movement actors and public dialogues in Germany and France', in K. Konrad, C. Coenen, A. Dijkstra, C. Milburn and H. van Lente (eds), *Shaping Emerging Technologies: Governance, Innovation, Discourse.* Berlin: AKA, pp. 67–82.

Seifert, F. and A. Plows (2014) 'From anti-biotech to nano-watch: Early risers and spin-off campaigners in Germany, the UK and internationally', *NanoEthics* 8: 73–89.

Snow, D. A. and R. D. Benford (1992) 'Master frames and cycles of protest', in A. D. Morris and C. MacCurg Mueller (eds), *Frontiers in Social Movement Theory*. New Haven, CT: Yale University Press, pp. 133–55.

Wohlsen, M. (2011) *Biopunk: DIY Scientists Hack the Software of Life*. New York: Current.

Yavuz, C. T., J. T. Mayo, C. Suchecki, J. Wang, A. Z. Ellsworth., H. D'Couto, E. Quevedo, A. Prakash, L. Gonzalez, C. Nguyen, C. Kelty and V. L. Colvin (2009) 'Pollution magnet: nano-magnetite for arsenic removal from drinking water', *Environ Geochem Health* 32(4): 327–34.

12 Rhetorics and practices of democratization in synthetic biology

Emma Frow

Introduction

Synthetic biology is an emerging sphere of practice concerned with trying to make biology easier, cheaper and more reliable to engineer.[1] Engineering is a key source of inspiration for this young and growing field – engineering principles and practices like standardization, modularization, and abstraction are being promoted as useful for 'building with biology', in much the same way as they facilitate the building of useful, reliable systems and artifacts out of non-biological materials. Early proponents of synthetic biology hope that the rigorous, systematic approach of engineering will succeed where they suggest traditional biotechnology and molecular biology have so far failed to deliver (Endy, 2005). Central preoccupations for synthetic biologists include managing the complexity of biology (a term practitioners often refer to as 'black-boxing' complexity), and developing principles or rules for designing robust, predictable, and scalable genetic 'circuits' out of smaller genetic components (Adrianantoandro, et al., 2006; Purnick and Weiss, 2009).

In terms of its technical foundations, synthetic biology draws together concepts, tools, and materials from biotechnology, engineering, and computer science – in this sense, it could be presented as a 'converging technology' that relies on technical advances from a number of different fields (Roco and Bainbridge, 2002). The rapidly growing international community of synthetic biologists is highly interdisciplinary, and their diverse expertise and research interests lead to lively and ongoing debates about the degree to which biology might be made to behave as an engineering substrate, and how best to integrate different knowledge systems and practices to advance the field (e.g. Kwok, 2010). But far from being a strictly technical enterprise, the synthetic biology agenda is also associated with broader ideas and ambitions about changing social order. As I will discuss, synthetic biology practitioners are working to challenge some of the institutional structures, funding models, and ownership regimes that currently underpin biotechnology industry and practice. I suggest that their activities are contributing to a form of convergence whereby new forms of biological engineering and sociocultural practice are being co-produced (Frow, 2013).

The desire to 'democratize' biotechnology through synthetic biology is an idea that surfaces routinely in public discussions about the ambitions of the field. Although often stated in straightforward terms, scrutiny of what is meant by this push to democratize reveals a number of overlapping ideas and practices in play. In this chapter I draw on literature from science, technology and innovation studies to help make sense of how democratization is being discussed and enacted in synthetic biology. In particular, I identify three interwoven strands of rhetoric and practice in the field. The first is associated with lowering the barriers to entry for synthetic biology, with implications for the identities and expertise of synthetic biologists. A second but closely related strand focuses more on the control and ownership of materials and tools for doing synthetic biology, working towards a less centralized and more distributed model of innovation. The third strand relates primarily to questions of transparency and accountability in the governance of synthetic biology, and to who has a say in shaping the direction and oversight of research and development.

I show that each of these strands is associated with somewhat different interpretations of 'democratization'. Arguably, each involves some call to broaden the notion of 'participation' in synthetic biology. But precisely what aspects of this technology are being opened up to broader participation, to whom they are being opened, and to what ends, differs in practice. Interpreting current practices through the lens of science studies, I suggest that the first two strands of activities are oriented towards the democratization of innovation through direct participation (von Hippel, 2005; see also Laird, 1993). The aspirations of this approach might be presented by practitioners in the field as somewhat subversive – aiming to reconfigure the biotechnology landscape, challenge expert-lay divides, and redistribute power through alternative ownership regimes – but it is nonetheless a model that prioritizes innovation, entrepreneurship, and individual freedom to create. It is one in which the underlying service of science and technology to society is not questioned. The third notion of democratization is not necessarily at odds with these ambitions, but it does speak to a different set of concerns; its focus is more explicitly at the level of the collective than the individual, and it prioritizes questions of governance and public good over individual freedom to innovate (Guston, 2004; Jasanoff, 2003). In what follows, I explore the relationship between the push to democratize innovation and the call to democratize governance in synthetic biology; at times in tension with one another, there are also possibilities for convergence that may yield both new technology and new identities for synthetic biologists.

Democratizing expertise? Engineers, undergraduates, and citizen scientists as synthetic biologists

> We're now thirty years into biotechnology. Are we ever going to get to the point where it's not an exclusive technology, it's not a technology that requires experts?
> (Drew Endy, quoted in Edge.org)[2]

The call for 'democratization' in synthetic biology is frequently associated with lowering the barriers to entry, with the hope that more participation = more innovation. This is a vision with strong parallels to von Hippel's presentation of democratized innovation (von Hippel, 2005). Increasing the scope of who is able to engineer with biology has been a central aim of synthetic biologists since their earliest funding proposals (e.g. Carlson and Brent, 2000). By codifying biological knowledge and restructuring bioscience workflows according to engineering principles such as standardization, decoupling, and abstraction, they promise to reduce the skills and knowledge of biology that a person needs to engineer biological systems at the genetic level (Endy, 2005). With this approach, proponents imagine that participation in synthetic biology will be opened up to individuals who might not have high-level training in molecular biology. Biological engineering is no longer to be left in the hands of elite biologists. In 2005, civil engineer and avid synthetic biology proponent Endy predicted that within about five years, 'Undergraduates and high school students, without prior training in biology or biological engineering, should, over a period of weeks, be able to design synthetic biological systems of their own invention ... and show [them] to work' (2005: 452).

Imagination of who the synthetic biologist of the future might be extends beyond the confines of traditional research and pedagogical domains to the amateur or citizen scientist. For example, in one of their first programmatic statements to the US Defense Advanced Research Projects Agency (DARPA), biologists Rob Carlson and Roger Brent advance a case for 'open-source biology', in which they envision a much wider and more distributed community of practice (Carlson and Brent, 2000). As bioengineering tools become more affordable and accessible, they discuss the possible emergence of 'garage' and 'kitchen' biology – biological engineering that takes place by citizens in increasingly domestic, rather than institutional, settings (see also Dyson, 2007; Wolinsky, 2009).

Over the past decade, several initiatives have been founded that are starting to broaden the participant and institutional base for biological engineering. An undergraduate competition in synthetic biology (the international Genetically Engineered Machine competition, or iGEM) was founded in 2004, and has grown rapidly into a global competition that in 2014 registered over 220 student teams.[3] Over 10,000 students have to date participated in iGEM, and this initiative has contributed much to the building of an academic synthetic biology community (Frow and Calvert, 2013). Alternative venues for bioengineering are also springing up, for example in the form of community laboratories like Genspace (New York) and BioCurious (San Francisco), in personal garage laboratories (Ledford, 2010), and in citizen science interest groups like do-it-yourself biology communities (DIYBio).[4]

The forms of citizenship being fostered through the push to open up participation in biological engineering are worth exploring. The citizen brought into being through this vision of democratization is defined by his or her direct participation in the doing of synthetic biology. (Importantyly, those who do not or choose not to participate are not included or represented here.) Furthermore, the action of participating in synthetic biology is associated with a notion of commitment to innovation through bioengineering. The nature of this relationship with innovation is not predetermined or identical across citizen scientists, but is rather forming in parallel with the development of tools and infrastructures for bioengineering. A number of science studies scholars are following and analysing academic synthetic biologists, iGEM, and the DIYBio movement (e.g. Aguiton, 2009; Balmer and Bulpin, 2013; Delfanti, 2012; Meyer, 2013; Tocchetti, 2012). Kera (2012) notes that it is difficult to generalize across these groups. This said, academic and amateur synthetic biologists share a certain entrepreneurial and 'frontier' spirit, one that prizes creativity and innovation. They will often draw comparisons between their activities and those of maverick Silicon Valley garage 'tinkerers' and 'hackers' who sparked the growth of the microprocessor industry in the 1970s (see Alper, 2009).

Kelty proposes a number of figures with which this generation of biological engineers could potentially be compared, including 'outlaws', 'hackers', 'Victorian gentlemen scientists' and 'Buffalo soldiers' (Kelty, 2010). He suggests that each can be said to have a different sense of community, a different relationship with the law, and a different approach to managing the flow of knowledge and expertise. Consistent with this diversity in possible personas, the relationships of synthetic scientists to the communities of which they are part are still being negotiated. In his study of DIYBio community labs, Meyer (2009: 1) notes how 'a distinct form of individuality is constituted by providing people access, transforming them into active makers of science'. He discusses it as a 'connected individualism', in that citizen scientists are dependent on common infrastructure and a communitarian ethos of sharing in order to be able to 'do-it-yourself' (Meyer, 2009: 19). Identifying a similar ambiguity, Delfanti (2012) suggests that DIYBio aims to challenge traditional biotechnology while simultaneously depending on its existing infrastructure and supporting similar entrepreneurial values.

As suggested in the quotation at the start of this section, the drive to open up participation is in part about challenging the boundaries between experts and non-experts in their capacity to engineer living organisms. At present, the reconfiguration of 'amateurs as experts'[5] is far from complete. The democratization of innovation, as von Hippel (2005) describes it – in which users of products and services have the opportunities and necessary expertise to create and to innovate for themselves – is a desired consequence of increasing access and participation, but has yet to become a visible part of democratization in practice in synthetic biology. The iGEM competition has certainly generated some innovative ideas (ones that have subsequently received funding from research councils and industry to develop), but Delfanti notes that 'right now garage biology is not a site of research and innovation' (2012: 165). Meyer similarly suggests that DIYBio is an amateur science in-the-making, one that promises but is not yet about deep citizen engagement in biological engineering (2013: 8). Much of the current effort among academic and amateur leaders of synthetic biology initiatives is focused on codifying and re-packaging biological knowledge to allow more actors – engineers, artists and designers, undergraduates, lay citizens – to work with biological materials and tools. Intriguingly, this democratization of knowledge is simultaneously a 'black-boxing' of knowledge, a restriction of the amount of biological knowledge and detail presented, so that it becomes more accessible to those with less training. In this regard, the need for expert knowledge has not yet vanished. Citizen science is imagined to innovate on the basis of 'toolkits' or 'Lego-boxes' of biological parts; it is not yet imagined to extend deep into the workings of biological systems. What knowledge and values become embedded in the information and toolkits being made available to citizen bioengineers thus become important considerations, as they will influence the types of innovations that amateur bioengineers might pursue (Frow, 2013). As Joly, Rip, and Callon note (2010: 29), 'there is no fully public science, there are always thresholds, circles of limited exchange'.

Democratizing ownership? Economic models and proprietary regimes for distributed innovation

The discourse of democratization around broadening participation in synthetic biology has a closely related strand, one concerned with models of access and proprietary regimes in biotechnology. The aim is more than reconfiguring expertise to promote the emergence of citizen bioengineers, it also relates to the rules and norms that structure their participation. A push for openness and the 'democratization' of information, materials and tools is being actively promoted among the academic and amateur synthetic biology communities. Some see openness as more than just desirable, but as a pragmatic necessity for widespread user-driven innovation in synthetic biology, required to prevent patent thickets or the concentrated ownership of core tools and technologies by institutions and industries (Carlson and Brent, 2000; Maurer, 2009). The push for openness is associated with the possibility of faster and more efficient innovation by a broader spectrum of individuals and institutions.

Patenting remains a core mode of intellectual property (IP) protection in biotechnology, but a 'diverse ecology' of open and proprietary models of ownership is being pursued among synthetic biologists (Calvert, 2012). There is a strong push to provide 'an alternative to the use of proprietary tools – a toolkit for biotechnology innovation that is affordable, accessible, and unencumbered' (Hope, 2008:105). Key proponents of parts-based synthetic biology such as the BioBricks Foundation hold that 'fundamental scientific knowledge belongs to all of us and must be freely available for ethical, open innovation'.[6] Through commons initiatives like the Registry of Standard Biological Parts,[7] and the development of intellectual property agreements for the free sharing of biological parts,[8] they are promoting open platforms for sharing tools and encouraging users to 'freely reveal' information (von Hippel, 2005). The IP framework for open-source software has been a key source of inspiration

(Calvert, 2008; Hope, 2008; Rai and Boyle, 2007), pointing to a possible convergence across ownership regimes in software engineering and in biotechnology. Whether materials, information and practices are close enough across software engineering and bioengineering for successful adoption of this model is not yet clear. As Calvert (2008) points out, the modularity of biological parts makes them well suited to both open-access and patenting regimes of commodification; the value of openness is not unambiguously embedded in these artifacts.

The open-source proposal for synthetic biology equates the democratization of technology with a growing and distributed community of users and innovators who use and contribute to common toolkits and resources for innovation – a prime example being the 'get and give' philosophy of iGEM promoted by founder Randy Rettberg (2009). Again, this is a model of democratization based on direct participation in the enterprise of synthetic biology. It is one that aims to rebalance power relations among individuals and institutions active in biotechnology, arguing that a commons-based approach to synthetic biology will allow greater participation, and lead to more efficient innovation than the private regimes that have dominated biotechnology to date. Indeed, synthetic biology commentator and proponent Rob Carlson predicts an inevitable triumph of distributed over centralized manufacturing, stating that 'distributed biological manufacturing *is* the future of the global economy' (2001: 17, emphasis added).

In attempting to redistribute agency, knowledge and power, distributed models of innovation promote not just a model for innovation but also a normative model of society (Joly, Rip, and Callon, 2010: 22). The ideal of more open and distributed innovation in synthetic biology emphasizes a particular relationship between the collective (relying on a community of like-minded individuals) and the personal (allowing individuals to innovate based on their own interests or needs).[9] Joly, Rip, and Callon (2010) discuss the need for 'hybrid organizations' and a diversity of public and private platforms and access arrangements to sustain open innovation. They also identify ambivalences in the degree to which citizens and interest groups might be enrolled as active innovators, and call for mechanisms to ensure collective experimentation and the promotion of learning across distributed regimes.

Furthermore, they note that 'democratizing innovation' (of the sort that von Hippel (2005) writes about and synthetic biologists embrace) is not a model of *political* democratization in which the public is listened to or granted more voice in the governance of technology (Joly, Rip, and Callon, 2010: 26). Identifying another important caveat in the push to democratize innovation, Hilgartner argues that the form of 'openness' being promoted through institutions like the BioBricks Foundation is one concerned primarily with promoting a conventional understanding of innovation – one in which innovation is uniformly understood to contribute positively to society and public good – rather than tackling broader concerns relating to the politics of technology (Hilgartner, 2012: 191). It is the broader politics of technology that I turn to next.

Democratizing debate? Processes for governing synthetic biology

As described in the previous two sections, early proponents of synthetic biology have been keen to promote democratization and openness with the aim of facilitating innovation in biotechnology. Democratization here consists of promoting the enrolment and direct participation of new innovators. In this interpretation, we see engineers, undergraduate students and citizen scientists being constructed as political subjects who are granted the right to participate and the freedom to innovate with biology (e.g. Presidential Commission, 2010: 142). This is a vision of innovation grounded in the entrepreneur, an individual whose imagination and creativity should be allowed to roam free.

However, there is also a strand of discussion about 'democratization' in synthetic biology concerned more with the democratization of governance than with the democratization of innovation. The democratization of governance is not focused on broadening access to the tools for *doing* synthetic biology, but rather denotes concern with who has a say in shaping the direction of its research and development, ensuring accountability in oversight, and promoting equitable distribution of risks and benefits. By and large, this is a discourse more prevalent among civil society organizations, social scientists and policy actors than it is among the scientists, engineers and citizens actively participating in synthetic biology (e.g. ETC Group *et al.*, 2006; Nuffield Council on Bioethics, 2012). Although not necessarily at odds with the 'open science' ethos that underlies the call for greater citizen participation in the practice of synthetic biology, it does speak to a different set of questions about the purposes of innovation and the nature of the social contract with science. Its focus is more explicitly at the level of the collective than the individual, and it prioritizes matters of representation, governance, and public good over individual freedom to innovate. Bioengineers are not the only 'relevant publics' in this interpretation of democratization.

Two examples can be used to illustrate how concerns over governance are being articulated in relation to the push to democratize innovation. The first relates to biosafety and biosecurity. As access to foundational technologies becomes easier and cheaper, and more citizens become active participants in bioengineering, it becomes harder to keep track of who is pursuing such work and what the purposes or intentions of their efforts might be. Bioengineers might in time come to include academic researchers, high school students, and a diversity of amateur biologists acting in diverse locales, with different degrees of training in biotechnology, and with different motivations for pursuing this work. Concerns have been raised about the possibility for synthetic biology to be used for illicit or 'rogue' purposes, and imaginations of a widespread and decentralized user group are regularly associated with challenges for biosafety and biosecurity (e.g. Bennett *et al.*, 2009; Schmidt, 2008; Wolinsky, 2009).

Acknowledging a tension between the democratization of innovation and possible threats to human and environmental health posed by opening up the community of practice, the still-fledgling academic synthetic biology community has been keen to try and limit the potential for misuse of this technology. For example, in 2006 they set about trying to develop a number of proposals for self-governance, which they were planning to vote on at the synthetic biology 2.0 conference in Berkeley in May of that year (Maurer, Lucas, and Terrell, 2006). As it turns out, this initiative was strongly objected to by a number of civil society organizations from around the world, who published an open letter prior to the conference expressing their concerns about this attempt at self-governance (ETC Group *et al.*, 2006). One of the key concerns they voiced was that self-regulation is anti-democratic, and that the purposes and directions of synthetic biology as a technology should be opened up to wider public and stakeholder debate (ETC Group *et al.*, 2006; Stemerding *et al.*, 2010: 158). In the end, the research community simply abandoned their plans to vote on the resolutions about self-governance (Campos, 2010).

A second example demonstrating possible tensions between the goals of democratizing innovation and developing technology in the public interest relates to the funding of citizen bioengineering projects. New approaches to funding synthetic biology projects are emerging that do not rely on traditional modes of industrial support or grants from government agencies or charities. For example, the crowdfunding platform Kickstarter has been used to sponsor synthetic biology-related initiatives including OpenPCR,[10] and recently – and somewhat more controversially – a project that aims to develop and distribute Arabidopsis and rose seeds that have been engineered to produce glowing light.[11] This 'Glowing Plant' project draws inspiration from previous iGEM team projects and was initially developed in community meetings of the 'BioCurious' hackerspace, based in the Bay Area. From an initial fundraising goal of $65,000, the developers quickly crowdsourced over 8,000 donations and raised more than $480,000.[12] Once completed, US-based donors who have contributed $40 or more to Glowing Plant are to receive a shipment of Arabidopsis seeds to grow their own glowing plants.

There has been both positive media attention as well as significant critique of the goals of the Glowing Plant project. The project's Kickstarter website assures that the project is 'legal' (in the US) and 'safe'. Others are concerned about the 'untested and unmonitored release of seeds', and about what seems to be a lack of clarity over which US agency has lead responsibility for evaluating this product (Cha, 2013). An online petition initiated by the ETC Group to prevent the release of the Kickstarter funds received nearly 14,000 signatures[13] (more than the number of project sponsors through Kickstarter), and has prompted Kickstarter to change its guidelines so that in future, 'projects cannot offer genetically modified organisms as a reward'.[14]

This emerging debate around the Glowing Plant project opens up a somewhat different narrative about the democratization of bioengineering. Developments such as these raise challenging questions about who should have a say in determining whether and how particular applications are pursued (or indeed whether the technology should be developed at all). Should the fact that a bioengineering project receives private donations and that it is not illegal mean that it should or must be allowed to proceed? Might there be a role for broader citizen deliberation or state intervention to steer research towards public good outcomes, or to prevent investment in particular technologies? What sort of participation or representation is being advocated by those concerned with democratization of governance?

STS scholars have made persuasive cases for democratizing the institutional context and governance of science, not simply opening up its detailed, daily practice to broader participation. For example, Guston (2004) argues that:

> Democratizing science does not mean settling questions about Nature by plebiscite, any more than democratizing politics means setting the prime rate by referendum. What democratization does mean, in science as elsewhere, is creating institutions and practices that fully incorporate principles of accessibility, transparency, and accountability. It means considering the societal outcomes of research at least as attentively as the scientific and technological outputs. It means insisting that in addition to being rigorous, science be popular, relevant, and participatory.

The apparent 'success' of such calls for greater transparency and accessibility has become manifest in particular through growing policy support for public dialogue and engagement around emerging technologies (e.g. House of Lords, 2000). Synthetic biology is no exception, and over the past few years there has been some visible implementation of formal, upstream engagement initiatives around synthetic biology. For example, in 2010 two of the UK Research Councils led a national public dialogue exercise on synthetic biology (BBSRC, 2010). Building on the model of sponsoring research into 'ethical, legal and social implications' of the Human Genome Project, research funders in the US and UK are also starting to funding social scientists as co-investigators on large science and engineering research grants for synthetic biology.[15]

In principle, such initiatives could potentially contribute a wider range of upstream inputs and expertise to the shaping and governance of synthetic biology. Jasanoff (2003: 243) notes that increased participation can improve accountability in decision-making, yet also cautions (ibid.: 237) that 'formal participatory opportunities cannot by themselves ensure the representative and democratic governance of science'. It is not clear at this stage whether the engagement opportunities in synthetic biology are contributing to the sort of change in *culture* called for by actors concerned with the accountability of democratic governance. This observation resonates with broader STS concerns regarding the institutionalization and perceived instrumentalization of public engagement (e.g. Delgado, Kjølberg, and Wickson, 2011), as well as questions about the types of citizens being constructed through such engagement activities (Irwin, 2001). It is not clear, for example, how the findings of the public dialogue exercise are influencing policy-level decision-making. Nor as yet do there seem to be inclusive, transparent mechanisms to address the tensions around self-governance and around funding models that are emerging from the parallel calls to democratize innovation and governance.

This said, perhaps the very identification of such tensions in the interpretations of democratization is itself an opportunity to try to open up meaningful discussion, and to experiment with building new forms of citizenship and practices of democratic governance (in the spirit embraced by Irwin, Jensen, and Jones, 2013). As this chapter shows, focusing on the elusive goal of democratization helps bring into relief key questions concerning participation and the nature of citizenship in innovation and governance. We see that in practice, democratization is not simply being enacted, but rather that its very meaning is being negotiated and remade.

Conclusions

Synthetic biology is a field still in the process of inventing itself. Yet its core ideas, tools, and technologies are beginning to be taken up in a diversity of venues, by a growing number of people with diverse experience and expertise. Bioengineering communities are forming in concert with changing material and information infrastructures, funding models, and ownership regimes. Many of its practitioners believe that synthetic biology is a technology full of promise; they imagine a reconfiguration and reinvigoration of biotechnology, and 'envision synthetic biology as a force for good in the world'.[16]

The notion of 'democratizing science' is popular in accounts of synthetic biology, but as this chapter explores, what the enactment of democratization entails is under active debate. The idea of broadening participation is a common thread across the different strands of democratization discourse associated with synthetic biology, but which aspects of the scientific process are being opened up to broader participation, to whom they are being opened, and to what ends, differ in practice. Does democratization relate to opening up the definition of who counts as a synthetic biologist, to promoting decentralized ownership of this technology, to broadening participation in upstream decision-making about the direction of research and activity, or to some combination of all three? And, if so, in what formulation?

The relationships among these different strands are not necessarily frictionless; for example, it's not clear that the culture of 'hacking' and 'play' so valued in the push to make synthetic biology a 'citizen science' is a framing that fits seamlessly with the drive for accountability emphasized in accounts of democratization more concerned with governance. Nor is it clear that systems of decentralized, distributed innovation guarantee the kind of learning seen as so central to democratic participation. Yet synthetic biologists hope that broadening participation in terms of who can practice synthetic biology will 'increase the number of citizens who have some sophistication on these issues and can participate in the political choices that increasing biological capability can bring' (Carlson and Brent, 2000: 2). In this way they present the democratization of innovation and the democratization of governance as interwoven. Laird similarly notes the profound effects of participatory activity on the engagement of citizens in democratic processes (1993: 345). And as Joly, Rip, and Callon point out (2010: 2), regimes of innovation are closely linked to the governance of innovation and to normative models of society.

Although calls for democratizing innovation and democratizing governance speak to somewhat different understandings of the social contract with science, there may be possibilities for these ambitions to converge in ways that offer new opportunities for collective experimentation. Their current fluidity in synthetic biology affords opportunities to rethink and recalibrate the rules that connect citizens, the scientific enterprise, and the state. Aspirations to reconfigure expertise and change the nature of innovation in synthetic biology (together with the identities of bioengineers) offer incentives for experimenting with and learning from participatory approaches to science – and vice versa: the development of new participatory approaches and citizen identities may fundamentally influence the nature of innovation in synthetic biology.

Notes

1 The term 'synthetic biology' is used to refer to a number of related research activities (O'Malley *et al.*, 2008); this chapter focuses primarily on 'parts-based' synthetic biology, which revolves around the design and construction of biological systems and organisms out of genetic components.
2 See http://edge.org/conversation/engineering-biology [accessed 20 January 2014].
3 See http://igem.org/Main_Page [accessed 20 January 2014].
4 See http://genspace.org/; http://biocurious.org/; http://diybio.org [accessed 12 January 2014].
5 This phrase refers to a project conducted by Grove-White and colleagues at the University of Lancaster; see www.lancaster.ac.uk/fss/projects/ieppp/amateurs [accessed 20 January 2014].
6 The BioBricks Foundation is a not-for-profit organization with a mission 'to ensure that the engineering of biology is conducted in an open and ethical manner to benefit all people and the planet' (http://biobricks.org [accessed 17 January 2014]).
7 See http://parts.igem.org/Main_Page [accessed 20 January 2014].
8 See e.g. https://biobricks.org/bpa/ [accessed 17 January 2014].
9 Kelty might refer to the synthetic biology community as a 'recursive public', a community 'constituted by a shared concern for maintaining the means of association through which they come together as a public' (2008: 28).
10 See http://openpcr.org [accessed 20 January 2014].
11 See www.kickstarter.com/projects/antonyevans/glowing-plants-natural-lighting-with-no-electricit?ref=live [accessed 20 January 2014].
12 The Glowing Plant project is also being backed by the start-up company Genome Compiler, whose mission is 'to democratize biology information' through the straightforward provision of DNA design tools; www.genomecompiler.com [accessed 20 January 2014].
13 See www.avaaz.org/en/petition/Tell_Kickstarter_not_to_allow_bioengineered_organisms [accessed 20 January 2014].
14 See www.kickstarter.com/help/guidelines?ref=footer [accessed 21 January 2014].
15 For example, social scientists have been included as partners in the Centre for Synthetic Biology and Innovation at Imperial College London, and the US Synthetic Biology Engineering Research Center. The negotiation of their roles, relationships,

and expectations is an ongoing and sometimes fraught activity (e.g. Calvert and Martin, 2009; Rabinow and Bennett, 2012).
16 This statement appears on the front cover of the programme book for the SB5.0 international synthetic biology conference, organized by the BioBricks Foundation and held in June 2011.

References

Alper, J. (2009) 'Biotech in the basement', *Nature Biotechnology* 27: 1077–8.
Andrianantoandro, E., S. Basu, D. K. Karig and R. Weiss (2006) 'Synthetic biology: New engineering rules for an emerging discipline', *Molecular Systems Biology* 2: 2006–28.
Aguiton, S. (2009) *SynthEthics: An ethical and sociological analysis on synthetic biology*. Paris: iGEM 2009 Team. Available at: http://2009.igem.org/wiki/images/b/b2/TeamParis-SynthEthics.pdf [accessed 22 January 2014].
Balmer, A. S. and K. J. Bulpin (2013) 'Left to their own devices: Post-ELSI, ethical equipment and the International Genetically Engineered Machine (iGEM) competition', *BioSocieties* 8: 311–35.
Bennett, G., N. Gilman, A. Stavrianakis and P. Rabinow (2009) 'From synthetic biology to biohacking: are we prepared?', *Nature Biotechnology* 27(12): 1109–11.
BBSRC (2010) *Synthetic Biology Dialogue*. Swindon: Biotechnology and Biological Sciences Research Council (BBSRC) and Engineering and Physical Sciences Research Council (EPSRC). Available at: www.bbsrc.ac.uk/web/FILES/Reviews/1006-synthetic-biology-dialogue.pdf [accessed 22 January 2014].
Calvert, J. (2008) 'The commodification of emergence: Systems biology, synthetic biology and intellectual property', *BioSocieties* 3: 383–98.
——(2012) 'Ownership and sharing in synthetic biology: A "diverse ecology" of the open and the proprietary?', *BioSocieties* 7(2): 169–87.
Calvert, J. and P. Martin (2009) 'The role of social scientists in synthetic biology', *EMBO reports* 10(3): 201–4.
Campos, L. (2010) 'That was the synthetic biology that was', in M. Schmidt, A. Kelle, A Ganguli-Mitra and H. de Vriend (eds), *Synthetic Biology: The Technoscience and Its Societal Consequences*. London: Springer, pp. 5–22.
Carlson, R. (2001) 'Open-source biology and its impact on industry', *IEEE Spectrum* May: 15–17.
Carlson, R. and R. Brent (2000) *DARPA open-source biology letter* [pdf]. Available at: http://synthesis.cc/DARPA_OSB_Letter.pdf [accessed 20 January 2014].
Cha, A. E. (2013) 'Glowing plant project on Kickstarter sparks debate about regulation of DNA modification', *Washington Post* [online], 4 October. Available at: www.washingtonpost.com/national/health-science/glowing-plant-project-on-kickstarter-sparks-debate-about-regulation-of-dna-modification/2013/10/03/e01db276-1c78-11e3-82ef-a059e54c49d0_story.html [accessed 21 January 2014].
Delfanti, A. (2012) 'Tweaking genes in your garage: Biohacking between activism and entrepreneurship', in W. Sützl and T. Hug (eds), *Media Activism and Biopolitics: Critical Media Interventions in the Age of Biopower*. Innsbruck: Innsbruck University Press, pp. 163–78.
Delgado, A., K. L. Kjølberg and F. Wickson (2011) 'Public engagement coming of age: From theory to practice in STS encounters with nanotechnology', *Science, Technology, & Human Values* 20(6): 826–45.

Dyson, F. (2007) 'Our biotech future', *New York Review of Books* [online], 19 July. Available at: www.nybooks.com/articles/20370 [accessed 20 January 2014].

Endy, D. (2005) 'Foundations for engineering biology', *Nature* 438: 449–53.

ETC Group, et al. (2006) 'Global coalition sounds the alarm on synthetic biology, demands oversight and societal debate', press release, 19 May. Available at: www.etcgroup.org/node/8 [accessed 20 January 2014].

Frow, E. K. (2013) 'Making big promises come true? Articulating and realizing value in synthetic biology', *BioSocieties* 8: 432–48.

Frow, E. and J. Calvert (2013) '"Can simple biological systems be built from standard interchangeable parts?" Negotiating biology and engineering in a synthetic biology competition', *Engineering Studies* 5(1): 42–58.

Guston, D. H. (2004) 'Forget politicizing science. Let's democratize science!' *Issues in Science and Technology* [online], Fall. Available at: www.issues.org/21.1/p_guston.html [accessed 20 January 2014].

Hilgartner, S. (2012) 'Novel constitutions? New regimes of openness in synthetic biology', *BioSocieties* 7: 188–207.

Hope, J. (2008) *Biobazaar: The Open Source Revolution and Biotechnology*. Cambridge, MA: Harvard University Press.

House of Lords Select Committee on Science and Technology (2000) *Third report: Science and society*. House of Lords papers 1999–2000, 38 HL. London: Stationery Office.

Irwin, A. (2001) 'Constructing the scientific citizen: Science and democracy in the biosciences', *Public Understanding of Science* 10: 1–18.

Irwin, A., T. E. Jensen and K. E. Jones (2013) 'The good, the bad and the perfect: Criticizing engagement practice', *Social Studies of Science* 43(1): 118–35.

Jasanoff, S. (2003) 'Technologies of humility', *Minerva* 41: 223–44.

Joly, P.-B., A. Rip and M. Callon (2010) 'Reinventing Innovation', in M. Arentsen, W. van Rossum and B. Steenge (eds), *Governance of Innovation*. Cheltenham: Edward Elgar, pp. 19–32.

Kelty, C. M. (2008) *Two Bits: The Cultural Significance of Free Software*. Durham, NC: Duke University Press.

——(2010) 'Outlaw, hackers, Victorian amateurs: Diagnosing public participation in the life sciences today', *Journal of Science Communication* 9(1): C03.

Kera, D. (2012) 'Hackerspaces and DIYbio in Asia: Connecting science and community with open data, kits and protocols', *Journal of Peer Production* [online] 2. Available at: http://peerproduction.net/issues/issue-2/peer-reviewed-papers/diybio-in-asia/ [accessed 20 January 2014].

Kwok, R. (2010) 'Five hard truths for synthetic biology', *Nature* 463: 288–90.

Laird, F. N. (1993) 'Participatory analysis, democracy, and technological decision making', *Science, Technology, & Human Values* 18(3): 341–61.

Ledford, H. (2010) 'Garage biotech: Life hackers', *Nature* 467: 650–2.

Maurer, S. M. (2009) 'Before it's too late: Why synthetic biologists need an open-parts collaboration – and how to build one', *EMBO reports* 10(8): 806–9.

Maurer, S. M., K. V. Lucas and S. Terrell (2006) *From understanding to action: Community-based options for improving safety and security in synthetic biology*. Berkeley: Goldman School of Public Policy, University of California Berkeley. Available at: http://citeseerx.ist.psu.edu/viewdoc/download?doi=10.1.1.132.8678&rep=rep1&type=pdf [accessed 27 January 2014].

Meyer, M. (2013) *Domesticating and democratizing science: A geography of do-it-yourself biology*. Paris: CSI Working Paper Series, No. 032. Available at:

http://hal.inria.fr/docs/00/78/46/85/PDF/WP_CSI_032.pdf [accessed 20 January 2014].
Nuffield Council on Bioethics (2012) *Emerging Biotechnologies: Technology, Choice and the Public Good*. London: Nuffield Council on Bioethics. Available at: www.nuffieldbioethics.org/emerging-biotechnologies [accessed 20 January 2014].
O'Malley, M., A. Powell, J. F. Davies and J. Calvert (2008) 'Knowledge-making distinctions in synthetic biology', *BioEssays* 30(1): 57–65.
Presidential Commission for the Study of Bioethical Issues (2010) *New Directions: The Ethics of Synthetic Biology and Emerging Technologies*. Washington, DC: Presidential Commission for the Study of Bioethical Issues.
Purnick, P. E. M. and R. Weiss (2009) 'The second wave of synthetic biology: From modules to systems', *Nature Reviews Molecular Cell Biology* 10: 410–22.
Rabinow, P. and G. Bennett (2012) *Designing Human Practices: An Experiment with Synthetic Biology*. Chicago, IL: University of Chicago Press.
Rai, A. and J. Boyle (2007) 'Synthetic biology: Caught between property rights, the public domain, and the commons', *PLoS Biology* 5(3): e58.
Rettberg, R. (2009) 'iGEM: International Genetically Engineered Machine Competition', in US National Academies, *Symposium on Opportunities and Challenges in the Emerging Field of Synthetic Biology*, Washington DC, 9–10 July. Washington, DC: National Academies.
Roco, M. C. and W. S. Bainbridge (2002) *Converging Technologies for Improving Human Performance: Nanotechnology, Biotechnology, Information Technology, and Cognitive Science (NBIC)*. Arlington, VA: National Science Foundation.
Schmidt, M. (2008) 'Diffusion of synthetic biology: A challenge to biosafety', *Systems and Synthetic Biology* 2(1–2): 1–6.
Stemerding, D., H. de Vriend, B. Walhout and R. van Est (2009) 'Synthetic biology and the role of civil society organizations', in M. Schmidt, A. Kelle, A. Ganguli-Mitra and H. de Vriend (eds), *Synthetic Biology: The Technoscience and its Societal Consequences*. London: Springer, pp. 155–76.
Tocchetti, S. (2012) 'DIYbiologists as "makers" of personal biologies: How MAKE Magazine and Maker Faires contribute in constituting biology as a personal technology', *Journal of Peer Production* [online] 2. Available at: http://peerproduction.net/issues/issue-2/peer-reviewed-papers/diybio-in-asia/ [accessed 20 January 2014].
von Hippel, E. (2005) *Democratizing Innovation*. Cambridge, MA: MIT Press.
Wolinksy, H. (2009) 'Kitchen biology', *EMBO reports* 10(7): 683–5.

Part V
Commentary

13 Considering convergences in technology and society

Steven Yearley

The chapters in this volume help us reflect on convergence in smart and distinctive ways. From the outset we can see that the very idea of convergence is attractive because it offers us the chance to think about innovation and technical change as occurring in a space. We all learned from studying Euclid in school that non-parallel lines must ultimately converge. Technological convergence is thus about the relative orientation of different trajectories and their tendency to come together and meet in one place. Seen in this way, part of the appeal of the idea of convergence is that it opens the possibility of hastening convergence or of getting to the point of convergence first. If technological trajectories are moving towards each other, then the innovators, clever investors and shrewd science-policy champions will be aiming to be the earliest to benefit from an upcoming convergence.

But Euclidean geometry is also implacable. Sooner or later, non-parallel lines simply will converge. Talk of convergence can thus serve as a form of language that makes certain kinds of change appear inevitable, perhaps 'historic' in a rather Hegelian sense. This is clear if one thinks about the then-well-known 'convergence theory' concerning development in the capitalist West and the Soviet zone in the 1960s and 1970s (Kerr, 1983). The idea then was that, despite their ideological differences and their insistence on being distinctive (indeed the very opposite of each other), the two ideological camps would find that the demands of industrial-technological society would force them to become more like one another. Hierarchical structures and managerial differentiation would arise even within state socialism; systems of state-backed welfare provision would grow even in the most market-based societies (Mishra, 1976). Straining to display their differences, the societies would none the less come to resemble each other. This may not have been an altogether good theory about its particular subject matter (Dunning and Hopper, 1966), but it conveys nicely the sense in which convergence is often taken as something that takes place whether one wills it or not. On this view, convergences are just going to happen, and society had better adapt to the process.

The key ideas presented and documented in this book are a response to both these senses of convergence: convergence as a trend to be spotted and exploited, and convergence as an ineluctable process. The analysis in the chapters contributes to our understanding by showing that mainstream accounts of technological convergence tend to marginalise certain groups of actors and therefore tend to downplay opportunities for engaging with them in shaping paths to convergence. For one thing, the studies collected here indicate that convergence is not so much an exclusive product of scientific and technical research, rather it is also an outcome of social practices – what several of the authors refer to as social convergence. The 'space' within which convergences take place is not only an intellectual realm but is also a zone populated with regulations and laws, firms and consumers, activists and ethical considerations.

Second, narratives about the historical inevitability of convergence are beset with the well known shortcomings of historicism. The familiar problem with stories about 'the end of history' is that they are nearly always entirely convincing, apart from the fact that they tend to overlook the rise of a kind of actor which has not hitherto been very influential but which comes to change the very terms on which history is assessed. The historical evolution of citizenship, for example, seemed perfectly well charted until feminists pointed out that the generalisations did not easily fit women's experience of trying to win and reshape citizenship rights (see Walby, 1994). Their intervention was not just about claiming full citizenship for women, but about changing the very idea of which kinds of equalities and expectations citizens had the right to demand. Similar oversights are documented here with historicist readings of convergence; convergence is disrupted, for example, by the emergence of new kinds of research practitioners and new types of stakeholders. Patients and their families become new kinds of partners in shaping medical research. Amateur scientists try to find new ways to do-it-themselves in advanced biology. It turns out that the path of convergence was not preordained, but can be redrawn, often through the interventions of new kinds of agents.

Some mainstream authors, such as the contributors to the National Research Council of the National Academies 2014 report on convergence, appear to want to retain the positive aspects of convergent technologies while avoiding any overcommitment to specific ideas about the direction in which technological change 'must' be heading. However, to save themselves from becoming hostages to history, they end up using convergence in an extremely broad sense, stating:

> The scientific opportunities enabled by convergence – the coming together of insights and approaches from originally distinct fields – will make fundamental contributions in our drive to provide creative solutions to the most difficult problems facing us as a society.
> (Preface to National Research Council, 2014 vii)

Described in these terms, convergence (as 'the coming together of insights and approaches from originally distinct fields') begins to sound simply like interdisciplinarity. Scientific convergence is suddenly all around us, but at the same time less important and less distinctive than we previously thought.

By contrast, for those who want to reserve the term for use with the more significant and far-reaching innovations in science and technology a subtle balance needs to be established when it comes to proposals for the governance of new knowledge and novel inventions (see the series of studies of regulatory controversies since Nelkin, 1979). Proponents are typically led to make strong claims about the novelty, excitement and potential impact of their emerging field or area of technological convergence. This may well reflect the genuine enthusiasm they feel for their projects, but also helps to mobilise funding and investment, and to stimulate political support (see Wright, 1994: 115). There is always competition for research funding and for investment by universities between the different fields and sub-disciplines, and new areas can only win significant backing through insistent and clear claims about the rewards they can bring. This is particularly true at times of economic constraints, such as most of the Western world experienced from 2008 to 2014; in these periods overall state funding for research tends to be frozen and new research areas find they can only gain support by taking that money away from existing fields. For this, one needs very forceful claims about the novelty of the research area and its economic, societal or security benefits. At the same time, the more novel the area, the greater the potential demands for regulatory intervention usually are (see Jasanoff, 1990: 2–9). Innovators are generally anxious about excessive regulation and therefore they commonly complement their claims about novelty with assertions to the effect that regulatory issues are negligible or have already been taken into account.

Of the topics covered by the authors in this volume, synthetic biology and aspects of nanotechnology seem to fit this generalisation very well. These areas can make a very plausible case for their innovative qualities. Of course, the science itself has great novelty. The idea of finding a minimal 'operating system' for life, for example, probably needs no exaggeration or rhetorical boosterism to appear highly significant. But there are also additional ways in which nanotechnology's and synthetic biology's novelty is manifest.

There is firstly the matter of the potential applications of the technology. Though the potential uses in the short term seem limited, proponents offer visions in which (for example) highly innovative biological systems are engineered to produce hydrogen or other fuels. There are also ideas about the engineering of biological systems to synthesise medically important molecules and even to deliver them to specific locations within living organisms. Other suggestions hinge on developing bacteria or other simple biological or nano-particle entities that can clean up environmental toxins or remediate contaminated land. In a period when governments the world over are concerned about finding technological routes to avoid carbon dependence, the idea of efficient biological factories for hydrogen production is inevitably attractive.

Alongside these ideas about practical interventions there is also a procedural novelty about synthetic biology: the way that it can take advanced genetic engineering to the 'garage' level. At least among some exponents – and in a sense institutionalised in the celebrated annual iGEM (international Genetically

Engineered Machine) competition which involves undergraduates and even high-school students across the world – one finds the idea that genuinely novel work can be done by relatively untrained people using commonly available equipment and materials. Just as in the world of IT and electronics where a number of powerful and commercially successful initiatives have been initiated outside the academy and beyond the walls of established corporations, synthetic biology can potentially be undertaken by enthusiasts in informal 'laboratories'. As commercial sources of oligonucleotides proliferate and as DNA synthesisers fall in cost and rise in speed, the feasibility of these claims has only increased (see Vriend, 2006).

The exact implications of this potential are contested and, in detail, unforeseeable but in the IT world such garage practitioners have given rise to enormously innovative firms and tremendous creativity, as well as to hackers and persistent distributors of viruses. There seems no reason to suppose that biological research could not develop along similar lines. And the already-demonstrated capacity to synthesise actual viruses from biological precursors suggests that the unwanted side of this move to 'garage production' is as likely as the positive one, even in the case of synthetic biology.

In the case of such converging technologies as synthetic biology and nanotechnology there are strong arguments about the scientific and intellectual novelty of the area, about the potential range of applications which could likely result, and even about the wide range of potential practitioners that could become involved. But directly corresponding to each of these is a kind of regulatory concern. If the entry barriers are low for a form of scientific practice with dramatic implications then – arguably – the need for regulatory control over access is great since no one wants unlicensed operators releasing experimental organisms. If there are likely to be extensive opportunities for application within the human body and in the open environment (for energy production or novel forms of bioremediation) then the release and safety-testing implications are potentially enormous. Lastly, if this technology does give people new power over the fabrication of entirely new forms of life then this might eclipse the ethical and moral concern over new reproductive technologies which have been so publicly contested over the last decade.

And the critical point is that, at present, little hangs on any of these claims about the intellectual or practical aspects of synthetic biology or other convergent technologies being correct or likely to take place; the point is that once these assertions about far-reaching novelty or widespread applicability are made the regulatory implications are hard to avoid. The more strongly the claims are put forward, the more powerful the apparent regulatory logic. Proponents of synthetic biology, nanotechnology or other new convergent technologies need to make claims about their startling novelty and wide-ranging implications if they are to win financial and other forms of support, yet they cannot make these claims without simultaneously raising questions about suitable safety and regulatory standards. The public life of converging technologies is far from straightforward.

Thus, to summarise the contributions of this book: by exploring the dynamics and logics by which converging technologies are thought to proliferate the authors in Part II have contributed to our appreciation of the rhetorics of convergence and of the flaws in historicist readings of convergence. The chapters in Part III have elaborated on the complicated questions around identifying suitable approaches to the governance of converging technologies. They have examined how regulatory and governance tools are adapted to convergence, and by whom. Finally, in Part IV – on amateurs and citizens – key questions are addressed about the new kinds of actors who can reshape the trajectory of technical change. As the editors proposed, the research discussed in this volume effectively poses an alternative to mainstream views of technological convergence, highlighting very different ways in which technical processes can converge. Above all, the chapters collected here stress the open-endedness and negotiability of convergences, expanding greatly the cast of players who have a say in the making of technological convergence.

References

Dunning, E. G. and E. I. Hopper (1966) 'Industrialisation and the problem of convergence: a critical note', *Sociological Review* 14(2): 163–85.
Jasanoff, S. (1990) *The Fifth Branch: Science Advisers as Policymakers.* Cambridge, MA: Harvard University Press.
Kerr, C. (1983) *The Future of Industrial Societies: Convergence or Continuing Diversity?* Cambridge, MA and London: Harvard University Press.
Mishra, R. (1976) 'Convergence Theory and social change: the development of welfare in Britain and the Soviet Union', *Comparative Studies in Society and History* 18(1): 28–56.
National Research Council (2014) *Convergence: Facilitating Transdisciplinary Integration of Life Sciences, Physical Sciences, Engineering, and Beyond.* Washington, DC: National Academies Press.
Nelkin, D. (ed.) (1979) *Controversy: Politics of Technical Decisions.* London: Sage.
Vriend, H. de (2006) *Constructing Life: Early Social Reflections on the Emerging Field of Synthetic Biology.* The Hague: Rathenau Institute.
Walby, S. (1994) 'Is citizenship gendered?', *Sociology* 28(2): 379–95.
Wright, S. (1994) *Molecular Politics: Developing American and British Regulatory Policy for Genetic Engineering, 1972–1982.* Chicago, IL: University of Chicago Press.

Index

23andMe 8, 51–53, 59–74, 111, 113

accountability 175, 180, 182–83
Action Group on Erosion, Technology and Concentration (ETC Group) 163–64, 166, 181
advertising 59–61, 113
Aebisher, P. 36
affect 45, 48–50
algorithms 50
Allen, D.E. 144
Allyse, M. 68, 70
Altman, M. 135
amaterialization 10, 143, 152
amateur biology 9–10, 125, 134–35, 142–46, 177, 180, 192, 195
amateurization 142–57
Amazon (retailer) 151
ambivalences 29–43
American National Academy of Sciences 5
ancestry testing 5–7, 59–60, 62, 111, 113
Angrist, M. 134
Animal Procedures Committee 97–98
Apple (company) 128
Arabidopsis 181
Ashcroft, R. 111
Asia 14, 112, 147
Audétat, M. 7–8, 29–43
Aull, K. 133, 135, 147
Australia 112, 114
Avey, L. 60, 69

backyard biology 125
Bacon, F. 32
Bainbridge, W.S. 32, 36, 47, 80, 86
Barber, M. 93–94
Barnes, B. 94
barriers to entry 175–76, 194

Baxter, A. 136
BBC Radio 4 7
Belgium 14
Bensaude-Vincent, B. 35
Bernal, J.D. 78–81, 83
best practice 61, 116
Big Bio 128–29
big data 30, 54
Big Pharma 152
big science 132
bioart 142, 147
biobanks 8, 59–74, 112
BioBricks 19, 178–79
biocapitalism 136–37
BioCurious 128, 133, 176, 181
biodiversity 93, 95, 98
biofuels 96, 147, 149
biofuturism 32
biohacking see hacking
Biohackspace 147
biohealth 131–35
bioinformatics 17, 36
Biologigaragen 147
biology types 125–57, 158–59, 174–87
biomaking 126–36
biomaterials 18
bioplastics 147
bioprinting 19
Biopunk Manifesto 131, 168
biopunks 125, 131, 148, 167–68
biosamples 50, 64
biotechnology 3–4, 12–14, 16–17; ambivalence 30–31, 35, 37; critical social movements 164–66, 168–69; democratization 159, 161–63, 174–87; governance 77, 95; logics 44, 47; promises 19
bioterrorism 167, 170
black-boxing 174, 178

Blair, T. 93, 100
blogosphere 33
Blue Transilluminator 149
Bobe, J. 128–29
Boots (retailer) 111
Border Agency (UK) 93, 98
Borry, P. 59–74
Borup, M. 30, 31
boundary objects 145–46, 153
Boy Scouts of America 129
Boys' Life 129
brain sciences 30
Brave New World 32, 85
Brent, R. 176
bricolage 143, 168
Britain see United Kingdom
BritainsDNA 7
British Medical Journal (BMJ) 111
British Synthetic Biology centres 18
Brockman, J. 82–83
Brown, N. 30–31, 50
Brown, W. 136
Bund für Umwelt und Naturschutz Deutschland (BUND) 164
bureaucracy 128, 169

Cabinet Office 94
Callon, M. 35, 145, 178–79, 184
Calvert, J. 179
Cambon-Thomsen, A. 59–74
Canada 147
Canton, J. 83–84
capitalism 79, 136–37, 166, 191
Carlson, R. 128, 147, 176, 179
case studies 4, 7, 9, 68, 106, 109–10, 132
Castells, M. 83
Centre for Converging Technologies 17
chimaeras 97
China 116–17
circuit design 20
citizen scientists 6, 9–10, 125, 132, 135, 137, 152–53, 175–78, 180–81, 183–84, 195
civic technologies 143
civil rights 158, 161, 192
civil society 9–10, 180–81
Clarke, A.E. 127
class 127
climate change 96, 168
clinical utility (CU) 52–53
clinician-patient relations 52, 54
co-construction 45, 54–55, 143
Coca-Cola 135
Cockbain, J. 59–74

Coenen, C. 8, 31, 77–91
cognitive science 3, 14, 17, 31, 44, 47, 77, 159
Coleman, G., 146
collaboration 5–6, 19, 36, 53, 144, 147–48
collective action frames 160–61, 164, 166, 169
commercialization 65, 67–69
Committee on Energy and Commerce 53, 55
commodification 33, 115, 179
Common Agricultural Policy (CAP) 101
community bio-labs 128, 132, 146–47, 176–77, 194
community building 142–43
computer science 19, 85, 130, 174
consent procedures 61, 63, 65–69, 71–72, 110, 112, 115, 134
contraceptive pill 134
convergence 12–25, 44–48, 50, 54–55, 59–74, 135, 137, 146–48, 153; considerations 191–95; critical social movements 158–73; democratization 184; diagonal 105–21; discontents 81–87; logics 44–58; messiness 12–25, 77–91; socio-technical 3–11, 44–45, 50–54, 191–95; UK 92–104
Convergence of Knowledge, Technology and Society 87
Converging Knowledge and Technologies for Society (CKTS) 14–15
Converging Technologies – Shaping the Future of European Societies 107
Converging Technologies (CT) 3–5, 7–10, 105–10; considerations 191–95; critical social movements 161–70; democratization 159–60, 174; dynamics 12–25; governance 115, 117–18
convivial tools 142, 152–54
copy-left 150
copyright 19, 148
corporatism 125, 128, 132, 152, 158, 164, 167–71, 194
cost-benefit analysis 49
counselling 61, 112, 114–15, 118
Cowell, M. 128–29
Craigslist 151
Creative Commons 148
critical social movements 158–73
crowdfunding/crowdsourcing 52, 70, 181
CTEKS report 13

198 Index

Cusenza, P. 60
cybernetics 35
Czech Republic 152

de-materialization 143, 145
deCODEme 53
Defense Advanced Research Projects Agency (DARPA) 135, 176
DEFRA 96, 98–99
Delfanti, A. 128, 132, 177
Delgado, A., 153
democratization 9–10, 33, 35; logics 51, 54; rhetoric 174–87; role 125–30, 132, 135, 137, 143, 152, 154, 166
Department for Business, Innovation and Skills (BIS) 96, 99
Department for Communities and Local Government (DCLG) 96–97
Department for Culture, Media and Sport (DCMS) 96–97
Department of Energy and Climate Change (DECC) 96
Department of Health 95–96, 99–100
Department for International Development (DFID) 96
dermatogenetics 60
Desmoulin-Canselier, S. 20
determinism 48, 50–51, 54, 83
DG Research 13
diagonal convergences 105–21
direct-to-consumer (DTC) genetic testing (GT) 59–74, 108–9, 111–17
discourse 3–5, 8, 10; ambivalence 30–31, 34–37; critical social movements 159, 162–69; democratization 126–28, 131, 137, 143, 146, 178; governance 77–81, 84–86, 89, 109, 111; promises 14
disillusionment 29–31
dissemination of knowledge 21
distributed innovation 178
divergences 167–70
DIYbio.org 128, 148, 151
DIYGenomics 71
DNA 4, 7, 17; ambivalence 29–30; biobanking 60, 62, 64; considerations 194; critical social movements 170; democratization 129, 132, 134–35, 147–49, 152; governance 93, 95, 97–99, 106, 110–11, 115; promises 19
do-it-yourself biology (DIY-bio) 9–10, 125–43, 145–49, 151–54, 158, 160–61, 163, 166–71, 176–77, 192
DremelFuge 147, 154
Drexler, E. 37

D'Silva, J. 21
Dupré J. 94
dynamics 7–8, 10, 12–25, 44, 46, 158–59, 195

eBay 151
e-book readers 44–45
earth systems 14
economic models 178
economy of promises 29–43
Eisenhower, D.D. 82
electronics 17
ELSI 40
emerging economies 33
emerging science and technology (EST) 31, 40, 182
Endy, D. 176
Engels, F. 79
engineering 16–17, 31, 49, 129–30, 174–78, 180
Engines of Creation 37
Enlightenment 47
entrepreneurs 34, 136, 152, 166–67, 175, 177, 180
Environment Agency 94
epistemology 44, 49, 77, 126, 143
equipment 142–57
eschatology 89
ESHG 71
ESRC 3
ethical, legal and social issues see ELSI
ethics 3, 8, 10; ambivalence 37, 40; biobanking 59, 61–62, 65–67, 72; considerations 192, 194; democratization 131, 145, 147–48, 152–53, 169, 178, 182; governance 77, 85–86, 88, 106–8, 110–12, 114–18; logics 44, 48–49;
ethics promises 12–14, 21–22
Euclid 191
eugenics 115, 117
Europe 4, 10, 32; ambivalence 34, 37; biobanking 68; democratization 142, 146–47, 162–63; governance 85, 95, 101, 105, 107–9, 111–12, 114
European Academies of Science Advisory Council (EASAC) 71
European Commission 13, 32, 101, 107
European Group on Ethics 14
European Parliament 13, 16
European Technology Assessment Group (ETAG) 13
European Union (EU) 34, 84, 96, 162
evidence-based policies 92, 100–101

Index

Farrimond, H. 115
Federal Institute of Technology (EPFL) 36
Federation of European Academies of Medicine (FEAM) 71
femininity 129, 132
feminism 9, 106, 109, 117, 125–41, 192
Ferrari, A. 13
First World War 79
Fletcher, I. 8–9, 92–104
folk theories 38
Food and Drug Administration (FDA) 112–13
Food and Environment Research Agency 98–99
food science 132–33
Food Standards Agency 96
Foreign and Commonwealth Office (FCO) 96
Forensic Working Group 98
forensics 5, 64, 93, 95, 98
Forest Research 98–99
Forestry Commission 98
Foucault, M. 9, 105
foundational tools 14
Framework of Principles for direct-to-consumer Genetic Testing 112, 114
France 18, 164–65
Franklin, B. 128
Freud, S. 78
Friends of the Earth (FoE) 164, 166
Frow, E. 10, 174–87
Fuller, S. 78
Future and Emerging Technologies 34
future research 127, 135, 137, 152–53, 169–71
futures studies 49
Futurism 32
futurology 33

Gandhi, M. 161
garage biology 125–41, 166–67, 176, 193–94
Garvey, C. 147
Gates, B. 130, 149
gender 125–27, 129–32, 134, 137
gene therapy 30–31
genealogy 59–60, 63, 135
General Public License (GPLv3) 150
Genethics 110
genetic exceptionalism 110–11
genetic testing (GT) 8, 29–30, 50, 59–74, 105–21, 133, 147
genetic-mapping kits 5

genetically modified organisms (GMOs) 35, 38, 40, 95–96, 162, 168, 181
Genetics and Public Policy Center 61
genome mapping 92–104
genome-wide association study (GWAS) 50
Genomera 71
genomics 3–4, 6–9, 18, 29–30, 44–58, 60, 92–102
Genomics Policy 35
geopolitics 33, 35
German Federal Institute for Risk Assessment (BfR) 165
German Nano-Commission 164
Germany 83, 164–65
Gibbon, M. 80
Ginkgo Bioworks 152
globalization 33, 105–21
Glowing Plant 181
GNU 150
Golob, J. 130
good practice 71
Google Ventures 61
Gottweis, H. 159
governance 4–5, 8–10, 12–14; ambivalence 37; considerations 195; democratization 135, 137, 175, 179–84; promises 21; role 77–78, 87–89, 92, 94, 99–102, 105–21
government policy 92–104
governmentality 9, 105, 136
grand narratives 7–8, 31
grant applications 34
Griesemer, J.R. 145, 153
Groves, C. 7–8, 44–58
Guardian 6
Guston, D.H. 182

hacking 10, 125, 128–29; considerations 194; democratization 131–36, 142, 145, 147–50; role 152–53, 167–68, 177, 181, 183
'Hacking Healthcare' 136
hacktivism 131
Haldane, J.B.S. 78
Hansson, M.G. 65
Hauskeller, C. 9, 105–21
health care professionals (HCP) 59–60, 62–63, 71, 112
Health Protection Agency 99
Hegel, G.W.F. 191
hemochromotosis 133
Henn, W. 115
HFEA 98

200   Index

Hilgartner, S. 179
Hitt, J. 128–29
hobby biology 125, 152
Holm, S. 111
home economics 132–33
Home Office 96–98
Homebrew Computer Club 130
House of Representatives 53, 55
Howard, H.C. 8, 59–74
Human Brain Project 36
human cloning 20–21
human enhancement 13–14, 21–22, 31–32, 35, 78, 84, 86–87, 89, 164
Human Fertilisation and Embryology Authority 95
Human Genetics Commission (HGC) 112
Human Genome Project (HGP) 3–4, 93, 110, 182
Human Provenance Pilot Project 97
human rights 110
human scale platforms 14
Human Tissue Authority 95
Huxley, A. 32, 85
hybridization 36, 78, 179
hype 29, 31, 127–30

Iceland National Human Genome Project 112
iconography 39
identity 5–7, 52, 110, 126–27, 142–43, 168, 175, 184
ideology 14, 80, 87, 191
Illich, I. 153
imperialism 106, 109
India 17, 116–17, 147
Indonesia 133, 147
industrial revolution 81
informatics 30
information and communications technology (ICT) 3, 13–14, 17; ambivalence 31–32; considerations 194; democratization 145, 147, 159, 166–67; governance 77, 83, 88, 102, 106, 111; logics 44, 46–47
informationalization 51, 54
initiator movements 161
innovation 16–17, 30, 33–35; ambivalence 37–39; considerations 193; critical social movements 158, 164, 169–71; democratization 125, 127–28, 130, 132–33, 144–45, 152, 154, 175–78, 180–81, 183–84;

governance 88, 92, 95–96, 98–101, 105; logics 46–49, 54
instructables.com 151
intellectual property (IP) 19, 23, 178
interdisciplinarity 14, 16–19, 36, 47, 87, 89, 127, 174, 192
International Center for Technology Assessment 166
international Genetically Engineered Machine (iGEM) 19, 176–77, 179, 181, 193–94
International Risk Governance Council (IRGC) 14
Internet 13, 32–33, 113, 153, 165
invisible hand 52
Ireland 147
Irwin, A. 183
Is It O.K. to Be a Luddite? 81
Israel 14
Israeli Academy 14
Israeli National Committee for Converging Technologies 14
Israeli National Science Foundation 14

Jane Collective 135
Jankowski, T. 148
Janssens, A.C. 67
Japan 17, 147, 162
Jasanoff, S. 46, 108, 182
Jen, C. 9, 125–41
Jensen, T.E. 183
Jobs, S. 128, 149
Johnson 79, 184
Jones, K.E. 183
Joy, B. 84

Katz, D. 134
Kelly, S. 115
Kelty, C.M. 128, 134–35, 146, 177
Kickstarter 149, 181
Kindle 45
kitchen biology 125–41, 176
Kitchen Science Investigators 132
'Knots and Strands' 105, 107
knowledge economy 34
Kohler, R. 144
Kraft, P. 67
Kumar, S. 19

labs-on-chip 37
Laird, F.N. 184
Lamarck, J.B. 79
Landrain, T. 151
Larsen, A. 144

LavaAmp 152
legislation 21, 96, 101, 110
Lévi-Strauss, J. 143
liberal democracy 158
licensing systems 148, 150, 152
life expectancy 31–32, 47
life sciences 35, 94–95, 100, 102, 110, 133, 162
LINUX 167
List of Ministerial Responsibilities 94
literacy 6, 137
literary genres 37–39
logics 7–8, 10, 44–58, 136, 152, 194–95
Lopez, J. 48
Luddism 81–82
Lyall, C. 9, 92–104

McAdam, D. 161
Macaulay, V. 6–7
Magic Nano 165
Maher, B. 134
Make 125, 128
maker culture 125–26
Maker Faires 125, 135–36, 151
Maker Media 125, 135
Making Perfect Life 16
market infrastructures 20
Marxism 80
masculinity 129, 132, 135–36
Massachusetts Institute of Technology (MIT) 16–17, 133
matchmaking 60
materials science 35, 37–38
Mechatronics 13
media 159, 163, 165, 181
mega cities 14
messiness of convergence 4, 77–91
Meyer, M. 9–10, 128, 142–57, 177
Michael, M. 30
micro-arrays 18
micro-electro-mechanical systems (MEMS) 36
micro-technics 38
Middle East 14
Miège, B. 36
military 35, 37, 79, 84–85, 135, 137
Milner, Y. 61
Ministerial (Bio-pharmaceutical) Industry Strategy Group (MISG) 99
Ministry of Defence (MOD) 93, 96
Ministry of Justice 96
minors 61, 71
mise-en-scène 39
misogyny 117

mobile phone industry 19
Moffat, A. 7
molecular biology 51, 82, 142, 147–49, 163, 174, 176, 193
Moore's law 30, 32
MPM Capital 61
Ms Science 131–35
multiculturalism 116
multidisciplinarity 16–19, 110, 114
Munro, W. 161
mutations 30

nano-bio-info-cogno see NBIC
nano-watch movement 163–65
nanomedicine 20, 39
nanoscale 36, 47, 49, 85
nanotechnology 3, 9, 12–14; ambivalence 29–32, 35–39; considerations 193–94; critical social movements 168–70; democratization 158–59, 161–66; governance 77, 83; logics 44, 46; promises 18
nanovectors 37
narratives/master narratives 8, 45–48, 51, 54–55, 125–41, 159
National Academies 192
National Bee Unit 98
National DNA Database 97, 100
National Health and Medical Research Council 112
National Institute of Advanced Industrial Science and Technology (AIST) 17
National Institute of Health (NIH) 112
National Nanotechnology Initiative (NNI) 31, 46, 55, 162
National Research Council 192
National Science Foundation (NSF) of Converging Technologies 31, 35, 80, 132
National Science and Technology Council 46, 83
National Wildlife Crime Unit (NWCU) 98
Nature 115, 134
Navigenics 53
NBIC 3, 7, 12–17; ambivalence 31–32, 36–37, 40; governance 77–78, 80, 83–87, 89, 105, 107, 114; logics 44–58; NBIC2 14; promises 21–22
NDPBs 92, 94–96
Nelkin, D. 193
neo-liberalism 135–37
Nerad, M. 132

Netzer, C. 115
neuroscience 17, 78, 83
New Atlantis 32
New Enterprise Associates 61
New Labour 93–94
New Public Management 93, 100
new social movements 10, 158–73
New York Times 29
NHS Blood and Transplant 99
No Longer Patient 106
non-governmental organizations (NGOs) 6, 163–65
non-institutional biology 125
non-invasive prenatal diagnosis (NIPD) 115–18
Nordmann, A. 22, 84–85, 87, 105, 107–8, 111, 114, 117
normativity 117–18, 136, 158, 179, 184
North America 4, 114
novum 48–49
Nowotny, H. 80–81

Office for Life Sciences 99
ontology 44, 46–47, 109
Open Gel box 148–49, 151
Open PCR 148–51, 154, 181
open source 10, 19, 35, 130, 143–47, 149–50, 153, 167–68, 176, 178–79
Openwetware 148, 151
opportunity costs 22
Organization for Economic Co-operation and Development (OECD) 66–67
Our Bodies, Ourselves 135
outlaw biology 125, 134–35, 177
ownership 174–75, 178–79, 183

Parkinson's Disease (PD) 67–68, 71
Partnership against Wildlife Crime (PAW) 98
patenting 19, 67–70, 152, 178–79
paternalism 37, 117, 134
Patterson, M. 125, 129, 131, 133, 135, 147
Pearl Biotech 148–49, 152
pedagogy 127, 132, 176
Peerbaye, A. 18
Perfetto, J. 148
performativity 29, 38, 44, 49
personal genomics *see* genomics
personal utility 52–54
personalized medicine 30, 51–52, 54, 100
Personalized Medicine Coalition (PMC) 53

pharmaceutical industry 30
pharmacogenetic testing 60
phenotypes 5, 50, 52, 59–61, 64–65, 110
photonics 17
Photonics-Electronics Convergence System Technology 17
Pièces et main d'oeuvre (PMO) 164–65
Pimp My Ride 130
PLOS Genetics 66
pluralism 109
Poland 161
Police and Criminal Evidence Act 98
policy narratives 159–60, 162, 165
policy-making 4, 159–60, 164
political economy 136
polymerase chain reaction (PCR) 95, 149
post-instruments 145
power relations 106, 109, 111, 118, 126, 170, 175, 179
Prainsack, B. 69
pregnancy testing 5
Presidential Commission for the Study of Bioethical Issues 166
Prime Minister's Delivery Unit (PMDU) 93
privacy 61–62, 89, 112
privatization 136
product development 17–22
production platforms 18
professionalization 144, 169–70
Progressive Era 132
promises 45–46, 48–51, 54; democratization 126–31, 133, 135–37, 154, 169; governance 95, 101; scientific 29–43; umbrella 12–25
proprietary regimes 178–79
proto-instruments 145
protocol-online.org 151
prototype testing 143
public goods 52, 70, 113, 175, 179–80, 182
public narratives 159–60, 162, 165–66
public policy 162
public sector 93
public sphere 158–59
Pynchon, T. 81–82

quality management 106, 115
quangos 95

Rabeharisoa, V. 145
Rader, M. 87
Rai, A. 19

Rajan, S. 136
Ratto, M. 145
Ravitsky, V. 115
re-materialization 142–57
Reade, W. 78
reconfigured narratives 131–35
Rede Lecture 81
Ree, R. 145
Registry of Standard Biological Parts 19, 178
regulation 20–21, 23, 52–55; biobanking 61, 63; considerations 191, 193–95; democratization 162, 169–70, 181; governance 92, 95–96, 109–15, 117
Reinhoff, H. 134–35
reputation 31, 160
Request For Comments (RFC) 148
research 16–22, 29–31, 37–38; biobanking 59, 61–72; considerations 192–93, 195; critical social movements 163, 166–67; democratization 125–27, 131, 133–35, 137, 144–45, 148, 175–77, 180–83; governance 81–82, 88–89, 97–101, 105, 108; logics 44, 46–53; public-private 125; regimes 33–35
research and development (R&D) 18, 31, 33, 82
Rettberg, R. 179
rhetoric 7, 14, 44–45, 50–55, 69, 95, 108, 169–70, 174–87, 193, 195
Richards, M. 6–7
Rip, A. 22, 35, 38, 178–79, 184
risk profiles 50–51, 54
risk society 39
RNA 148–49
Robinson, D. 7–8, 12–25
Roche Venture Fund 61
Roco, M. 32, 36, 47, 80, 86
Rodrigues, E. 3–11
Royal Academy of Engineering 166

Sassen, S. 146
Schloendorn, J. 134–35
Schmitz, D. 115
Schummer, J. 36
Schurman, R. 161
Science 29
science fiction (SF) 32, 78, 85
science, technology, engineering and maths (STEM) subjects 129–32, 137
Science and Technology Options Assessment (STOA) 16

Science and Technology Studies (STS) 4, 45, 50, 54, 109–10, 117–18, 182
scienceandfood.org 133
scientific equipment 142–57
Scott, P. 80
Second World War 32
segregation 132
Seifert, F. 10, 158–73
self-quantification 51, 53
semiconductor industry 20
Shaping the World Atom by Atom 47
Sherwin, S. 106, 109, 111, 117–18
Silicon Valley 177
Singapore 133, 147
single nucleotide polymorphisms (SNPs) 50, 60, 64
sites of origin 126, 128, 130–31, 133, 135
situational analysis (SA) 127
slow science movement 40
Slusser, G. 78
Smalley, R. 37
Smith, A. 52
Snow, C.P. 81
social construction 50, 54
social media 45, 51–52
social movements 158–73
socialism 80, 191
societal-scale platforms 14
sociocultural differences 117–18
sociology of expectations 7, 29–31, 33, 48–49
Solidarity Movement 161
source codes 19
South 164
South America 14
Soviet Union 191
Sparrow, R. 48
speculative ethics 21–22
spin-off movements 161, 163, 165–66, 169
Star, S.L. 145, 153
stem cells 30
Stenger, I. 40
Sterckx, S. 59–74
strong convergence 44–48, 50, 54
susceptibility testing 50
Swierstra, T. 13
Switzerland 36
synergy 5, 16, 102
synthetic biology (SynBio) 4, 9–10, 17–19; considerations 193–94; critical social movements 168–70; democratization 129, 147, 158–59, 161–66, 174–87; promises 21

Task Force on Genetic Testing 112
technicians 18
technology agglomeration 18
Technology Strategy Board 96
Teilhard de Chardin, P. 79
Third Culture 82–83
Thomas, M. 6
Tobin, S.L. 67
totalitarianism 39
transdisciplinarity 17, 89
transhumanism 8, 35, 77–80, 84, 86–87, 89
transparency 59, 62–63, 65, 68–72, 175, 182
trust 59, 63, 65, 68–72, 112
Tutton, R. 52, 69
The Two Cultures and the Scientific Revolution 78, 81–82

UK Biobank 112
uncertainty 45, 48–50, 55, 106
undergraduates 175–78, 180
UNESCO 97
United Kingdom (UK) 3, 8–9, 92–104, 116, 144, 162, 182
United States (of America, USA) 5, 8, 13; ambivalence 31, 34; biobanking 61; critical social movements 166; democratization 125–31, 133–35, 137, 142, 147, 161–64, 176, 181–82; governance 80, 83–85, 93, 105, 107–8, 111–12, 116; logics 46, 50, 55; promises 16
unity of science 8, 47, 77, 79–80, 84, 86, 88–89
University of California, Los Angeles (UCLA) 133
University of Cambridge 80
University of Edinburgh 3–4, 77, 87
University of Rajasthan 17

University of Reading 21
university science departments 132–33
utopianism 85, 125, 136

value chains 20
Vinck, D. 36
vision assessment 77, 79, 81, 85–89
Von Hippel, E. 144, 176–77, 179

Warhol, A. 149
Warwick, K. 21
weak convergence 44–48, 54
Wellcome Trust 93
Wells, H.G. 78
West 109, 115, 136, 146, 158, 163, 191, 193
What Works network 94
White Paper on Nanotechnology Risk Governance 14
Wienroth, M. 3–11
Wikipedia 167
Wild Open PCR 150–51
Wired 128
Wojcicki, A. 60
Wolinsky, H. 134
women's health movement 133–34, 137
women's studies 126
workarounds 147, 166
Working Group on Nanoscience, Engineering and Technology 83
The World, the Flesh and the Devil 78
World Heritage designations 97
World Trade Organization (WTO) 162
WTEC conferences 22

xenotransplantation 30

Yearley, S. 9–10, 92–104, 191–95
YouTube 151